Faith, Life, and Learning Online

Faith, Life, and Learning Online

Promoting Mission across Learning Modalities

Edited by
BRANT M. HIMES and JOHN W. WASHATKA

Foreword by David S. Dockery

CASCADE *Books* • Eugene, Oregon

FAITH, LIFE, AND LEARNING ONLINE
Promoting Mission across Learning Modalities

Copyright © 2022 Wipf and Stock Publishers. All rights reserved. Except for brief quotations in critical publications or reviews, no part of this book may be reproduced in any manner without prior written permission from the publisher. Write: Permissions, Wipf and Stock Publishers, 199 W. 8th Ave., Suite 3, Eugene, OR 97401.

Cascade Books
An Imprint of Wipf and Stock Publishers
199 W. 8th Ave., Suite 3
Eugene, OR 97401

www.wipfandstock.com

PAPERBACK ISBN: 978-1-6667-0568-3
HARDCOVER ISBN: 978-1-6667-0569-0
EBOOK ISBN: 978-1-6667-0570-6

Cataloguing-in-Publication data:

Names: Himes, Brant M., editor | Washatka, John W., editor.

Title: Faith, life, and learning online : promoting mission across learning modalities / Edited by Brant M. Himes and John W. Washatka.

Description: Eugene, OR: Cascade Books, 2022 | Includes bibliographical references and index.

Identifiers: ISBN 978-1-6667-0568-3 (paperback) | ISBN 978-1-6667-0569-0 (hardcover) | ISBN 978-1-6667-0570-6 (ebook)

Subjects: LCSH: Web-based instruction. | Distance education. | Internet—Religious aspects.

Classification: LB1044.87 F50 2022 (paperback) | LB1044.87 (ebook)

04/04/22

Contents

Foreword   vii
    David S. Dockery

Acknowledgments   xiii

Contributors   xv

Introduction   xvii

PART 1 | CONTINUING THE LEGACY

Chapter 1: The Current State of Online Spiritual Formation   3
    Scott D. Edgar

Chapter 2: A Holistic Approach to Christian Faith, Life, and Learning   20
    Brant M. Himes

Chapter 3: Building a Culture of Collaboration   35
    John C. Reynolds

Chapter 4: Assessing Faith, Life, and Learning   47
    Wayne R. Herman

Chapter 5: Faith, Life, Learning, and Institutional Identity   61
    John W. Washatka

CONTENTS

PART 2 | FAITH, LIFE, AND LEARNING IN THE CURRICULUM

Chapter 6: Christian Worldview — 77
John W. Washatka

Chapter 7: God's Story — 90
Brant M. Himes

Chapter 8: Diverse Faith Perspectives — 102
Lisa D. Phillips

Chapter 9: Faith through Academic Disciplines — 118
Shannon N. Hunt

PART 3 | FAITH, LIFE, AND LEARNING ACROSS THE UNIVERSITY

Chapter 10: Coaching for Faith Formation — 135
Carrie M. Akemann

Chapter 11: Incarnational Practices for Faith Formation — 152
John W. Washatka

Chapter 12: A Call to Cultivate Mission across Modalities — 166
Wayne R. Herman

Bibliography — 173

Foreword

DAVID S. DOCKERY

DAVID S. DOCKERY *has been involved in leadership of Christian higher education for nearly three decades in his service as President of Union University; as President of Trinity International University/Trinity Evangelical Divinity School; and as President of the International Alliance for Christian Education. He previously served as board chair for the Council for Christian Colleges and Universities and as President of the Evangelical Theological Society.*

Those serving in the world of Christian higher education have been asking important questions over the past three decades, since the rise of the internet, related to educational methodology and delivery systems. What began in the minds of many as the next step beyond correspondence studies has developed into a multifaceted educational enterprise. This observation is not to suggest that full support for the innovations known as online education were readily present across the board in higher education. In fact, much pushback was experienced by those technologically savvy early adopters. Several institutions began to offer online courses, but few dared to enter into the territory of online degree offerings.

With new initiatives in the realm of social media and the expanded opportunities that came with widespread internet service in the early years of the twenty-first century, things started to change. More and more institutions entered the world of online learning, forcing accrediting agencies to make decisions about the possibility of online degree programs. Could such programs be offered in every discipline? Should these programs be designed primarily for undergraduate students or graduate students? Nontraditional students or traditional students? Christian institutions often entered the field with reluctance since their understanding of education extended beyond the delivery of information, focusing on the importance of personal formation and campus community.

Within the last decade, Christian educators began to explore ways to bring together their passion for spiritual formation with faithful pedagogy in online formats. The road was not easy and reluctant administrators (not unlike yours truly) needed to be convinced that faith formation and personal transformation could take place in a digital educational context. I served as a campus president at two institutions for nearly a quarter of a century and I can assure you that I was not alone in raising questions about the credibility and viability of such programs. While most in recent years had moved toward embracing and supporting online initiatives, there remained serious doubters and holdouts until 2020. When COVID-19 issues became front and center, everyone became an online educator, at least in some sense.

Over the past decade in particular, I and others have been helped by the writings of Kristen Ferguson (*Excellence in Online Education: Creating a Christian Community on Mission*), Steve and Mary Lowe (*Ecologies of Faith in a Digital Age: Spiritual Growth through Online Education*), and Timothy Paul Jones and others (*Teaching the World: Foundations for Online Theological Education*). Now the book you hold in your hand, *Faith, Life, and Learning Online*, courageously and convictionally offers a proposal for serious and faithful Christian education not just by providing occasional courses or even full degree programs, but by establishing an entire online institution. Moreover, they have convincingly made the case that faith, living, and learning can be brought together in virtual format to advance institutional mission. Their contention is that faith and learning are essentially matters of mission not modality.

I have watched with great interest as Los Angeles Pacific University has developed, pioneering new territory for Christian higher education. Not only are these innovative educators committed to "excellence in online education," to borrow the phrase from my friend Kristen Ferguson, they are also deeply dedicated to bringing the Christian faith to bear on every subject across the curriculum. It is a bold undertaking and most likely paves the way for many other Christian institutions to follow in the days ahead.

While Los Angeles Pacific University (LAPU) is pointing the way forward in the digital space, they are also calling others to take seriously the work of bringing together faith and teaching as well as faith and learning, highlighting and distinguishing the priority of mission. Doing so makes their space in the educational world doubly distinctive. By this I mean that they are not just seeking to create an environment in which the implications of the Christian faith are allowed to exist; they are seeking to offer distinctive content in a full-orbed digital delivery system.

If indeed the primary question that the contributors to this fine volume are seeking to answer is primarily one of mission and not modality, we must ask, "what is meant when we talk about the work of faith and learning?" The words of Jesus in the first and greatest commandment (Matt 22:36–40) make it quite clear that the followers of Christ are to love God with our minds, as well as our hearts. Learning to think Christianly, to be a thoughtful Christian, to ask how faith bears upon and informs teaching and learning, shapes the way we think about every academic discipline as well as all aspects of life. To love God with our minds means that we think differently about the way we live and love, the way we worship and serve, the way we work to earn our livelihood, the way we learn and teach.

Such thinking means being able to approach every discipline from business to biology, from English to economics, from art to zoology from the vantage point of the Christian faith made known to us in God's general and special revelation. It means thinking in accord with the pattern of Christian truth. Such an approach to education involves recognizing that all knowledge flows from the one Creator to his one creation. Specific bodies of knowledge relate to each other not just because scholars and students work together in community, not just because interdisciplinary work broadens our knowledge, but because all truth has its source in God, composing a single universe of knowledge.

Genuine Christ-centered education involves more than the passing on of content to our students. It also means the shaping of character and moves toward the development and construction of a convictional way of seeing the world by which students are able to see, learn, and interpret life from the vantage point of God's revelation to his people. Such an approach to education fosters intellectual seriousness, encouraging students to grow in their understanding and appreciation of God, of his creation and grace, and of humanity's place of privilege and responsibility in the world.

Those who serve and those who study at faithful Christ-centered institutions, whether more traditional institutions or online institutions like LAPU, are called to explore and engage subject matter in a way that questions autonomous reason, recalling instead Augustine's model of faith seeking understanding. This distinctive approach to teaching and learning recognizes that wherever truth is found, it is the Lord's, even as men and women struggle with the great ideas of the past and the pressing issues of today, carrying on debate in pursuit of this truth. Such a lofty aspiration can only take place in learning communities in which our minds and hearts are renewed by God's Spirit (Rom 12:1-2). This understanding of education is accompanied by an authentic sense of humility that acknowledges that God, the source of all truth, knows all things and we do not.

This task will be intellectually challenging, with great implications for all aspects of life. The best of the Christian tradition points today's educators in this engaging direction. Intentional Christian thinking is derived from the unifying principle that God is Creator and Redeemer. It seeks answers to the fundamental questions of human existence. It calls for educational efforts across the curriculum to flow from a coherent and comprehensive way of seeing the world. While it looks to the past to reclaim key aspects of the Christian intellectual tradition, it emphasizes the need to be aware of contemporary cultural, societal, and ecclesiastical trends.

An approach to teaching and learning from the vantage point of the truth once and for all delivered to the saints includes both an engagement mindset as well as the humility to acknowledge that we wrestle with complex and challenging issues, which are often filled with ambiguities. Even with the help of Christian Scripture and the Christian tradition, we recognize that we are finite humans who see as through a glass darkly. Ultimately, Christian thinking grows out of a commitment to sphere-sovereignty, confessing the lordship of Jesus Christ, whether in the arts, the sciences, the humanities, the social sciences, or professional studies.

A commitment to faith and learning, whether in a single online course or in an entire online curriculum, will help students develop a way of seeing and engaging God's world in such a way as to joyously contemplate a wide range of ideas. Such an approach holds out hope for restoring the endangered virtues of kindness, humility, love, grace, truth, beauty, goodness, honor, justice, and purity (Phil 2:1-4; 4:8). Learning to think Christianly is not just an expression of one's personal piety. Rather, it is an all-consuming way of life, applicable to all spheres of life. Helping faculty and students think in this way has never been, and will not be, easy, but the rewards for doing so are great for faculty members, students, for institutions, as well as for church and society.

To the extent that this approach to Christian education can be put into practice, guiding students in these important matters, we will begin to see a holistic development of intellectual, moral, and character formation take place. At the heart of this distinctive Christ-centered approach to education is the belief that God has revealed himself to us in creation, in history, in our conscience, and ultimately in Christ, and that this revelation is now primarily available to us in Holy Scripture. This revealed truth is the foundation of all we believe, teach, and do at Christian institutions. This framework enables students and faculty to interpret the world, the great ideas of the past, the issues of the present, the events of human history, as well as our responsibilities toward God and one another in this world. We pray that in doing so we will see a new generation of students, a new generation of online learners, who have been informed, formed, and transformed in the educational process, becoming thoughtful followers of the Lord Jesus Christ who love God with heart, soul, strength, and mind.

Faithful Christ-centered institutions of higher education are needed today as never before, and we certainly need institutions like Los Angeles Pacific University to help lead the way in the online space. We commend John Reynolds, Wayne Herman, Brant Himes, and John Washatka for their initiative and efforts related to this project. Let us pray that the essays found in this book will lead to the development of a new generation of engaged students who will become instruments for establishing a Christian presence in the world. May this timely book become a means for renewing hope and for renewing minds and hearts, as well as for extending God's kingdom in this world, even as we pray for all involved in the work of Christian higher education, especially in these new, developing, and expanding online contexts.[1]

---

1. I have benefitted from and drawn from the following sources: Cartwright et al., *Teaching the World*; Lowe and Lowe, *Ecologies of Faith*; Ferguson, *Excellence in Online Education*; Dockery, ed., *Faith and Learning*; Dockery, *Renewing Minds*; and Dockery and Morgan, eds., *Christian Higher Education*.

Acknowledgments

This book is an example of the power of collaboration (and of the consequences of running with ideas). The initial idea for the book emerged in December 2017, when Los Angeles Pacific University faculty gathered in San Dimas, California to participate in extended meetings that were held in conjunction with commencement ceremonies. During one of the meetings, John Washatka tossed out the idea that "we should write a book" about online learning. This led Scott Edgar, Wayne Herman, Brant Himes, and John to meet for breakfast before commencement at Flappy Jack's on Route 66 in Glendora for further brainstorming. After sketching out some ideas, the four agreed to meet monthly to continue the conversation.

"The Book Project," as it was dubbed, gained further momentum in April 2019 when Brant met with Michael Thomson, acquisitions editor at Wipf & Stock, at the Kuyper Conference and the Henry Symposium on Religion and Public Life at Calvin University, where they discussed the need for a book about faith formation and online education. The relevance and timeliness of the book were heightened even more with the onset of the coronavirus pandemic in the spring of 2020. With higher education institutions scrambling to migrate quickly to online learning, it was clear it was time to pull all of our ideas together and write the book.

The project would not have been possible without the support and assistance of many people. While we cannot list everyone individually, we are grateful for all the help and encouragement which helped to bring this idea to a reality. In particular, we want to thank a few groups of people whose help was critical to the success of the project. University president John Reynolds provided valuable resources and support and contributed the chapter on building a culture of collaboration. Scott Edgar and Wayne Herman provided foundational suggestions and ideas in the brainstorming stage of the project, and they each contributed chapters. In his role of chief academic officer, Wayne provided ongoing advocacy for the duration of the project. Wayne also deserves an honorary editor title for his feedback, edits, and comments as the manuscript was being produced.

The chapter contributors who provided the book content were invaluable, as were survey and interview participants consisting of LAPU faculty, staff, and students, and scholars and practitioners from other institutions. The book was edited to provide a consistency of tone and voice throughout, while striving to preserve the unique style and expertise of each individual author. We hope the finished product represents well both the ideas of each author and our overall collaborative efforts to share our passion and commitment to faith and learning. We also wish to thank Michael Thomson, Rodney Clapp (our editor at Cascade Books), and the capable team at Wipf & Stock. We know the book would not be in your hands or on your screen without their gracious guidance and work.

BRANT HIMES, *Bend, Oregon*
JOHN WASHATKA, *Mason, Ohio*

Contributors

CARRIE M. AKEMANN, Senior Success Coach at Los Angeles Pacific University.

SCOTT D. EDGAR, Adjunct Professor in Humanities at Los Angeles Pacific University.

WAYNE R. HERMAN, Vice President, Chief Academic Officer at Los Angeles Pacific University.

BRANT M. HIMES, Associate Professor in Humanities at Los Angeles Pacific University.

SHANNON N. HUNT, Assistant Professor in Psychology at Los Angeles Pacific University.

LISA D. PHILLIPS, Assistant Dean at Los Angeles Pacific University.

JOHN C. REYNOLDS, President of Los Angeles Pacific University.

JOHN W. WASHATKA, Associate Professor in Humanities at Los Angeles Pacific University.

Introduction

DISRUPTION

An international conversation is taking place about the increasing disruptions, challenges, and opportunities facing higher education. While there is a steady stream of books, articles, conferences, and blog posts about the shifting state of postsecondary education, David Staley and Dennis Trinkle captured many of the poignant issues in their 2011 article aptly titled, "The Changing Landscape of Higher Education."[1] The authors identified and described ten changes that were taking place at the time, using language like "disruptively" and "dramatic," and employing the metaphor of an earthquake by using terminology such as "seismic" and "tectonic." Even though the article was written over ten years ago, there appears to be no slowing of the changes nor a diminishing of their impact.

Three forces of disruption, one of which is identified by Staley and Trinkle, bear further attention. The first is the rise of what is now understood to be "post-traditional students" (what the authors described as "the changing 'traditional' student").[2] The term is explained in more detail in chapters 2 and 3 of this book, but generally refers to students with a profile that substantially differs from traditional students. Universities finding post-traditional students in their population are being forced to grapple not only with curricular issues (e.g., andragogy v. pedagogy), but with student support issues as well.

---

1. Staley and Trinkle, "The Changing Landscape of Higher Education," 16.
2. See also Soares, "Post-traditional Learners," 1–2.

The second disruptor is the trend of shifting enrollments, due in part to the circumstances of post-traditional students, whose responsibilities and commitments hinder them from enrolling at a traditional, campus-based institution. A brief analysis of enrollment data (both undergraduate and graduate) of Title IV institutions from 2012 to 2018 shows that while overall enrollment decreased by 7.1 percent, the number of students studying via distance education (those enrolled in any distance education courses) increased by 27.2 percent, and students enrolled in any distance education increased to a total of 35.3 percent of all enrollments.[3] Notably, these trends are before the COVID-19 pandemic, as Integrated Postsecondary Education Data System (IPEDS) data for the past two years is not yet available. However, the National Student Clearinghouse has produced a report showing that enrollment dropped by 2.5 percent from fall 2019 to fall 2020.[4] Other data for spring 2021 shows undergraduate enrollment is down 5.9 percent over the same time last year, but the exception to that decline was online institutions, which saw undergraduate enrollments increase by 2.2 percent.[5] What remains unclear, however, is how the pandemic specifically affected enrollment (correlation is not causation). Overall enrollments are trending away from traditional students attending college in a campus environment.

When it comes to Christian institutions specifically, overall enrollment in Christian higher education institutions (HEIs) declined by 0.4 percent (with undergraduate decreases offset by graduate increases) from roughly the same period (2013 to 2018). However, enrollments of students taking online classes (some or only) increased by 46.1 percent, fueled by a 71 percent increase of undergraduate students. Chapter 12 provides a broader context and more information regarding this data. Those institutions, faith-based or otherwise, that depend on enrollments generally, and traditional students specifically, are being forced to rethink enrollment strategies.

Christian HEIs may be particularly interested in the third disruptor: the rise of "post-Christian culture."[6] A post-Christian culture is the follow-up to a postmodern culture, and provides the predominant cultural and

---

3. National Center for Education Statistics (NCES), "Fast Facts"; and Ginder and Stearns, "Web Tables." The NCES reports are based on data from the Integrated Postsecondary Education Data System (IPEDS).

4. National Student Clearinghouse Research Center, "Current Term Enrollment Estimates." Note the explanation for the discrepancies in their numbers compared to IPEDS numbers on page 22.

5. Tableau Public Research Center, "Undergraduate Enrollment in Its Steepest Decline So Far Since the Pandemic Began." See also tab 7, Primarily Online Institutions, figure 15, of the same report.

6. Veith, *Post-Christian*.

worldview backdrop of today's students. Gene Veith sees a post-Christian culture as the result of a growing global pluralism generally relativistic in nature. The resulting post-Christian culture's regard for Christianity ranges anywhere from indifference to outright antagonism. Developing a learning environment that is supportive of post-traditional students also requires anticipating the worldview of enrolling students. The concept of worldview is developed and applied more fully in chapter 6.

All three disruptors—changing students, changing enrollments, and changing culture—are requiring administrators to develop new strategies in order to attract and support students. These disruptions have created obstacles when it comes to Christian HEIs fulfilling their missions to integrate faith, life, and learning, especially for those educators having a reluctance for anything other than a traditional, campus-based environment. However, those obstacles also created opportunities for universities willing to consider a paradigm shift when it comes to offering an education. The shift could be the result of philosophical considerations of how best to fulfill their mission, or it could be the result of the more practical considerations such as university survival. In any case, disruptions can be the stimuli for universities to consider how best to adapt in the face of these and other changes in higher education.

OPPORTUNITY

In this present disruptive context, *Faith, Life, and Learning Online* is an invitation for faith-based institutions to take bold steps toward integrating a holistic mission of spiritual formation into the online learning environment. For Christian higher education, faith integration is a matter of mission, not modality. Regardless of whether learning happens in the traditional classroom, through hybrid models, or exclusively online, Christian universities have a missional mandate to continue their long legacy of forming students of competence and character. While traditional campuses continue to provide unique and meaningful opportunities for students to grow in their faith, online learning has opened new avenues for engagement and development of spiritual formation. As such, Christian universities are now called to take advantage of this unique technological moment to continue to offer transformative opportunities for the holistic integration of faith, life, and learning in the online environment.

Los Angeles Pacific University (LAPU) has developed a holistic approach to faith, life, and learning that recognizes the artificiality of separating faith and spiritual formation from academic rigor, personal growth, and career preparedness. The very expression "faith, life, and learning" attempts to articulate and recognize the idea of development of the entire person by the entire community. Such holistic integration occurs in the context similar to what is described by Mary Lowe as "an ecological perspective of spiritual formation."[7] Lowe uses the metaphors of ecology and ecosystem to describe how the student's entire community (within and without the university) influences spiritual development. For Lowe, development of the entire person includes all aspects of formation, including "spiritual, social, and intellectual."[8] Holism, then, refers both to the development of the individual and the development of the community.

This book explores the challenges and realities of integrating and sustaining a commitment to faith formation in the online university. It offers an account of how one Christian HEI has addressed the challenge of integrating its worldview throughout the experience of its students and staff and reflects on topics related to the university's identity as evangelical Christian, the nature of its students, and the online environment. While the book focuses on one particular university, LAPU is used for illustrative purposes only, providing a framework that can be adapted to other institutions, even those that are primarily traditional.

Throughout, the book asks questions, offers ideas, and contributes to the conversations Christian HEIs have revolving around best practices of delivering a faith-based education in an online environment. Such conversations remain relevant due to institutions turning to online education as a means of extending their missions and remaining sustainable through adverse circumstances and disruptive forces. Adapting to and developing post-traditional education strategies—including effective development of faith, life, and learning—remains university dependent, guided by each institution's unique identity. An institution's identity provides a foundation for discerning solutions that best fit its particular context. As an illustration, chapter 5 explores how the identity of LAPU provides a foundation that enables it to thrive in a time of changing students, enrollments, and cultures.

This book, then, addresses some of the changes that are occurring within Christian higher education and provides ideas and guidance for institutions as they navigate through challenges they may face. It is designed to be another, hopefully helpful, voice in the ongoing conversation of how colleges, universities, and seminaries can engage with the disruptions and opportunities taking place within higher education. In this regard, the book is for administrators, faculty, course developers, and student support

---

7. Lowe, "Spiritual Formation," 58.
8. Lowe, "Spiritual Formation," 60.

personnel at Christian HEIs who are navigating philosophical and practical questions of integrating spiritual formation concepts and activities into online learning environments.

Specifically, administrators responsible for creating a structure for faith integration within the context of online delivery will find practical strategies for organizational collaboration. In addition, faculty will find resources for integrating holistic faith formation concepts and practices into their online courses, and they will be encouraged to leverage university-wide resources in the service of their students. Those responsible for developing material for faith integration will discover how cultivating university-wide partnerships is essential for creating a culture of holistic faith formation that extends beyond the boundaries of online courses. Indeed, the book recognizes that many individuals, including those serving in enrollment, advising, and marketing, play critical roles in institutional efforts of faith formation. Practically speaking, the book could be used as a guide for professional development opportunities for various groups and by individual faculty members working online. Finally, there are undoubtedly those readers who may be skeptical of the ability to provide an education that is both academically challenging and spiritually rich via an online modality. For them, this book can be viewed as another voice (perhaps somewhat of an apologetic) in the ongoing conversation of contemporary postsecondary, post-traditional education.

A WAY FORWARD

This book approaches faith, life, and learning as a holistic, university-wide endeavor. Rather than offering insights and tips for how individual faculty members can integrate faith into their online classrooms, the book describes a comprehensive effort across the university to infuse faith formation into all aspects of the learning experience for its students. The first section, Continuing the Legacy: Faith Formation for Online Christian Higher Education, sets the current state of online spiritual formation within the context and faith-formation tradition of Christian higher education. After a survey of current practices and insights from various universities (chapter 1), the focus turns to how LAPU is navigating its commitment to faith, life, and learning in an exclusively online learning environment (chapters 2 through 5). This part recognizes that the university is a participant in a wider movement across Christian higher education and attempts to locate the university within that movement.

The second section, Faith, Life, and Learning in the Curriculum, explores how faith formation concepts can be integrated into the online classroom, organized according to four themes: Christian worldview (chapter 6), God's story (chapter 7), diverse faith perspectives (chapter 8), and faith through academic disciplines (chapter 9). These chapters provide concrete examples of how concepts and practices of faith formation can be included in a variety of online courses.

The last section, Faith, Life, and Learning across the University, explores how faith formation is facilitated across the larger university community, outside the classroom. After describing a unique model for student support (chapter 10) and presenting a framework for incarnational practices and additional resources for faith formation (chapter 11), the book concludes (chapter 12) with a call for Christian universities to rely on their institutional identities, resources, and creativity to further develop their own commitment to holistic faith formation in their online learning endeavors.

The book describes three characteristics of Los Angeles Pacific University, the combination of which has resulted in a fairly seamless and holistic approach to faith, life, and learning. First, the university utilizes a shared governance model, rather than a faculty governance model. The model, described in chapter 3, facilitates communication and collaboration between various departments. Second, the university uses standardized curriculum throughout all its academic programs. The approach, described in chapters 2 and 3, enables a more consistent approach and feel students can expect, regardless of class. Lastly, the university uses a success coach model, described in chapter 10, that enables comprehensive support of the students. The integration of all three characteristics has provided a comprehensive implementation of faith, life, and learning at LAPU. Overall, the book describes how the entire university is involved in faith, life, and learning. It is not just an academic effort, nor does it belong only in the chaplain's office. Practices have been threaded throughout the university, and involve all of its employees.

Finally, what is clearly articulated throughout the book is the central role hope plays in the life of the university. Hope is a principal part of LAPU's identity, purpose, and mission. As a result, the university is committed not only to preparing individuals with skills and attitudes to thrive in their community and workplace, but also to pointing to something bigger than what can be found in an educational program—to the ultimate hope that is in Jesus Christ. Such a hope replaces the despair of hopelessness with a view of the future that has the redeeming work of Christ at its center and that is robust and life-giving—a hope that is foundational to a vibrant new life for all who embrace it.

PART 1

Continuing the Legacy

Faith Formation for Online Christian Higher Education

PART 1 *sets the current state of online spiritual formation within the context and faith-formation tradition of Christian higher education. After a survey of current practices and insights from various universities (chapter 1), the focus turns to how Los Angeles Pacific University is navigating its commitment to faith, life, and learning in an exclusively online learning environment (chapters 2 through 5).*

Chapter 1

The Current State of Online Spiritual Formation

SCOTT D. EDGAR

SCOTT EDGAR, *Adjunct Professor at Los Angeles Pacific University, explores the legacy of spiritual formation in Christian higher education, and argues that faith formation is a matter of institutional mission, not learning modality. His chapter addresses key questions surrounding the feasibility and efficacy of holistic faith formation in the online environment, such as: How can online learning facilitate spiritual formation? What are the challenges and opportunities? How can online and mobile learning modalities break down barriers for faith formation?*

Online learning is here to stay. Indeed, it appears that most every Christian higher education institution is launching online courses and programs. Whether central or peripheral to their institutional strategies, the opportunities for extending missional impact with online learning are rapidly expanding. As these efforts continue in earnest, Christian colleges, universities, and seminaries are working to create online programs that not only reflect a Christian worldview, but also intentionally facilitate spiritual formation among their students. Indeed, the concepts of Christian worldview and spiritual formation work together to provide the student with both a Christian perspective of the world and the capacity and motivation to live and function Christianly within it. These are not two separate, abstract concepts for students. Rather, the work of constructing a biblically informed Christian worldview provides the foundational knowledge for the process of spiritual formation. Since many readers are already deftly skilled in presenting a Christian worldview in the educational process, this chapter will explore the current state of online spiritual formation by focusing on the second concept—the desired outcomes and best practices for facilitating spiritual formation online, as proposed in the literature and modeled by several Christian universities.[1]

SPIRITUAL FORMATION IN ONLINE EDUCATION

The challenge of cultivating authentic, holistic spiritual formation is one of the most pressing concerns for Christian higher education online learning today. To tackle this issue and explore the efficacy and potential for how online learning can support spiritual formation, Stephen and Mary Lowe conducted a three-year study examining various aspects of online learning and spiritual formation. The conclusion: spiritual formation is unequivocally possible in online education. Their research demonstrates that virtual learning communities can be as effective in facilitating spiritual formation as physical, face-to-face learning communities commonly associated with traditional on-campus experiences.[2] The key ingredient is the cultivation of genuine networks and communities, what the Lowes describe as "ecologies of faith," in helping to provide an environment of learning and growth. Spiritual formation is less about modality (online or face-to-face) and more about creating communities that support the process of "whole person transformation into the fullness of Christ."[3] The Lowes demonstrated that

---

1. The concept of promoting "faith, life, and learning" at Los Angeles Pacific University will be explained and extrapolated at length throughout this book. Faith, life, and learning is in reality a synergy of integration of faith and learning (worldview formation) and the personal response to this truth (spiritual formation). Hence, in this chapter, LAPU's terminology of faith, life, and learning will be used interchangeably with the concept and practice of holistic spiritual formation. For an example of this view, see Plantinga, *Engaging God's World*.

2. Lowe and Lowe, "Absent in Body," 14–15.

3. This definition of spiritual formation comes from the Erskine Seminary National Consultation on Spiritual Formation in Theological Distance Education. See Lowe and Lowe, "Absent in Body," 15.

such whole-person transformation was just as possible in online learning communities as it was in on-campus environments.

For the Lowes, a holistic ecology of spiritual formation includes six developmental and interconnected dimensions of human development: moral, social, emotional, intellectual, physical, and spiritual.[4] Similarly, Diane Chandler proposes a model of whole-person formation that draws from the Genesis narrative of being created in the image of God. This model incorporates seven dimensions: spirit, emotions, relationships, intellect, vocation, physical health, and resource stewardship. Chandler sees this model as providing desired outcomes for the church, academy, and ministry.[5] Both Chandler and the Lowes offer models of spiritual formation that are necessarily connected to other areas of human development. Christian universities—committed as they are to whole-person development—should then also be promoting spiritual formation in a holistic manner. This means faith formation needs to be intentionally connected to a wide range of learning activities and academic disciplines and not limited to adding a specialized course in spiritual formation to the curricula. Spiritual formation, even in online education, includes desired outcomes connected to holistic human development that are much broader than traditionally understood in Christian education.

In addition to widening the scope of outcomes for spiritual formation in online education, Christian universities are broadening the environment in which formation takes place in order to move beyond the roles of faculty and the curriculum. Spiritual formation in Christian online education is not limited to the individual initiatives of faculty, administration, course developers, or student affairs alone. Rather, building an educational environment that facilitates spiritual formation involves university-wide partnerships.[6] Emerging from this understanding is the need for Christian institutions to increase their scope of influence with online students, creating a holistic environment to facilitate spiritual formation among students.[7] Current research and best practices show that Christian higher education institutions' efforts in this regard fall into four broad categories: (1) online learning communities, (2) engaging faculty presence, (3) educational partnerships, and (4) curricular components. Exploring these four areas provides insight and application for Christian higher education institutions seeking to promote learning environments conducive for holistic spiritual formation.

4. Lowe and Lowe, *Ecologies of Faith*, 17–18.
5. Chandler, "Whole-Person Formation."
6. Balzer and Reed, eds., *Building A Culture of Faith*, 3–20.
7. Edgar, "Toward an Ecosystem of Spiritual Formation," 3.

FACILITATING SPIRITUAL FORMATION IN ONLINE LEARNING

Online Learning Communities

Online learning communities provide a central structure for the cultivation of holistic faith formation in the online environment. While the concept of "online learning communities" is not new, Rena Palloff and Keith Pratt helped popularize the concept. Their foundational research and best practices for creating online learning communities sought to address concerns that online learners were isolated and lacked a critical learning dimension. Moving beyond the question of whether online learning communities were legitimate, they argued that such communities provided a critical setting for multidirectional connections, self-reflection, and engagement with fellow learners.[8] Indeed, Palloff and Pratt describe online learning communities as virtual spaces where learners "form new relationships," "acknowledge different ideas," and "acquire new knowledge." This multidirectional process results in new learning at both individual and group levels and is described as "transformational" in nature—connecting this process to Jack Mezirow's transformational learning theory.[9]

Similarly, the Lowes' research builds on their holistic understanding of spiritual formation and views online learning communities as creating a social context for spiritual formation—in reality, providing an "ecosystem" for spiritual formation.[10] The Lowes set forth a theological foundation for online learning communities as a legitimate and compelling context for biblical spiritual formation.[11] In addition, the research of Ronald Hannaford affirms and validates the effectiveness of online learning communities that are composed of members residing in diverse global contexts. As such, online learning communities offer promising opportunities for spiritual formation for student populations that are at a distance and are multicultural in composition.[12]

The research of Heidi Campbell offers additional confirmation that online learning communities can and do facilitate the process of spiritual formation. Her findings describe six positive components of online religious

---

8. Palloff and Pratt, *Building Online Learning Communities*, 129.

9. Palloff and Pratt, *Building Online Learning Communities*, 129. Mezirow's theory describes how transformational learning can take place as adults make meaning of the learning experience. See Mezirow, *Transformative Dimensions*.

10. Lowe and Lowe, *Ecologies of Faith*, 68–71.

11. Lowe and Lowe, *Ecologies of Faith*, 131–225.

12. Hannaford, "A Model of Online Education," 150–56.

THE CURRENT STATE OF ONLINE SPIRITUAL FORMATION   7

communities, including (1) the development of close relationships; (2) practicing mutual care and support; (3) the experience of being heard, validated, and accepted; (4) a safe place for transparency and accountability; (5) an environment that accelerates spiritual growth; and (6) the development of a shared understanding of Christian faith and practice.[13] Pam Vesely and colleagues then identify five common elements for successful online learning communities, including (1) a shared understanding of purpose, (2) a clear understanding of member roles and responsibilities, (3) mutually agreed upon group norms and behaviors, (4) mutual interaction between members, and (5) an environment of trust, respect, and support among group members.[14] As evident, learning communities are an important element in creating an online ecosystem for spiritual formation.

Extending the boundaries of the online ecosystem, Liberty University connects online students with the broader community through a university-wide online network called Yammer.[15] This network provides access to resources and personnel in the LU Shepherd office, creating opportunities for growth for online students well beyond those at the course or program level.[16] Although using social media would appear to be beset with potential challenges, such initiatives should be responsibly leveraged as possible tools to enlarge and strengthen the online community outside online courses.[17]

When it comes to best practices for spiritual formation in online learning communities, Mark Maddix is helpful. He describes best practices in four broad areas, and while these are important for any online learning community, they take on additional significance in the context of creating an environment to foster holistic faith formation. The first area of focus is to *develop clear guidelines for online discussions* by setting expectations for online communication, modeling effective communication as an instructor, and providing personalized and focused feedback.[18] Next, Maddix encourages instructors to *develop a supportive learning environment* by monitoring the tone, frequency, and quality of interaction in the forum, and intervening when necessary, to enforce netiquette and encourage balanced participation. A related area of focus in online communities is *to foster online presence and faculty involvement*, which includes being active in the forums, providing biographical information, and being intentional in making relational

13. Campbell, *Exploring Religious Community Online*, 181–86.
14. Vesely et al., "Key Elements in Building Online Communities," 3.
15. Liberty University, "Yammer."
16. Liberty University, "LU Shepherd."
17. Lowe and Lowe, *Ecologies of Faith*, 87–103.
18. Maddix, "Developing Online Learning Communities," 144–45.

connections with students. A fourth area essential in online learning communities is *to create learning activities that foster interaction and dialogue*, such as collaborative learning assignments, organizing learning teams, and contextualized assignments to encourage students to interact with others.[19] As Maddix maintains, faculty are embedded and embodied agents for spiritual formation—especially as they function in an online learning community.[20] This connection between online learning communities and faculty engagement provides a natural segue into the next element of facilitating spiritual formation in the online environment: faculty presence.

Engaging Faculty Presence

Faculty play a critical, mediating role in the cultivation of holistic faith formation in the online environment. In this regard, universities need to recruit faculty who demonstrate both subject matter expertise and a commitment to the holistic integration of their faith into the online classroom. After the hiring process, faculty should receive regular opportunities for professional development specifically related to the facilitation of spiritual formation among online learners. For example, Indiana Wesleyan University has a specific strategy for recruiting and training online faculty, including a mission-fit interview on issues related to spiritual formation and, upon hiring, a robust process for faculty development, supervision, and evaluation. New faculty receive training in online pedagogy and the integration of faith and learning, and are assigned a faculty mentor who guides, supervises, and evaluates them on a wide range of competencies, including modeling and facilitating spiritual formation.[21] Ongoing training opportunities include specific guidance in living and modeling a vibrant Christian walk for students.[22]

Once in the online classroom, faculty can employ six touchpoints to promote the holistic integration of faith, life, and learning. The first is *informal forums*, which are sometimes optional. Courses that better facilitate community, and subsequently spiritual formation, are those that include opportunities for students and faculty to introduce themselves by providing biographical information and answers to personal questions designed to help learners build relationships. This introductory forum is often called a cybercafe or community forum. During the first week of the course, an

---

19. Maddix, "Developing Online Learning Communities," 145–47.
20. Mark Maddix, interview by author, October 1, 2020.
21. Paul Garverick, interview by author, October 13, 2020.
22. Garverick, "Remaining Christ-Centered and Mission-Focused."

instructor can ask students to introduce themselves and share what they hope to learn. Responding to each introductory post helps to establish a relationship and can open doors to further connections and conversations. The community forum is also a place where instructors can share their own background and faith journeys, as they affirm the journey of others.[23] Throughout the term, the community forum can also be a place where students ask each other questions and share prayer requests.

A second touchpoint includes *posting weekly announcements*. A primary means that faculty can use to enhance learning, facilitate the integration of faith and learning, and promote spiritual formation is in the introduction of each week (module) of learning in their online courses. Many online instructors use this space to post video or written greetings, provide short summaries of the topics for discussion, and remind students of upcoming assignments. However, additional elements can include a brief introduction to the subject and a conceptual or topic map showing where the material fits into the course. Weekly announcements can be used to introduce students to relevant issues in the discipline (academic, worldview collision points, and life application), highlight key concepts, and point students to additional resources to facilitate more in-depth learning. This is also a place to share life experiences and biblical principles to promote understanding, worldview development, and spiritual formation. Note that authentic biblical integration related to spiritual formation requires more than just adding biblical references to online course materials or offering students prayer. Integration is best facilitated by practitioner faculty who have wrestled with the primary biblical integration and spiritual formation challenges related to their academic disciplines.[24]

A third touchpoint is *discussion forum participation by faculty*. There is no shortage of ideas and approaches when it comes to faculty participation in the discussion forum. There are different schools of thought on how faculty can facilitate discussions that enhance learning, affirm students' contributions, and keep conversations on track. One such method, Socratic questioning, can be very useful in facilitating biblical integration and spiritual formation in discussion forums. Online faculty can enhance student learning (both cognitive development and spiritual formation) by scaffolding the discussion process through the use of Socratic questions. To do this, when responding to a student discussion post, instructors can (1) *affirm* the student's answer (identify a positive insight), (2) *build* on the content in the post (enriching or adding insight from life experience), and (3) *extend*

---

23. Edgar, "Facilitating Spiritual Formation," 6.
24. Edgar, "Facilitating Spiritual Formation," 7–10.

the discussion by asking an additional question (at a higher level of learning or requiring personal reflection). In particular, the Socratic method's extending element is a most useful strategy to move a discussion focusing on an academic discipline toward one focusing on biblical integration and spiritual formation.[25]

A fourth touchpoint includes posting *discussion summaries* at the end of the week. Anyone teaching online can attest to the fact that discussion forums sometimes take on a life of their own. Even with carefully crafted forum questions and faculty participation during the week, online conversations may inadvertently veer off course. Discussion summaries help to bring focus and clarity back to the topic at hand. In addition to summarizing significant concepts related to the forum objectives, these posts can make additional connections or examples to illustrate the topic, clarify confusion and misinformation that surfaced in the forum, and provide final thoughts related to biblical integration and spiritual formation. In essence, the discussion summary offers a fitting conclusion to the topic first introduced in the weekly announcement and explored throughout the week.[26]

A fifth touchpoint is leveraging the area of grading and *providing feedback to promote spiritual formation*. In his article "The Ministry of ... Grading?" Richard Ramsey expands on the critical role of faculty in the grading process. Ramsey maintains that through grading Christian educators have a developmental mission in guiding students in holistic growth, a biblical call of evaluation, a mentoring ministry, a role in spiritual discernment, and an opportunity to help students exercise discernment in research. Ramsey identifies a litany of student benefits, educationally and spiritually, when faculty view grading as a formative ministry.[27] Although his work is not directed toward online teaching per se, those who teach from a distance should take advantage of this means of shaping students' lives not only academically but spiritually as well. The seemingly mundane activity of grading can certainly be an opportunity for faculty to impact students' lives.

A sixth touchpoint, and often the most rewarding in the online environment, is having *crucial conversations with students*. To set the tone, faculty can post an announcement during the course inviting students to connect one-on-one by phone or video call. Typically, at least a few students will take advantage of the opportunity to chat about learning and life, and such conversations can lead to lasting mentoring relationships. These conversations are often the highlight of the teaching session.

25. Edgar, "Online Discipleship," 13–15.
26. Edgar, "Facilitating Spiritual Formation," 7–10.
27. Ramsey, "Ministry of ... Grading?," 409, 415.

Finally, online faculty should leverage teachable moments that arise while teaching their courses. Such moments can be positive or negative. Even talking and praying with a student who has failed the class can prove to be transformative. The learning opportunities are everywhere, and students and faculty alike can be uplifted and can make new connections to their faith through genuine, caring conversations.[28] Indeed, it is evident that faculty are essential workers of spiritual formation. As Aliel Cunningham proposes, online learning should take advantage of every method and means for spiritually vibrant faculty to express an authentic Christian presence with students and move them on in their faith journey.[29]

Educational Partnerships

In *Building a Culture of Faith*, Cary Balzer and Rod Reed describe how university-wide partnerships can be formed to facilitate spiritual formation.[30] Although an abundance of literature is available on the issue of student development and spiritual formation, this work sets forth a holistic approach by demonstrating specifically how university-wide partnerships can create an institutional environment for fostering the spiritual formation of students. The book provides a rich collection of contributions written by practitioners in the field, explaining how university presidents, faculty, and student development personnel can work together, leveraging their unique roles and opportunities to promote a healthy ecology for spiritual formation in their universities. The volume presents a unified philosophy and a team-centered approach to student spiritual formation. The work advances a conceptual framework for understanding how spiritual formation can be facilitated in a Christian university and provides practical models for strengthening the role of faculty and others in the process. For example, Balzer and Reed argue that faculty and student development professionals should make the spiritual formation of students a priority by intentionally integrating and infusing spiritual formation into their academic curricula and leveraging faith mentoring opportunities and conversations with students. The authors also describe the importance of service learning, internships, and cross-cultural experiences in student spiritual formation.[31] Indeed, educational programs for online learners should be intentional in

---

28. Edgar, "Facilitating Spiritual Formation," 23.
29. Cunningham, "Envisioning Christian Presence and Practice."
30. Balzer and Reed, eds., *Building A Culture of Faith*, 141–86.
31. Edgar, Review of *Building a Culture of Faith*.

helping students connect to their local contexts—yet another environmental factor for learning and spiritual formation.

In terms of Christian universities with online programs, the use of students' local contexts can be a powerful factor in facilitating learning in general and spiritual formation in particular, especially if students are connected to mentors and supervisors who demonstrate a vibrant spirituality. Online students in professional programs can also benefit from mentors who know them personally and in their local contexts. Mark Maddix and James Estep describe such a structure in how mentors are selected for graduate students in the spiritual formation program at Northwest Nazarene University. Such mentors have a strategic role in supporting students in their programs by providing timely wisdom, modeling authentic spirituality, and challenging learners to progress in their spiritual formation.[32] In addition, writing from the perspective of online theological education, John Cartwright and colleagues acknowledge that online programs for ministry have the advantage of convenience, flexible work schedules, and allowing students to pursue their training without uprooting their families. In theory, online students' local context would appear to provide an ideal context for what they are learning in their online studies. The question, however, is whether educational institutions are adequately leveraging this context for their students enrolled in online programs.[33]

Christian higher education institutions can also dedicate chaplain and advising resources to support holistic faith development. For example, Indiana Wesleyan University provides care and promotes spiritual formation for online students through a network that includes part-time regional chaplains and a full-time online chaplain. Operating out of the department of Spirit Care, the university extends its reach to minister to online students in times of crisis (face-to-face when possible) and on a regular basis through pastoral care and the provision of resources to facilitate spiritual formation.[34]

A distinctive feature of Los Angeles Pacific University (LAPU) is the success coach ministry—a team of individuals who focus on student success and spiritual formation. All students are paired with a success coach who offers encouragement and guidance and serves as an advisor on learning techniques, financial aid, academic progress, course selection, career guidance, motivation, strengths counseling, and spiritual development. This partnership ensures personal support and promotes success of learning in a

---

32. Maddix and Estep, "Spiritual Formation," 431.
33. Cartwright et al., *Teaching the World*, 133–36.
34. Bob Burchell, interview by author, October 13, 2020.

virtual community.[35] Although success coaches could be seen as merely one element in an online learning community, the reality is they focus on intervention, problem-solving, and providing timely assistance (both academic and spiritual) when a student is in need.

As is evident, educational institutions can use various approaches to support student learning and spiritual formation, intervening at strategic moments to help learners advance in their personal development and spiritual formation. Notably, such approaches often—and as a best practice—utilize a collaborative approach by coordinating and resourcing key stakeholders and facilitating university-wide partnerships.

Curricular Components

Over the past decade and a half, there have been significant contributions related to spiritual formation in Christian higher education. Most of the research has focused on worldview formation and the integration of faith and learning. For example, Robert Harris's *The Integration of Faith and Learning: A Worldview Approach* provides philosophical and practical resources for connecting one's Christian faith with academic learning.[36] In addition, Roger Lundin's edited volume, *Christ Across the Disciplines: Past, Present, and Future*, has guided a generation of Christian educators in exploring the relationship between faith and the life of the mind.[37] *Faith and Learning: A Handbook for Christian Higher Education*, edited by David Dockery, has also proved to be a resource rich in theological insight and practical application.[38] More recently, James K. A. Smith's *Desiring the Kingdom: Worship, Worldview, and Cultural Formation* has moved the conversation closer to the concept of "faith, life, and learning" that is thoroughly explored throughout this book. This concept comes into focus through two lenses: the integration of faith and learning (worldview formation) and the personal response to this truth (spiritual formation).[39] These contributions are now finding more serious consideration and application within the sphere of Christian online education.

As was mentioned earlier, Balzer and Reed's edited volume argues that Christian universities should seek to infuse spiritual formation throughout their curricula, both at the content and process levels. Within this volume,

35. Los Angeles Pacific University, "Student Support Services."
36. Harris, *The Integration of Faith and Learning.*
37. Lundin, ed., *Christ across the Disciplines.*
38. Dockery, ed., *Faith and Learning.*
39. Smith, *Desiring the Kingdom.*

James Wilhoit and colleagues contribute a chapter entitled, "Soul Projects: Class-Related Spiritual Practices in Higher Education." The chapter presents a wide variety of class-tested ideas for facilitating spiritual formation with students. Although the methods have successfully been used in a traditional class setting, they can certainly be modified and implemented in online learning settings.[40]

Focusing more specifically on practices that foster spiritual formation, Adele Calhoun sets forth specific spiritual practices that can be incorporated in online courses. These practices are broader than those traditionally understood as spiritual disciplines, and could be used with students who would not necessarily consider themselves Christian or religious.[41] Point Loma Nazarene University (PLNU) encourages faculty to incorporate these spiritual practices into their courses as learning experiences and/or assignments. Specific examples of faculty incorporating spiritual practices into courses can be found at the PLNU Center for Teaching and Learning.[42]

In addition, institutions can strengthen the educational synergy between what is learned in the online classroom and a student's local context. Liberty University, for example, revised certain courses in its divinity school programs. Their new emphasis on content (biblical) to context (local) is intended to bridge student learning with experiences, mentors, and opportunities for further learning in their own contexts.[43] For its part, LAPU has adopted the expression "faith, life, and learning" in recognition that spiritual formation and development is holistic—that is, it involves the entire person and the entire community. It is not merely cognitive or affective, or only for students; rather, it engages the entire person and the entire university for the whole of life. As such, in addition to the use of elements that facilitate spiritual formation within the parameters of online courses (i.e., curricula, faculty, etc.), the university's goal is to create spaces for the entire community to speak into the holistic development of faith, life, and learning using tools like a website and mobile app, and by facilitating connections between faculty, staff, and students.

More broadly, since faculty teaching in online programs typically operate within a set curriculum defined both in content and teaching methodology, the processes of course design and delivery are critical for incorporating a holistic approach to faith formation. As a start, the work of Joanne Jung is helpful in providing conceptual and practical guidance for designing

---

    40. Wilhoit et al., "Soul Projects."
    41. Calhoun, *Spiritual Disciplines Handbook*, 13–26.
    42. Point Loma Nazarene University, "Christian Practice."
    43. Mary Lowe, interview by author, December 11, 2020.

courses and utilizing online methodologies that foster spiritual formation in the online classroom.[44] Toward this end, Indiana Wesleyan University has since 2007 revised online curriculum at least five times, attempting to implement new designs and practices to better facilitate spiritual formation in their curricula.[45] Designing courses that include objectives related to the integration of faith and learning and spiritual formation necessitates that assignments include rubrics that measure and evaluate student work in these areas.[46] Although many Christian universities have taken steps to assess assignments in the area of faith integration, the concepts set forth by Jung should challenge them to develop processes that measure and evaluate spiritual formation even though it is often more subjective.[47] In addition to assessment at course levels, effective assessment of these desired outcomes includes assessment at the program and university levels. Chapter 4 explores specific strategies and considerations for assessing faith formation in the online learning environment.

Finally, there are also specific tools that can aid institutional efforts at exploring and better understanding the spiritual growth of students. Kendra Bailey and colleagues of Biola's Rosemead School of Psychology conducted research using the Relational Spirituality Interview in order to explore numerous domains of spiritual experience from a relational spirituality perspective.[48] Additional research conducted in partnership with the Council of Christian Colleges & Universities (CCCU) led to the Spiritual Transformation Inventory, an assessment tool to help institutions strengthen their spiritual formation programs.[49] The inventory may prove valuable when conducted as a pretest and posttest to measure online programs' effectiveness in facilitating spiritual formation. The Duke University Religion Index (DUREL) is another instrument that can be useful in assessing spiritual formation. This assessment is a five-item measure of religious involvement, and was developed for use in large cross-sectional and longitudinal observational studies. Point Loma Nazarene University uses this instrument with students in their first two years at the university and has found it helpful in measuring more broadly spiritual formation among students who may lack

---

44. Jung, *Character Formation*, 25–62.
45. Paul Garverick, interview by author, October 13, 2020.
46. Maddix et al., *Best Practices of Online Education*, 155–81.
47. Jung, *Character Formation*, 113–27.
48. Bailey et al., "Spirituality at a Crossroads."
49. Spiritual Transformation Inventory.

an understanding of the terminology and practices of faith that are associated with the Spiritual Transformation Inventory.[50]

CHALLENGES AND OPPORTUNITIES: FROM SURVIVING TO THRIVING

Enlarging the Ecosystem

For the past decade, many Christian higher education institutions have viewed online learning programs as an essential supplement to increase revenue streams to support their primary work on the traditional campus. Online programs are seen as necessary, albeit not a priority. Despite an investment in technology and course development resources, most online programs are not allocated comparable resources and are but a bare-bones version of their on-campus siblings. Online programs lack the many amenities that contribute to a holistic learning environment on campus. This reality was first identified over a decade ago by James Watson, who noted that Christian universities were not incorporating in their programs for online students "intentional ethos enablers" that have long been considered best practices in traditional, on-campus programs.[51] Unfortunately, many schools have not taken tangible steps to correct this reality first called out by Watson.

During the time of unprecedented change brought on by the coronavirus pandemic in 2020, many universities have tried to survive by relying on minimally innovative online programs until they can return to business as usual, with the main focus on the traditional campus. However, others are likely to take advantage of this season of disruption to embrace online learning as a viable educational reality for the future and a modality that can be strategically used to fulfill their institutional missions—even in spiritual formation. Toward this latter option, colleges, universities, and seminaries will need not only to implement ideas presented in this chapter and book, but will need to take bold and costly steps to enlarge their ecosystem for online programs.

Toward this end, LAPU is now offering virtual chapel services three times throughout an eight-week session. This venue for interacting and

---

50. Mark Maddix, interview by author, October 1, 2020.

51. Watson, "Inclusion of Ethos Enablers." The author identifies core ethos enablers including: (1) provision of a faculty that is available to counsel with and model Christian living for students; (2) maintenance of a student services cadre; (3) coordination of a program to facilitate and regulate chapel/worship attendance; (4) oversight of and coordination of ministry formation/field experiences; (5) employment of admissions personnel; and (6) supervision of the implementation of community life standards.

sharing the university's life with online students enlarges the ecosystem to promote spiritual formation. As another example, Fuller Theological Seminary has launched Formation Groups. Offered initially in a face-to-face context, the groups were embedded within MA and MDiv programs and focused on vocational calling and spiritual formation. Currently, formation groups are facilitated virtually and are intentional in helping students engage in their local contexts around the world. Formation groups are asynchronous in nature with optional face-to-face meetings. In addition to weekly assignments and exercises, participants receive personal mentoring from seasoned leaders.[52] On a broader scale, such groups could be offered to online students virtually and/or even face-to-face where there is a significant population of localized students. Formation groups could be offered for credit or simply be an extension of an institution's mission.

Enlarging the ecosystem for spiritual formation may include adding new elements to engage students. These may consist of virtual chapel services, a chaplain, spiritual formation groups, optional workshops and conferences, local and virtual meet-ups, programs with optional face-to-face components (hybrid), and a proprietary social media network for university faculty, staff, students, and alumni. If Christian universities view online programs as legitimate means of fulfilling their institutional missions, they must take tangible steps to enlarge the educational ecosystem.

Extending the Growing Season

In addition to enlarging the ecosystem for spiritual formation, Christian higher education institutions should take steps to stay connected with and cultivate ongoing relationships with graduates. Informing this idea is a wealth of research on lifelong learning. Richard Edwards and Robin Usher convincingly argue that lifelong learning is a postmodern condition of education, in that it acknowledges the limits of traditional knowledge, emphasizes knowledge production, decentralizes learning, and maintains that learning must be flexible in responding to the needs of an ever-changing world.[53] Furthermore, they argue that the goal of lifelong learning is not content mastery, but preferably using skills for learning throughout the life span.[54] Elaborating on this point, Peter Jarvis defines formal education as initial education—reiterating the mantra that formal education is

52. Amy Drennan, interview by author, November 3, 2020.
53. Edwards and Usher, "Lifelong Learning." The authors maintain content mastery is no longer the goal of education, but rather skills in utilizing the process of education.
54. Edwards and Usher, "Lifelong Learning."

insufficient to prepare members of technologically advanced societies for life.[55] Linda Cannell, commenting on theological education, then maintains that seminaries have not taken seriously the role of lifelong learning in ministry preparation. Cannell argues that Christian education should embrace lifelong learning because it reflects biblical values of continued growth and transformation.[56]

Programmatically, educational institutions can facilitate lifelong learning by offering postgraduate seminars and continuing education. They can also assist graduates in establishing learning networks, keeping them current on issues related to faith and their professions, while equipping graduates with additional competencies for self-directed learning. In short, educational institutions can provide both internal (motivational) and external (structural) resources in facilitating opportunities for lifelong learning.

Indeed, according to Yukiko Inouye and colleagues, online education has now evolved from a marginal form of learning to a commonly accepted and increasingly popular means of providing lifelong learning opportunities to a wide range of learners.[57] Extending the growing season will require an investment in energy and resources. This investment will produce spiritual results. However, it will also produce results in creating a pipeline for student enrollment, additional streams of revenue for continuing education, and an active network for student internships and employment. With this in mind, LAPU is directing resources toward educational offerings that reach beyond the traditional parameters of degree programs to include opportunities for professional development (micro-credentials) and continuing education.

Mobile and Micro-Learning: Breaking Down Barriers for Faith Formation

Currently, LAPU is launching a new initiative designed to extend access to its programs and pioneer new methods of learning. Spearheaded by George Hanshaw, Director of eLearning Operations at LAPU, the university is working to provide all courses and communication in mobile-first format, thus reaching students who may not have access to a laptop or desktop computer.[58] In addition to access and financial advantages for students, mobile learning will expand and extend the classroom by reaching students in their own learning environments, 24/7. This can enhance a sense

---

55. Jarvis, *Adult Education*, 39–40.
56. Cannell, *Theological Education Matters*, 302–5.
57. Inoue, ed., *Online Education*, 7–9.
58. George Hanshaw, interview by author, September 23, 2020.

of connectedness between students and faculty and foster the development of relationships critical for the online learning community. In many ways, this initiative will enlarge the ecosystem of learning and spiritual formation discussed earlier in this chapter.[59]

A commitment to mobile learning also provides the opportunity to incorporate new instructional methodologies—such as micro-learning—into the online classroom.[60] Built on the research of just-in-time learning, micro-learning presents content in smaller pieces, allowing students more time to reflect on topics and respond throughout the online week. An implication of this approach, for example, would be courses that include four or five smaller discussion forums available throughout the week.[61] This is in contrast to the common practice of interacting in a single, lengthier forum that students complete after significant preparation and when they have access to their computers. As evident, mobile learning provides a more consistent learning community for students and enhances learning. The implications for spiritual formation are conspicuous!

CONCLUSION

This chapter highlighted the current research and best practices that Christian universities are using to facilitate spiritual formation in their online programs. Research and practices fall, for the most part, into four broad categories: (1) online learning communities, (2) engaging faculty presence, (3) educational partnerships, and (4) curricular components. Moving beyond this survey of the research and best practices, the chapter explored opportunities for enlarging the ecosystem in which spiritual formation can take place by extending the growing season for spiritual formation toward lifelong learning. The chapter makes clear that all Christian higher education institutions can take concrete, bold steps toward further supporting their missions of faith formation in the online context. By way of example, the next chapter provides a closer look at the holistic approach to faith, life, and learning for online students at Los Angeles Pacific University.

---

59. Wang et al., "Efficacy of Microlearning."
60. Jahnke et al., "Unpacking Design Principles."
61. Hanshaw and Hanson, "Using Microlearning."

Chapter 2

A Holistic Approach to Christian Faith, Life, and Learning

BRANT M. HIMES

BRANT HIMES, *Associate Professor at Los Angeles Pacific University, describes how the university carries out its institutional mission as it relates to faith formation. The chapter addresses several key questions that relate to LAPU's Statement of Faith, Life, and Learning: How are institutional commitments to faith formation connected to concrete practices? What is unique about a "holistic approach to faith, life, and learning" versus more traditional language and practices of "faith integration"? How does the course development process facilitate a commitment to holistic spiritual formation?*

Certainly, a hallmark of Christian higher education is a commitment to helping form Christ-centered character among students. This vision is not unique to Los Angeles Pacific University (LAPU). As chapter 1 illustrated, holistic faith formation is indeed a unifying goal and commitment across all institutions of Christian higher education. While this commitment is broad, each institution's strategy and methods for attaining the goal are different and attuned to their various contexts and theological traditions.

LAPU is no different. It is a Wesleyan school in the Free Methodist tradition, broadly evangelical, and committed to the transformative truth of the life, death, and resurrection of Jesus Christ. Where it is unique in comparison to most other Christian institutions is its 100 percent online modality. Imagine: no weekly chapel gatherings, no dorm hall Bible studies, no service clubs, and no worship nights. By its online nature, LAPU lacks the traditional infrastructure to facilitate so many of the tried-and-true Christian formation practices that are prevalent and celebrated on Christian campuses across North America and the world.

In addition, the make-up of LAPU's student body falls outside the mainstream eighteen- to twenty-three-year-old demographic of traditional campuses.[1] Its post-traditional students are likely in their thirties, working full time, raising a family—perhaps as a single parent—and many are first-generation collegiates. Chapel service at ten in the morning on Tuesdays and Thursdays is simply not an option for these students, online or not.

And yet, as a Christian school, LAPU is committed to the spiritual formation and growth of its students. Being online cannot be an excuse to abdicate this responsibility. Being online also cannot be an excuse to sprinkle some Bible verses throughout the curriculum and say that is sufficient for doing Christian formation. If a school is going to do this, it has to go all in. This means its approach must be holistic. It must be holistic in what it teaches students about faith—that it connects to all of life; and it must be holistic in how everyone at the university takes responsibility for the care and formation of students. A phone call with the financial aid office can be an opportunity for spiritual engagement and formation just as an assignment exegeting a Bible passage can. Since the touchpoints with online students are less organic than at a typical campus, they must be that much more deliberate and intentional.

As such, this chapter explores how LAPU's Statement of Faith, Life, and Learning guides the work of holistic faith formation across the entire university. With a shared understanding and commitment to faith, life, and learning, the university collaborates across departments, courses, and

---

1. The National Center for Education Statistics uses seven characteristics to describe nontraditional students, one of which is financial independence. In a footnote, they explain, "Independent students are age 24 or over and students under 24 who are married, have dependents, are veterans or on active duty, are orphans or wards of the courts, are homeless or at risk of homelessness, or were determined to be independent by a financial aid officer using professional judgment. Other undergraduates under age 24 are considered to be dependent." For our purposes, dependent students under age twenty-four are considered traditional while independent students age twenty-four and older are considered post-traditional. See Radford et al., "Demographic and Enrollment Characteristics," 7.

programs in an effort to help students realize the ultimate hope of Jesus Christ in their lives. The statement provides a grounding and a blueprint for how the university engages both curricular and extracurricular efforts for cultivating Christian life and faith:

> Los Angeles Pacific University (LAPU) teaches and serves from a Christian worldview through a holistic understanding and practice of promoting faith, life, and learning. We believe the entire LAPU community is called to contribute to cultivating hope through learning and we accomplish this through our core values of being Exemplary, Caring, and focused on Learning. We are committed to preparing individuals not only with the skills and attitudes to thrive in their community and workplace, but also to point the way to something bigger—to the ultimate hope that is in Jesus Christ.
>
> As it relates to students, LAPU conceives the promotion of faith, life, and learning as engaging students in learning (through curriculum design, instruction, and student support) that reflects the Christian worldview of LAPU and culminates in the realization of hope in our students. As a result of this process, through their interactions and study at LAPU, our students will be able to:
> - apply a Christian worldview to their life and work in the world;
> - articulate how and in what ways their life journeys connect to God's story;
> - engage with diverse faith perspectives within the learning community at LAPU; and,
> - recognize God's work in the world through all academic disciplines.[2]

If the university wants students to be able to do these things—apply a Christian worldview, articulate how God's story in the Bible connects to their life, engage with diverse faith perspectives, and recognize God's work through all academic disciplines—then it has to be very intentional about designing specific opportunities for learning and engagement. In order to design and guide the learning, the university also has to be clear about what it means by each of the four points in the statement.

---

2. Los Angeles Pacific University, "Commitment to Faith, Life, and Learning."

1. APPLY A CHRISTIAN WORLDVIEW TO THEIR LIFE AND WORK IN THE WORLD

The world is a complex place with many competing ideas, practices, and philosophies. As it always has been, college is an ideal time to wrestle with diverse ideas in order to discover and synthesize one's own beliefs and commitments. Like other Christian universities, LAPU teaches from a distinct Christian worldview perspective. LAPU relies on its Wesleyan and evangelical heritage to guide students through the building blocks of the faith and to challenge them to assess their own beliefs and assumptions about their place in the world. This can be an interesting and exciting journey because LAPU students come from a wide variety of backgrounds, ages, and experiences.

Indeed, it is this question of *who* the students are that drives so much of the learning design and engagement. In any given class, there may be an eighteen-year-old who just graduated from a Christian high school; a thirty-four-year-old single mom who is working full time, grew up Catholic, and hasn't been to Mass in ten years; a forty-two-year-old dad who is a cultural Muslim; and a sixty-year-old grandmother who has led Bible studies in her church for thirty years and wants to set an example for her grandkids to earn a college degree. In such a diverse environment, helping students to articulate a Christian worldview and then apply it to their life and work in the world is not an easy task.

First, the university cannot assume that each of its students is a Christian. While unapologetically a Christian school, LAPU does not require students to sign a statement of faith (employees do sign a statement of faith). Because of this open admissions policy, students from all sorts of religious backgrounds enroll. While some open admissions schools are divested of overt religious instruction so as not to exclude or offend, LAPU sees an opportunity to present a distinct Christian worldview perspective and then ask students to engage with this perspective, whether they fully agree with it or not. In this sense, the university has to be clear in what it means by "Christian worldview," and then it has to provide the context for sincere reflection and engagement.

In other words, in order for a commitment to faith, life, and learning to thrive in its context, LAPU has to provide robust learning around foundational Christian worldview concepts and it has to make space for students to engage this learning on their own terms. The university expects every student to be able to apply a Christian worldview to their life and work in the world, whether they are Catholic, Protestant, Muslim, agnostic, or anything else. Even the non-Christian should be able to talk about the distinctives of a Christian worldview and show how such a perspective could connect to their own unique life and situation. This means LAPU has to be open about who it is as a university and it has to be open about who its students are—and then create generous spaces for learning, dialogue, and application.

Second, LAPU makes sure its content is relevant by continuously asking students to connect their learning to their own experiences. When relevant content connects to relevant experiences, transformation can take place. So, for example, when talking about moral decision-making from a Christian worldview perspective, the university presents distinct Christian ethical frameworks and then asks students to apply this framework with examples from their own life and work experiences.

Admittedly, this focus on application is not novel; it is just good pedagogy (or, in the post-traditional context, good andragogy). But the larger point is that those in the online environment have to be very intentional about leading students through this process of learning and application. It cannot be assumed these things will happen organically. Rather, course design and student interactions are intentional with these very specific outcomes in mind.

Chapter 6 takes a deeper look at how Christian worldview is integrated into the curriculum across LAPU.

2. ARTICULATE HOW AND IN WHAT WAYS THEIR JOURNEY CONNECTS TO GOD'S STORY

The second faith, life, and learning goal at LAPU is to help each and every student to articulate how their life journey connects with God's story. The university believes an important part of the LAPU experience is giving students a lens to see how God's work in the Bible has continued through history to impact the world around them in profound ways. This means students encounter the key narrative of creation, fall, and redemption as they study the Bible. As before, students are challenged to apply the continuation of this narrative to their lives and in the world.

A focus on the biblical narrative makes explicit LAPU's commitment to its theological and evangelical heritage. It also helps establish a baseline for all students to enter in and engage with a shared narrative and theme. With students coming from such a wide range of religious experience and commitments, it is critical to introduce the Bible in a way that invites everyone into its wondrous story. By adopting the language of "God's story," the university can use similar and agreed-upon language throughout the curriculum and even in student services. In this way, the biblical foundations set in the two required Bible courses are continuously reinforced in other

A HOLISTIC APPROACH TO CHRISTIAN FAITH, LIFE, AND LEARNING

classes and in interactions with faculty and staff across the university. This means the shared narrative must also permeate faculty and staff training and interactions. So, for example, staff members may be invited to open a meeting by sharing about how their story connects to God's story. This simple exercise not only fosters trust and relationships among faculty and staff, it also continues the thread of the biblical narrative from classes and into university operations. In other words, the entire community is on this learning journey—students, faculty, and staff together.

LAPU's shared narrative goes something like this:[3] In the Bible, Genesis 1 and 2 describe God's good creation: sea, stars, land, plants, animals, and more are all made by a creative God and display his glory. Creation then culminates with humans, made in the very image of God. God placed them in the world to cultivate and create, to care for, and to help God's world thrive. But then, in Genesis 3, paradise is lost; humans—in their pride, wanting to be like God—chose to rebel by going against God's instructions not to eat from the tree of the knowledge of good and evil. This breaks the intimate relationship and oneness that humans had with God. They are kicked out of the garden; the tree of life is now out of reach, protected by angelic swirling swords. The consequences of sin permeate all aspects of life: the ground is hard, relationships suffer, and pain disrupts even the most fundamental of human endeavors. Yet there is a promise even now: the serpent who instigated the humans' rebellion will one day be crushed, even as it strikes at the heel of the Savior.[4]

The rest of the Bible, from Genesis 4 through Revelation, tells the story of God's great efforts toward the redemption and restoration of humankind and the rest of creation. Exodus and Deuteronomy, for example, recount how God rescues his people from Egypt under the leadership of Moses, Aaron, and Miriam. God implores his people to follow him in faith and obedience, as he establishes the Ten Commandments through Moses, and leads them to the promised land. Yet, even in their rescuing and redemption, God's people continue to rebel and forget about God's goodness and faithfulness.[5]

Then, in the New Testament, the story dramatically changes. Here, the Gospels introduce the most consequential person in history: Jesus of Nazareth. Luke, for example, describes how Jesus came to heal, set captives free, and proclaim the good news that God's kingdom has arrived, on earth

---

3. The following reflection is part of LAPU's Faith, Life, and Learning resource web page shared with all students and staff. See Himes, "Connecting Our Story to God's Story."

4. See Bonhoeffer, *Creation and Fall*, 141–44.

5. See Bartholomew and Goheen, *Drama of Scripture*, 39–43.

as it is in heaven. Jesus himself comes as the Son of God, fully human and fully divine. The Old Testament time and again recounts how the human propensity toward sin and rebellion continued to keep people out of close relationship with God. In the New Testament, God himself comes through Jesus as a bridge to connect to humanity. The oneness that was broken in Genesis 3 could now be restored in the person and work of Jesus.[6]

Jesus changed everything. He saw the suffering, pain, sin, and confusion of the people; and he reached out and healed, spoke truth into their lives, and forgave them for their sins. His radical love turned the world upside down. The lowly were raised up; the mighty were sent to the back of the line. Jesus disrupted the religious culture so much that he was killed, hung on a cross to die.[7]

But that old rugged cross—that tree of life that had been protected by angelic swirling swords since humans left the garden—would usher in new life for the world. Jesus died and was buried; but three days later he appeared to his friends and followers, very much alive. Jesus' death on the cross had been defeated through his resurrection. The reality of the world changed; death no longer had the final say—it had lost its sting.

The book of Acts then describes how Jesus' friends and followers started to share and spread this good news of Jesus through the power of the Spirit of God. After Jesus ascended into heaven, the Holy Spirit became manifest among those early believers. The Spirit empowered them to speak, travel, and share the news of Jesus' life, death, and resurrection with all who would listen. First, their message reached only the ears of the Jews; but soon the Spirit led the disciples to the Gentiles, as well. God's good news continued to spread, changing lives.

People began to see hope for their lives and for the world. Because of Jesus' power over death, and his ministry of healing and redemption, people from all walks of life realized they could live differently. They could live life with an orientation toward hope, redemption, and reconciliation. Just as God reconciled himself to the world through Jesus, those who follow Jesus could be reconciled with others. Oneness can be restored.

While lives can now be oriented toward hope, the world is still suffering under the effects of sin. Jesus conquered the grave, but the final abolition of sin must wait until Jesus comes one last time, to usher in God's ultimate kingdom.

So, Christians live in a world between the already and the not-yet. Already, Jesus has redeemed and he invites his followers to live lives fully

---

6. See McKnight, *Blue Parakeet*, 66–79.
7. See González, *Story Luke Tells*, 29–44.

devoted to him. When Christians recognize this redemption for their own lives, they can participate in the continuing work of redemption that God is doing in every corner of society. But the world is not yet restored. Sin still wreaks havoc, ruining lives, spoiling the creation, and mocking the hope of Jesus. God's grace works tirelessly to restrain the full effects of sin, allowing his people to experience beautiful glimpses of God's kingdom on earth; but not until Jesus returns one more time will the serpent's head ultimately be crushed.

Until that time, followers of Jesus are on a mission to proclaim the good news of Jesus and to live lives that are fully devoted to ushering in the goodness and graciousness of God in all the world. In other words, followers of Jesus are invited into the story of redemption and hope.

For LAPU, this means the university community is always seeking to engage the power of the gospel in the world around it. The community members ask each other: Where will you shine a light on God's redemptive grace in the world? How will you live a life of hope? How will your faith make a difference in your family, among your friends, and toward your neighbors? The university navigates these questions all together—as students, staff, faculty, and administration—in their classes, through conversations, and in their daily interactions with each other. They can then piece together their disparate experiences of faith, and thread connections to God's work in their lives and through their learning. Each person is part of God's redemptive story, and as a community, the university commits to discovering and living out the meaning and implication of this story in everything they do.

This means the LAPU community shares a collective mandate: whatever their job, vocation, or station in life—indeed, wherever they find themselves—they know that Jesus is calling them to walk alongside him in showing the world his grace, creativity, love, goodness, and salvation.

Chapter 7 further explores how the thread of God's story is connected across various courses and programs throughout the university.

3. ENGAGE WITH DIVERSE FAITH PERSPECTIVES WITHIN THE LEARNING COMMUNITY AT LAPU

Diversity is a defining characteristic of LAPU, particularly given the post-traditional demographic of its students and the diversity of the population in general in Southern California, where many of the university's students and staff reside. The university has a unique opportunity to engage with the beauty and variety of the different faith experiences and perspectives of its students, which are reflective of the image of God. So, on the university's Faith, Life, and Learning website, John Washatka explains the meaning and implications of hosting a diverse community in the context of LAPU's faith commitments. His writing is quoted at length as it articulates both basic philosophical and practical frameworks for engaging diversity within the LAPU learning community. He writes:

> It should be no surprise LAPU is a diverse community, one which cultivates "God-honoring diversity." Generally, colleges encourage diversity (whether the diversity consists of different ideologies, opinions, religions, ethnic groups, political affiliations, etc.) because experiencing diversity is part of what it means to be educated. In a broader context, diversity thrives in American culture because of the nation's commitment to pluralism.
>
> Cliques, factions, and divisions are a threat to diversity in that they work counter to the value of diversity—which includes the consideration of perspectives we would not otherwise consider, regarding others unlike ourselves with equality and equity, and recognizing God's hand at work in the world. Such diversity is reflected in the culmination of God's kingdom.
>
> Additionally, a real danger to diversity is reducing genuine differences to a sort of relativism that embraces "what is true for you is not necessarily true for me" and "what is moral for you is not necessarily moral for me." Essentially, the danger is being intolerant of those with whom we genuinely disagree, and subsequently not permitting those disagreements to be heard or addressed. Practicing tolerance with those with whom we disagree is recognizing their right to be heard, and the possibility that we might be wrong. I think what we are after here at LAPU is a kind of "mindful diversity" that cultivates God-honoring diversity while being intolerant of a path that leads away from truth and moral behavior.
>
> The saying, once attributed to St. Augustine, "in essentials, unity; in doubtful matters, liberty; in all things, charity" is good advice as we recognize each other's differences in the context of a learning community. At the very least, we are called upon to be civil and practice civil discourse when we have conversations and engage with those with whom we disagree. Don't look for offense, or take offense if none is offered, or even if it is.
>
> Since most communication in the classroom occurs via posts and emails, LAPU provides guidelines for online communication to help students and instructors be kind to one another, even in the midst of disagreements and differences.

> To participate in a diverse learning community requires thinking the best about others and extending courtesy to all while expecting the best of ourselves. In this way, LAPU can experience and model diversity that is reflective of God's kingdom.[8]

Washatka continues:

> Our curriculum is presented from a Christian worldview perspective, while being welcoming to students from all faith backgrounds. Instructors have the responsibility of cultivating trust and respect for all in their classrooms, so all students have the opportunity to share their ideas and experiences without fear of being censored. One of the benefits of sharing diverse ideas and experiences is the learning that occurs in such a context. We are confident our classroom environments are richer as a result.
>
> Outside the classroom, all employees at LAPU share common beliefs and values and extend the same culture of trust and respect as our students interact with staff members from different departments. Our desire is that all university stakeholders witness a deep respect for others and their various faith perspectives modeled by all LAPU employees. Engaging in faith, life, and learning culminates in the realization of hope for our students—a practical hope for students through earning a degree, and an eternal hope through a relationship with Jesus Christ.[9]

Chapter 8 provides an additional focused exploration of the importance of diversity, equity, and inclusion in fostering holistic faith formation in courses and programs throughout the university.

4. RECOGNIZE GOD'S WORK IN THE WORLD THROUGH ALL ACADEMIC DISCIPLINES

Perhaps the greatest hallmark of Christian higher education is the commitment to helping students recognize God's work in the world through every avenue of study and academic pursuit. There are not "Christian" majors and "non-Christian" majors; those studying theology, for example, are not more spiritual than those studying business. Some students may enter the university thinking or wondering about these things, but Christian universities largely take great efforts to emphasize the wonders of God's work through

---

8. Washatka, "Practicing Tolerance in Diversity."
9. Washatka, "Diverse Faith Perspectives."

each of the academic disciplines. This is part of the responsibility Christian universities have to help students realize and connect to their vocation, or calling, as it relates to their academic study and career goals.

Like the other three points of LAPU's Statement of Faith, Life, and Learning, this last commitment must be pursued with clear intention across the university. Each major and course presents unique opportunities to explore the intersection of knowledge and God's gracious work in the world. Since "all truth is God's truth," each course opens up new possibilities for discovery and the integration of faith, life, and learning.[10]

Chapter 9 provides further illustrations for how faith connects to all academic disciplines across the university. Throughout the book, there will be additional examples which illustrate how each of the four points from the statement are pursued in various classes and through university resources.

DESIGNING FOR INTENTIONAL LEARNING ACROSS THE UNIVERSITY

Teaching in the online university requires a massive paradigm shift away from what has been considered as the accepted educational norm of classroom face-to-face instruction. A teaching-focused paradigm—necessitated at times on traditional campuses where large classes are conducted in lecture-orientated classrooms—can contrast with a learning-focused paradigm, where the focus is less on who is doing the teaching and more on how students are learning. In this way, an online university learning experience will not be successful if the goal or practice is merely to shift what happens on a traditional campus to an online platform. If the rapid race to distance learning required by the onset of COVID-19 in the spring of 2020 taught higher education anything, it is that—more often than not—simply putting an in-person lecture class online in videoconference format does not generate the desired student engagement and learning outcomes. Many will say this proves online learning does not work.[11] But that misses the point. Remote teaching is not the same as online learning. What sets online learning apart from the experience of a "Zoom class" is the intentional and complex learning design process that goes into creating the highest quality online learning courses.

---

10. See Dockery, ed., *Faith and Learning*, 5–8 for a foundational perspective on the place of the Christian faith in relation to academic disciplines.

11. See, for example, Lederman, "Virtual Learning Will Be Better This Fall. Right?" and McMurtrie, "Are Colleges Ready for a Different Kind of Teaching This Fall?"

A HOLISTIC APPROACH TO CHRISTIAN FAITH, LIFE, AND LEARNING

The chapter earlier mentioned how learning design must start with the *who* question: Who are the learners that will be participating in this course? This is indeed a foundational question, but it is also just the first step in an eight-step iterative design process LAPU has adopted and adapted from what is known as Dialogue Education. Jane Vella and Global Learning Partners, among others, have pioneered and honed this approach to teaching and learning for use in any variety of learning environments—from meetings and trainings, to support and learning for communities in the developing world, to formal classrooms in K–12, college, graduate school, and beyond.[12] When paired with principles of adult learning theory, the Eight Steps of Design provide a strategic, holistic, and very effective framework for building and implementing online (and of course in-person) learning opportunities.[13]

The Eight Steps of Design should feel familiar to anyone who has put together a syllabus; in many ways, the questions are obvious and intuitive. What makes the process so effective, however, is the intentionality of forcing reflection and planning around each of these questions. The eight questions make explicit the assumptions of the purpose and design of a course, and help faculty and course developers think critically and creatively about what they hope to achieve through designing and offering the course:

1. Who? Who are the participants involved in the course? What do we know about the students, including their age, demographics, previous knowledge or experience in the subject? What about the instructor(s)? What is their background?

2. Why? Why is this course being offered? How does it fit into the curriculum, both in the major and across the university?

3. When? When will this course be offered? How long will each session be? Is this course synchronous or asynchronous? How much time each week will students be expected to engage in learning?

4. Where? Where will the course be offered? Via Zoom? In the university's Learning Management System (LMS) like Moodle or Canvas? Are there other locations required for learning, like site visits?

5. So That? These are the transfer objectives. What will students do differently back in their lives and workplaces as a result of this course?

---

12. See, for example, Vella, *Learning to Listen*; Goetzman, *Dialogue Education*; and Global Learning Partners.

13. See for example, Knowles, *Adult Learner*; Dweck, *Mindset*; and Duckworth, *Grit*.

6. What? This is the content of the course, and includes the knowledge, skills, and attitudes students will acquire. Notice that the content question comes after considering things like Who, Why, and When. Perhaps the plan was to structure the class around a particular textbook, but after reflection on the earlier design questions, it becomes clear there is not enough available time to really dive in as expected. Or, there is the realization that students already had this content in another course, or that they are not ready for it yet. Holding back on this question of content is often the biggest challenge for faculty. After all, they have subject matter expertise and often have strong feelings about particular textbooks and course content. Faculty can have a sense that the content should drive the course, as opposed to the content being pushed around by other course factors. Be assured the content still takes primary focus; it is simply integrated with the other seven design questions in mind. In the end, the learning will be more effective if the content is delivered within the larger design questions.

7. What For? These are the achievement-based objectives, also known as the course learning outcomes. What will the learners do with the content? How will we know they have accomplished the required learning?

8. How? These are the learning tasks. How will students accomplish the objectives or learning outcomes? Typically, faculty think of learning tasks like listening to lectures, reading texts, and writing papers. The advantage of online learning is that the world of learning tasks opens up many more creative and effective opportunities. This is where the expertise of instructional designers can really enhance a course. For example, instead of faculty filming themselves talking into a computer for an hour from an awkward angle and with bad lighting, they could work with an instructional designer to produce an engaging video and animated presentation. The content still gets across, but maybe the main idea can be explained in a fifteen-minute video, and then additional information can be explored through other forms of learning. Online learning sets itself apart from face-to-face instruction with the ability to harness technology and collaborate with other creative professionals to design unique and effective learning opportunities. It need not be "better" or "worse" than in-person instruction; at their best, both mediums promote transformational learning when pursued to their full potential.[14]

---

14. See, for example, Chen et al., "How Online Learning Compares"; Holmes and Reid, "Comparison Study"; and Pei and Wu, "Does Online Learning Work Better?".

The Eight Steps of Design also include guidance on how to conduct a Learning Needs and Resources Assessment, planning for evaluation and assessment, fostering dialogue by crafting open questions, integrating Bloom's Taxonomy into objectives, and incorporating principles of adult learning theory.[15] Of course there are numerous effective frameworks for learning design. Whatever the go-to resources, the challenge is to think holistically about learning in the online format. Faculty should take their best knowledge and intuitions about teaching and learning, and then consider what paradigms and practices may need to shift in order to ensure students receive the best learning possible—no matter the medium.

FAITH, LIFE, AND LEARNING ACROSS THE CURRICULUM, AND BEYOND

As a university, LAPU has integrated the principles and practices of learning design, dialogue education, and adult learning theory into a standardized program and course development process. This allows for a consistent and centralized process and committee (the Curriculum and Academic Policy Committee) to implement best practices in each course. This process also provides an avenue to advocate and design for the integration of faith, life, and learning principles across the curriculum. Through the centralized course design process, the university can effectively share and disseminate best practices across departments, including the strategy for faith, life, and learning. As chapter 4 will discuss, this intentional design and incorporation of faith, life, and learning within courses means the university can effectively measure and assess to what extent students are actually learning and exhibiting the spiritual formation outcomes it claims graduates will experience. In this way, faith, life, and learning is not just aspirational; the university is held accountable to its own unique institutional identity.

Part 2 of the book explores each of the four stated outcomes of LAPU's Statement of Faith, Life, and Learning—apply a Christian worldview; connect to God's story; engage with diverse faith perspectives; and recognize God's work in all academic disciplines—in greater detail as they relate to specific strategies for implementation across the curriculum. Part 3 of the book looks beyond the curriculum to university-wide efforts to cultivate holistic faith formation, particularly through success coaches and with additional resources such as the Faith, Life, and Learning website. Before examining these examples, however, it is important to establish how LAPU's unique collaborative culture enables an initiative such as faith, life, and

15. See Goetzman, *Dialogue Education*.

learning to flourish. In addition, the remaining chapters of Part 1 address issues of collaboration, assessment, and institutional identity. Throughout, the "four points" of the Statement of Faith, Life, and Learning guide holistic, collaborative, and university-wide endeavors toward the ultimate realization of hope in students.

Chapter 3

Building a Culture of Collaboration

JOHN C. REYNOLDS

JOHN REYNOLDS, *President of Los Angeles Pacific University, describes how a shared governance model facilitates the online university's holistic approach to faith formation. The chapter addresses the key question: How does collaboration provide creative and effective solutions to the challenges of online faith formation?*

// Shared Governance has few defenders, or at least, few people who support it publicly," states Derek Bok in describing "The Trouble with Shared Governance."[1] In analyzing the legacy challenges of the "administration," disaffected faculty, and trustees often more interested in expansion, reputation, athletics, and financial sustainability, Bok opines that there is ample opportunity for improving the academic quality of institutions "through the *cooperative* [emphasis added] effort of presidents and faculties with enlightened boards of trustees." This ideal of cooperation or intentional collaboration is a complex and multifaceted challenge in most higher education institutions (HEIs), gaining further complexity in an online university where most often a managerial culture is dominant, financial sustainability is driven by enrollment, faculty are geographically distributed, and

---

1. Bok, "Trouble with Shared Governance," 19.

the majority of the teaching is through practitioner adjunct faculty.[2] Collaboration and cooperation between those responsible for academic quality, student success, and financial sustainability through growth and market relevance require a unique design and organizational culture that creates an environment that supports functional outcomes, expectations, and goals, while being holistic in the identity and mission of the university—in essence building and nurturing a collaborative culture.

THE TRADITIONAL UNIVERSITY MODEL

The traditional academic journey for a faculty member is primarily a solo and individualistic journey. The path to faculty status, although influenced by academic scholars and mentors, is generally an independent accomplishment recognized academically through a terminal credential. Doctoral dissertations are not team projects. The journey is a clear professor/student relationship even when an academic peer is segmented again by rank and title. This pathway, or model, cultivates an excellent scholar, a strong critical thinker, an expert in a specific area of research, and an asset to any university as a lecturer, researcher, and knowledge contributor to their field of study. This pathway, over at least a decade, does not generally nurture attributes of collaboration (outside of academia) within the university structure. This is further reinforced by the appointment to faculties, schools, or colleges in their field such as Business, Applied Science, etc. In many ways, academia is not designed for a collaborative model; it is indeed a collegial model by choice, but not by intention.

This siloed effect is extended to curricular and cocurricular activities within the institution. As an example, the Academic Senate seldom collaborates with Student Affairs, faculty with athletics, etc. The terms clearly convey separate domains—curricular and cocurricular. Students navigate these two environments as they journey through their pursuit of a degree, and after graduation accept this as the norm. If continuing their academic path, they will practice this culture from their experience. The traditional academic model is not broken and has been the foundation of the university model for generations. The challenge in the twenty-first century is the evolving plethora of university models where the online university is a prime example. The evolving transition of a legacy faculty-centric model to a student-centric model, where the student expects support, effectiveness, immediacy, and connectedness from the institution, knowing the financial burden they will bear for many years to come, will demand a common face

2. Bergquist et al., *Engaging the Six Cultures of the Academy*, 3.

and voice from the institution. The future student (and their patrons) will not expect silos or being passed between the academy, the administration, and the student affairs/support functions; rather, they will expect a common and collaborative model regardless of rank, title, or function.

The model of the future will require a holistic approach to student learning and experience in the attainment of an academic credential. The challenge will be leading all areas of the university into that collaborative and equitable culture that has not been the culture, model, process, or experience of the current university stakeholders. This is not a management change, but a leadership challenge. Administrators, the academy, and functional leaders will be required to rethink, reset, and reimagine a university environment where collaboration and cooperation are the authentic and intentional norms and behaviors of the institution.

Many institutions have begun this process of change, triggered by external stakeholders who are demanding accountability, transparency, value, and relevancy for their graduates. This has been influenced by the growing number of proprietary institutions, changing demographics of students already in the workplace, and the convenience of the online modality. These institutions might be regarded as post-traditional institutions.

THE POST-TRADITIONAL UNIVERSITY MODEL

Traditional model institutions have evolved over time to focus on a specific demographic of students who continue their education from secondary school into the tertiary level as a continuum. In the twenty-first century the student population, particularly in North America, has bifurcated into traditional students (normally identified by the age of eighteen to twenty-three) and post-traditional students, defined as "individuals already in the work force who lack a postsecondary credential yet are determined to pursue further knowledge and skills while balancing work, life, and education responsibilities."[3] This definition encompasses roughly 98 million people, according to the U.S. Census Bureau's 2016 Current Population Survey, and also creates a new student population of individuals who have not yet achieved any postsecondary education credential, and are not in a place in life where attending a traditional college is feasible or affordable. This need and demographic, first recognized by John Sperling and the launch of the University of Phoenix in 1976, was the genesis of the proprietary

---

3. Soares, "Post-traditional Learners," 1–2. See also Radford et al., "Demographic and Enrollment Characteristics," 7.

(for-profit) university model.[4] The model evolved in the twenty-first century with the adoption of the internet as a tool of the people for education and commerce. The convenience of attending university where class times were scheduled by the student, no physical presence was required, federal funding was available, the tuition was affordable, and where employers recognized the diploma while remaining agnostic to the modality, launched the creation and conversion of many universities to the "for-profit" model addressing primarily the post-traditional student population. Other private institutions, not-for-profit, such as Southern New Hampshire University, Brandman University (now UMass Global), and Los Angeles Pacific University, adopted the business model and provided similar delivery models—growing with the ease of accessibility, convenience, and affordability when compared to traditional university alternatives.

A post-traditional university model requires a different organizational structure and approach to course development, faculty, quality assurance, student support, and learning cycles. Post-traditional students do not seek or require many cocurricular activities or the traditional campus experience. As working adults, their greatest need is support systems and services to achieve a marketable diploma from a quality (i.e., accredited) educational institution, in the shortest time possible and at the least cost (generally they are personally funding their education). In the online university model this generally implies more frequent start dates, asynchronous engagement and teaching, and a full-quality academic experience in a virtual environment. From the institution's perspective, this mode requires quality course development, teaching, and services with the maximum personalized student support possible.

Philosophically, post-traditional institutions are, as described by Ernest Boyer in his four models of scholarship, heavily invested in the scholarship of teaching.[5] In essence, the scholarship of teaching involves innovative strategies and the application of best practices to develop skills and facilitate learning. It is a model of collaboration in teaching, advising, mentoring, and learning. The online university model, utilizing the scholarship of teaching and learning in a cooperative process, requires processes and systems that integrate the various facets of the student's engagement, thus eliminating traditional faculty and staff organizational boundaries. Enrollment volumes, individualized support, open enrollment, and high mobility of students demand an agile teaching workforce. This, for economic, practitioner, and sustainability reasons, normally results in a higher proportion of adjunct

4. Sperling and Tucker, *For Profit Higher Education*.
5. Boyer, *Scholarship Reconsidered*, 129–39.

faculty than in traditional universities and higher numbers of class sections for popular courses. Demanding academic quality and high standards has in many post-traditional institutions resulted in faculty-developed, institutionally managed academic programs and courses. Once an academic course is developed, the course is then standardized for teaching until a needed refresh or updating for relevancy. This required collaboration is at the highest level between faculty, student engagement staff, instructional designers, and eLearning production teams. In order for the post-traditional online university model to be effective, collaboration must begin at the essence of a reputable university, the academic community.

THE ONLINE UNIVERSITY MODEL

The concept of an online university or college is not well defined in academic literature. The value of online programs, online courses, and online delivery is generally understood operationally, but there are few clear definitions of the university in which there are no synchronous requirements, all teaching and engagement is virtual, all student resources such as library, financial aid, and remedial support are online, and the faculty member and student do not require any physical contact or presence to teach or graduate. The key characteristic of asynchronous (time agnostic) both complicates and differentiates "online" learning and universities. In remote synchronous teaching, utilizing the internet is interactive, situational, and immediately collaborative. On the other hand, asynchronous teaching utilizes the internet but is not immediately interactive, it is not situational, and requires intentional interventions and techniques to cultivate a collaborative culture. For the purposes of this topic, the online university will be defined as an institution that offers academic programs that can be completed entirely via asynchronous teaching and learning with robust student support services that students can similarly access without ever physically going to a campus.

This model of university tends to be more attractive to a certain demographic of students. Traditional-aged students (high school to college in the same calendar year) typically seek a full on-campus college experience. Residential community, cocurricular options, and intramural sports/activities are a significant draw to complement their academic journey. The primary focus of the university, where the student progresses and graduates successfully in a meaningful time frame with specific competencies, is the academic journey.

For an online university, the post-traditional student is the typical profile of the student body. These students, many of whom are working professionals, are seeking not only a diploma but pragmatic application to their daily work. Faculty who are practitioners in the discipline and can authentically engage students in both theory and practice are essential for student persistence and success. For this primary reason, the academically qualified practitioner or contingency/adjunct lecturer is a significant factor in the delivery and engagement of students in an online university.

This fundamental factor—a larger contingent teaching workforce than more collegial/traditional university models—requires a unique academic governance, curriculum, and teaching model. With a larger part-time faculty, inclusion and collaboration in all academic systems and processes is not an option, but a requirement.

THE ACADEMIC COLLABORATIVE MODEL IN AN ONLINE UNIVERSITY

The disaggregation of the traditional faculty's role in all areas of the academic system into specific areas of expertise—such as curriculum development, teaching and student engagement, assessment, advising, support services, and student success—may be simple conceptually and in the design of the universities' organizational structure, but must be perceived as holistic and integrated to the student. This need, complemented by a higher ratio of adjunct faculty, requires collaboration in all aspects of the academic system in an online university model.

Curriculum Development

"The role of curriculum in higher education is sine qua non for the provision of quality and relevant educational programs and services to the current and potential learners in the USA and elsewhere in the world."[6] Curriculum, both its design and planning, involves implementing instructional strategies and methods in a course or module that are focused on achieving specific outcomes or competencies that optimize the student's development in a course of study. In an online university, as in any university, curriculum is the purview of the faculty/academy. In an online university this design and planning generally cannot be owned and developed by one faculty member for several reasons: (1) part-time faculty are larger in number and are transitional in employment—the academy must manage the continuity of curriculum and quality; (2) the number of sections taught

---

6. Khan and Law, "Integrative Approach to Curriculum Development," 66.

for the same course is generally greater than the full-time faculty can teach and for consistency, institutional curriculum must be standardized at the content and assessment level to accommodate a mobile part-time faculty base; (3) programs and courses, especially in the professional disciplines, require constant review for relevance and a consistent and frequent process of refresh; and (4) the essence or mission of the institution, such as in faith-based institutions, is a signature that must be evident in all curriculum and with a singular or part-time faculty this is more complex to ensure.

For these and other unique reasons, the online university typically adopts a collaborative curriculum development model. Collaborative curriculum development takes several forms, but as practiced, for example, at Los Angeles Pacific University (LAPU), includes at least five different roles collaborating in the development and final design of a curriculum: the subject matter expert (an active academic faculty member in a university context), the instructional designer, the program design coordinator (an individual who audits the Program Learning Outcomes and consistency between program courses), the academic administrator overseeing the program, and the academic committee responsible for the quality and effectiveness of the curriculum. This curriculum development team works together toward the common goals of developing the best curriculum feasible to promote academic quality, enabling the students to demonstrate their knowledge and skills related to the subject, incorporating effective instructional practices, and establishing fair and reliable standards for the assessment of student achievement.

Teaching and Student Engagement

When teaching and engaging with students at the tertiary level, the process is often didactic and bilateral. The image of the traditional lecture venue with a sole lecturer and an amphitheater of students is often what is considered university teaching. For many HEIs, specifically private and faith-based, the faculty-to-student ratio is a differentiator in promoting a more personalized experience. In an asynchronous and virtual online university model, this paradigm is not possible or replicable. Teaching is informed through student engagement, individually, as a group, and as peers between students. Students collaborating, or working jointly, to achieve the course objectives not only encourages active engagement by the students, but also promotes important career-related competencies.

Assessment, Advising, and Student Support

Although assessment and advising appear to be non-collaborative processes, in an online university where students are physically distant, instructors are part-time, and the institution's reputation is at stake, a collaborative effort to assess and support the student is nonnegotiable. The student's academic success depends on the integrated efforts of the instructors, the academy, and the student success model. The traditional university model promotes an environment where students have access to faculty members, both current and past, on a daily basis. In an open enrollment, online university setting utilizing part-time faculty, access and support must be collaborative and have continuity for the student. There are few institutions that have shown success in this tri-stakeholder effort; however, LAPU has utilized a collaborative model for more than a decade with success (as determined by its students and alumni).

The collaborative model integrates the instructor, the student, student support, and the academy into a seemingly single support model for the student's success. As an online university founded on a student-centric paradigm, the starting position is how best to support the student to be successful in their academic aspirations. Serving post-traditional students, many of whom are working adults with multiple college transcripts, institutions have a practical and ethical obligation to provide the best possible environment for fast and constant support. The link between the student and the university cannot in an online environment be limited to the academy. In the LAPU model, every student is assigned on enrollment a student success coach. As far as feasible over the life of the student at the university, the student will keep the same coach until graduation. (There are obvious exceptions for personnel changes, etc.) The first stakeholder is then the success coach who partners with the student from enrollment to graduation over several years in a continuous relationship. In the student's academic journey toward a specific major, the assistant deans are full-time academic leaders who have overall accountability for the quality and delivery of the curriculum and the instructors contracted to teach in the majors within their span of academic oversight. This is the second stakeholder in the student's journey to a completed degree. The third stakeholder is the course instructor, who teaches, engages, energizes, and assesses the student for a single academic course. The number of instructors could be as many as thirty to complete a bachelor's degree from enrollment to graduation. Collaboration between the student, the student success coach, the instructor, and the assistant dean is the signature ingredient to the student perceiving the full institution's support toward their academic credential. Integrating missional (faith and learning) and other key student success strategies such as career guidance, Clifton Strength's coaching,[7] financial aid support, etc. as a one-stop service to the student is not feasible without an intentional and effective collaborative model between the academy, the student success coach, the instructor, and the student.

Design to Culture

Sandra Jones and colleagues argue for a new model of leadership in higher education, stating "that there is a need to develop a more distributed and collaborative leadership approach for the sector to continue to provide leading edge change. This collaboration will be best achieved if it includes academics, executive, and professional staff."[8] The authors also posit that, "while multiple theories of leadership exist, the higher education sector requires a less hierarchical approach that takes account of its highly specialized and professional context."[9] As effective a strategy, organizational structure, system, or process is, the leadership challenge is how to evolve the intention of collaboration to an organizational culture where collaborating is the norm. What then is a framework for a cultural shift from a traditionally autonomous and hierarchical model, normally demonstrated by siloed activities centered on the unique but separate skills and gifts of faculty, staff, or administrators, to a collaborative and synergistic culture that is focused on the students and their success?

According to William Powell, "simply defined, collaboration takes place when members of an inclusive learning community work together as equals to assist students to succeed in the classroom."[10] For online universities, the "classroom" is pragmatically the total engagement process experienced by the student that integrates teaching, peer interaction, interacting with the instructor, and the support of their student support staff member. Working as a community toward that common goal of student success is more than a system, it is the natural style and expected/normal behavior and model of the university. When this value of work ethic is preferred and is the intrinsic behavior and style of working, a collaborative culture becomes a reality.

However, as posited, this is generally not the experience or behavior of faculty or staff recruited to the online university. Explaining the university's

7. Rath, *StrengthsFinder 2.0*.
8. Jones et al., "Distributed Leadership," 74.
9. Jones et al., "Distributed Leadership," 67.
10. Powell, "Collaboration."

valuing and expectation of collaboration often requires some form of rubric. What then is a culture of collaboration? Lynn Cook and Marilyn Friend list the defining characteristics of successful collaboration, particular to teaching at secondary school, but pertinent to higher education with conditions such as voluntariness, parity among participants, mutual goals, shared responsibility for participation and decision-making, shared resources, and sharing accountability for outcomes. Practiced in a collaborative online university, these might be expanded as follows:[11]

1. *Voluntary participation.* Including collaboration in job descriptions, performance management models, organizational procedures, and policies are good management practices, but do not change the culture. When university stakeholders, intent on a student's success, volunteer to work together regardless of the management framework, collaboration becomes the culture.

2. *Parity among participants.* The most challenging issue in the university talent model is the stratified classification of academics, administrators, and staff. There are few university organizational models that do not frame their organizational structure, policies, employment, benefits, etc. utilizing a segregated system of classification. Collaboration in this organizational culture is challenging, if not impossible. Identifying formal and informal systems to communicate parity as it pertains to student success is critical.

3. *Mutual goals.* A common and mutual goal is the foundation of any form of collaboration. To what end are we collaborating? A clear, articulated, and repeated vision is essential to developing any organizational culture. For the online university, the student and their success must be the common purpose and goal. If all stakeholders in the university have a common goal of student success, collaboration will become the natural vehicle for success, and natural behavior defines the culture.

4. *Shared responsibility and empowerment.* Leading an online university, and being intentional in nurturing a collaborative culture, requires trust and transparency. Promoting an organizational structure that empowers student-engagement stakeholders to work together through delegated decision-making is expedient, empowering, and effective in developing a collaborative culture.

---

11. Cook and Friend, "Educational Leadership," 422–23.

5. *Shared resources.* The sharing of resources through common access to all areas of the university, professional development opportunities, and funding, signals to the stakeholders that there is equity in considering the needs of the student—the common purpose.

6. *Shared accountability.* Organizations are managed well when there are clear roles and responsibilities. Every individual is responsible for their particular role and outcomes. Collaborative cultures synergize these individual responsibilities and identify a shared accountability for the university's purpose. In the online university model, the purpose of shared accountability is students—most of whom will never physically be present with a university representative or on campus—being successful in attaining their academic dream.

Supporting, recognizing, and rewarding these six core practices will result in the natural shift to a culture of university-wide collaboration. The challenge will be how this changing model of collaboration and shared governance will influence colleges and universities who are missionally Christian and regard faith as centric to their academic model, specifically in the online context.

COLLABORATIVE GOVERNANCE: AN EFFECTIVE MODEL FOR FAITH FORMATION

Consistently integrating faith and learning is a significant process for confessing institutions, universities, and colleges where the infusion of faith in a holistic social and academic framework is a foundational commitment and one of their core functions. As institutions engage more contingent faculty, factors such as consistency, alignment, and support of the institution's faith values become more complex. In the online university model where contingent faculty are the norm, the integration of faith and learning must be viewed as an institutional priority or core value, and as such cannot be delegated or executed in isolation or without collaboration. The importance, intention, and infusion must be considered throughout the institution. To be a cultural imperative, the commitment to faith formation begins with governance and is holistic in design—a shared responsibility of principles, discourse, collective support, and ownership of this essential part of the Christian university's identity. In the academic context this impacts curriculum design, assessment, hiring of faculty, and student engagement. The biblical principles of community, collaboration, inclusion, and valuing all stakeholders can only be manifested in a model that does not delegate the inclusion of faith, but embraces and infuses it into the purpose, process, and principles through shared understanding, debate, and values. Shared understanding and principles lead to shared language and outcomes. At LAPU, a nondenominational institution with a clear Christian identity, promoting a culture of faith, life, and learning is not the responsibility of a department or one person with an appropriate title. *Governance*, as the term implies, refers to systems and processes that ensure accountability, transparency, impact, and participation. *Collaborative* governance assumes common ownership and support through a process of shared thinking and discussion. In *a faith-based institution*, collaborative governance has at its core the integration of the mission and its discerning inclusion in the academic journey. In an *online* faith-based institution, collaboration is not an option—shared understanding, language, principles, and even theology are essential for meaning and engagement.

CONCLUSION

Collaboration in any organization is a process and, if desired, must be built and nurtured not only by leadership, but by every university representative who is accountable for the student's success. This is not a natural process in the academic world where autonomy and individuality are the path to faculty with systems, governance, and traditional models enabling the process. However, in the modern university—and specifically in the online university model with online, typically post-traditional, and high-risk students engaged in asynchronous learning—collaboration is essential for university effectiveness and a positive student experience. Managing and implementing collaborative systems and procedures is important and necessary, but alone will not infuse a natural set of behaviors and norms to create a collaborative culture. Building a collaborative culture requires leadership that nurtures, recognizes, and rewards behavior and interventions where individuals, regardless of their specific role in the academy or student support function, mutually work together in engaging the student to be successful. As with any cultivation of organizational culture, this is not an event but a continual process of clear purpose and the expectation that the student is only successful if the entire university works together. Collaboration is the key to a student's experience and success.

Chapter 4

Assessing Faith, Life, and Learning

WAYNE R. HERMAN

WAYNE HERMAN, *Chief Academic Officer at Los Angeles Pacific University, asserts that formal assessment of learning outcomes related to faith formation is possible, and can be done. The chapter addresses the key questions: Why assess faith formation? How do we value what cannot be assessed?*

Most Christian higher education institutions formulate mission and/or identity statements that articulate their expectations regarding how students will engage with issues of faith. A few examples from several institutions in Southern California accredited by the WASC Senior College and University Commission illustrate this point:

> The mission of Biola University is biblically centered education, scholarship and service—equipping men and women in mind and character to impact the world for the Lord Jesus Christ.[1]

> Since the university's founding in 1899, APU [Azusa Pacific University] has incorporated our religious beliefs into every aspect of university life. We are transparent about our *God First* approach to higher education as it reflects our mission-driven

---

1. Biola University, "Mission, Vision and Values."

identity, including our commitment to diversity. Rigorous curriculum across academic disciplines explores topics infused by faith. In the residence halls, during chapel, and in discipleship groups, students unpack God's call upon their lives and witness His transformation. To uphold this distinction, APU employs faculty and staff who share the Christian faith across denominations.[2]

California Baptist University believes each person has been created for a purpose. CBU helps students understand and engage this purpose by providing a Christ-centered educational experience that integrates academics with spiritual and social development opportunities. Graduates are challenged to become individuals whose skills, integrity and sense of purpose glorify God and distinguish them in the workplace and in the world.[3]

A similar statement is found on the website of Los Angeles Pacific University:

Los Angeles Pacific University teaches and serves from a Christian worldview through a holistic understanding and practice of promoting faith, life, and learning. We believe the entire LAPU community is called to contribute to cultivating hope through learning and we accomplish this through our core values of being Exemplary, Caring, and focused on Learning. We are committed to preparing individuals not only with the skills and attitudes to thrive in their community and workplace, but also to point the way to something bigger—to the ultimate hope that is in Jesus Christ.[4]

These statements all reflect an institutional goal of engaging students in a transformative process aligned with a Christian commitment. This goal is expressed variously as "a biblically centered education," curriculum that "explores topics infused by faith," "a Christ-centered educational experience," and "promoting faith, life, and learning." Such statements illustrate that Christian institutions typically believe learning happens best in the context of faith. In other words, learning within the context of a Christian higher education institution should be informed by or infused with faith in such a way that it can be recognized as distinctively Christian.

---

2. Azusa Pacific University, "Faith and Learning Community."
3. California Baptist University, "Mission."
4. Los Angeles Pacific University, "What We Believe."

FAITH, LIFE, AND LEARNING: A CASE STUDY

The faculty and academic administrators at Los Angeles Pacific University (LAPU) have recently undertaken a review of the role of faith in the learning experience of students, largely due to the recommendation of an initial accreditation site review team. LAPU, which was birthed by Azusa Pacific University (APU) in 2011 as Azusa Pacific Online University (APOU), was intended by the APU board of trustees to be a spin-off institution. That is, the original vision for the institution was that it would become a separately accredited institution that would retain some form of relationship with APU. Although it was established with a separate board, separate faculty, separate leadership, and separate staff, it remained under APU's accreditation for its first six years. In 2017, the APU board of trustees approved APOU's pursuit of separate accreditation with the Western Association of Schools and Colleges (WASC) Senior College and University Commission (WSCUC), which was granted by the WSCUC in February 2018. One of the recommendations included in the accreditation letter sent by the WSCUC to LAPU was:

> Develop a shared understanding of the role of faith as the institution continues to grow. A shared understanding of the role of faith in the culture of LAPU and in the design and delivery of educational programs will be essential as the institution continues to grow, adds additional degree programs and other educational options, and serves a broader range of students, many of whom will embrace other faith traditions or have no faith tradition of their own.[5]

This recommendation resulted in the formation in October 2017 of a Faith Integration Task Force at LAPU, later renamed the Faith, Life, and Learning Task Force, which was charged with addressing these concerns.[6] As the task force met, its members conceived its primary duties as discerning the implications of LAPU's Christian faith commitment and creating points of engagement based on those implications for its curricula, faculty, students, and the broader LAPU community. Although each of these is important, the focus on how a faith commitment is reflected and assessed in the curricula of an institution is most germane to this chapter.

---

5. WASC Senior College and University Commission, "Action Letter," 2.

6. In July 2021 this task force became the Faith, Life, and Learning Committee, in recognition of its continued importance in addressing a vital element of LAPU's mission.

The first step in this process was to revisit LAPU's commitment to faith integration. Although this had been part of LAPU's identity from its foundation, the maturing of the institution and the prompting of the accreditation letter recommendation provided an opportunity to revisit this commitment and formulate it in a new way. This commitment, which features prominently on LAPU's website and in its academic catalogs, states:

> Los Angeles Pacific University teaches and serves from a Christian worldview through a holistic understanding and practice of promoting faith, life, and learning. We believe the entire LAPU community is called to contribute to cultivating hope through learning and we accomplish this through our core values of being Exemplary, Caring, and focused on Learning. We are committed to preparing individuals not only with the skills and attitudes to thrive in their community and workplace, but also to point the way to something bigger—to the ultimate hope that is in Jesus Christ.

As it relates to students, LAPU conceives the promotion of faith, life, and learning as engaging students in learning (through curriculum design, instruction, and student support) that reflects the Christian worldview of LAPU and culminates in the realization of hope in students. As a result of this process (through their interactions and study at LAPU) students will be able to:

- apply a Christian worldview to their life and work in the world;
- articulate how and in what ways their life journeys connect to God's story;
- engage with diverse faith perspectives within the learning community at LAPU;
- recognize God's work in the world through all academic disciplines.

This statement needs to be placed within the broader context of LAPU's mission and ethos.[7] As an institution that states its vision as existing "to serve people around the world who desire education delivered in the context of faith, excellence, and flexibility, removing the barriers to affordability and accessibility," LAPU conceives its mission as including open admissions, accepting students of all faith traditions or no faith tradition. LAPU's goal is not primarily to produce Christian workers (i.e., pastors, missionaries, and youth leaders). Instead, LAPU seeks to help students (1)

---

7. Chapter 5 addresses the identity, vision, and purpose of the university in greater detail.

engage in learning experiences that are grounded in a Christian worldview; (2) connect their stories to God's story; (3) respect diverse faith perspectives; and (4) see God's work in the world holistically. Thus, the statement noted above expresses several key components of LAPU's understanding of its faith commitment and how that commitment relates to students' learning experiences:

- The faith commitment is grounded in a Christian worldview.
- This Christian worldview gives shape to the development of learning experiences.
- Faith-infused learning experiences are intended to cultivate hope in students.

These components could be conceived as sequential in nature: LAPU's Christian worldview informs the development of faith-infused learning experiences that in turn give rise to hope among students.

One implication of this is that LAPU's Christian worldview—as expressed in its mission, vision, and core values—is the foundation for and permeates the university's identity, mission, and practice. In order to operate from a perspective that is grounded in a Christian worldview, LAPU hires only faculty and staff who affirm the Christian faith and agree to live according to Christian community standards. This foundational Christian commitment enables the university to develop programs and curricula that reflect a Christian worldview and include specific faith-related course and program learning outcomes. Although LAPU admits students from diverse backgrounds, experiences, and worldviews, the focus on faith, life, and learning ensures that students understand what a Christian worldview is and how it relates to their academic disciplines and work. Among employees this focus on faith also helps establish an institutional culture that seeks to honor God through actions. One of the key desired outcomes of these efforts for students is the realization of hope, which includes graduating from a program, personal growth, spiritual growth, community engagement, and gainful employment.

Such statements about the importance of faith and learning no doubt have aspirational value to students, prospective students, faculty, and other stakeholders, who value an education informed and infused with the Christian faith. However, such statements remain only aspirational unless institutions also have a robust assessment system and are committed to assessing the achievement of such goals. Such a system needs to include relevant and achievable learning outcomes at various levels of the curriculum, well-aligned assessment rubrics, instructors who are adept at using rubrics and providing meaningful feedback to students, and assessors who regularly measure the students' achievement of such outcomes. While students are likely to experience faith formation activities through their personal engagement with instructors and advisors or coaches, intentionally incorporating faith-related outcomes and learning activities in the curricula is a vital aspect of making students' learning experiences truly Christian.

At LAPU one institutional learning outcome (ILO) is devoted to faith, life, and learning: "Students who complete degrees at Los Angeles Pacific University shall be able to relate a Christian worldview to academic disciplines, life, and work; articulating ways life journeys connect to God's story in the Bible."[8] This broad statement of purpose is intended to encompass the salient points noted above in the commitment to faith, life, and learning. Each program at LAPU translates this ILO into one or more program learning outcomes (PLOs), such as the following:

Associate of Science in Health Sciences

- PLO 1: Apply key elements of a Christian worldview to personal and professional values, ethics, and commitments.
- PLO 2: Articulate contextually informed interpretations of biblical texts through key themes.

Bachelor of Science in Information Systems

- PLO 1: Demonstrate the ability to integrate biblical concepts and principles with discipline specific topics and domains.

Master of Business Administration

- PLO 5: Apply a Christian worldview to decision-making processes and outcomes.

These few examples demonstrate how the overarching ILO is translated into specific learning outcomes at the program level, each of which is tailored to the target students, academic level, and vision of the individual programs. Such an approach provides room for faculty responsible for the academic quality of individual programs to develop PLOs that appropriately guide the development of course learning outcomes (CLOs) for the individual courses that comprise each specific program.

While PLOs are important, they are only meaningful if there are well-formulated CLOs that correspond to them in the courses that comprise the program. Another way of describing this correspondence between PLOs

8. Los Angeles Pacific University, "Institutional Learning Outcomes."

and CLOs is in terms of *alignment*, that is, how closely connected CLOs and PLOs are. Well aligned CLOs will translate the PLOs into specific learning outcomes for each course. Without PLO and CLO alignment, it is difficult to assess the achievement of the PLOs. Again, it is helpful to see some specific examples of this as LAPU has attempted to develop an assessment system related to faith, life, and learning. Using one of the same programs and PLOs identified above, here is a specific CLO from the course that has been identified as a mastery-level assessment course for the PLO:

Bachelor of Science in Information Systems

- PLO 1: Demonstrate the ability to integrate biblical concepts and principles with discipline specific topics and domains.
    - Course: MGT 380 Information Systems Management
    - CLO 4: Students will be able to apply principles of ethical leadership from a Christian worldview.

The above-mentioned CLO is developed as part of the course vision in LAPU's curriculum design process, is approved by the Curriculum and Academic Policy Committee (CAPC), and then is linked to a specific assignment as the course design is completed. The intention is that the assignment linked to such a CLO will have clearly developed grading rubrics that provide instructors the opportunity to assess whether students have satisfactorily achieved the CLO. The following example illustrates this intended alignment of CLO, assignment, and grading rubric. In the Bachelor of Science in Information Systems program, PLO 1 and CLO 4 are assessed via the Emerging Technologies Workgroup Proposal Part 3 assignment. One performance criterion in the grading rubric for this assignment (allocated 25 percent of the assignment grade) is, "Comprehensively summarizes the ethical and moral considerations of the implications of the proposed business plan. Alternative viewpoints are acknowledged within the context of the proposed recommendation." While this performance criterion does not specify that the student must address this issue from a Christian worldview, prior to this exercise students are provided with resources about Christian ethics for reading and discussion. Specifying a Christian worldview perspective for this analysis would tie the assignment grading rubric more closely to both the CLO and PLO.

In the process of reviewing several programs, courses, and assignments for the purpose of writing this chapter it became apparent these three assessment elements can become misaligned. For example, in reviewing a similar PLO for the Bachelor of Science in Supply Chain Management and a CLO that states, "Students will be able to evaluate ethically sound business decisions through the lens of servant leadership," it became clear the assignment grading rubrics did not include any specific performance criteria related to the evaluation of ethically sound business decisions or servant leadership. The grading rubrics tended to focus on process rather than content, that is, how the student summarized, analyzed, evaluated, and presented the content, rather than on the content itself. While methodology is, no doubt, important, focusing exclusively on methodology makes it difficult to assess faith-related learning activities.

When such misalignment between PLOs, CLOs, and assignment grading rubrics occurs, it is important to have a well-developed process in place for identifying and correcting such problems. At LAPU, this occurs as part of the annual program assessment cycle, in which two or three PLOs from each program are reviewed by a team of faculty assessors. The Bachelor of Science in Supply Chain Management is a relatively new program at LAPU and PLO 1 is scheduled for review for the first time in 2021. This explains why this particular misalignment had not been resolved. But, in the course of conducting the annual PLO assessment process for programs, misalignments such as this would be identified and would result in a recommendation to make a change to the PLO, CLO, assignment, and/or grading rubric to ensure an appropriate alignment.

LEARNING DOMAINS

One of the challenges of assessing faith, life, and learning ILOs, PLOs, and CLOs is determining the appropriate learning domain that one should assess. When developing learning objectives, LAPU instructors tend to rely on Bloom's Taxonomy, which addresses learning within the cognitive domain.

The six levels of this familiar taxonomy—remember, understand, apply, analyze, evaluate, and create—identify different levels of students' thinking about issues of faith, life, and learning. The Association of American Colleges and Universities VALUE rubrics provide helpful guidance and examples of different ways to assess students' achievement of learning outcomes at each of these levels.[9] One advantage of assessing a student's learning about the Christian faith via the cognitive domain is that such assessment does not necessarily require a personal faith commitment by the student. As long as the student can recall, explain, interpret, examine, apprise, or develop perspectives from a Christian worldview, their learning about the Christian faith can be assessed.

9. Rhodes, *Assessing Outcomes and Improving Achievement*.

But what about the affective and psychomotor domains? David Krathwohl and colleagues developed a taxonomy to describe learning in the affective domain that includes (from lower-order to higher-order learning) subdomains of receiving, responding, valuing, organizing, and characterizing.[10] This taxonomy reflects levels of learning related to attitudes, beliefs, emotions, feelings, and values progressing through awareness, commitment, self-identification, assimilation, and integrous behavior related to affective responses. Certainly, much of what people commonly experience of faith lies within the affective domain.

Similarly, Elizabeth Simpson developed a taxonomy for learning in the psychomotor domain, which is concerned with learning related to the development of physical behaviors, skills, and tasks.[11] The seven levels of Simpson's taxonomy progress through increasingly complex levels of learning to do things: perception, readiness to act, guided response (or imitation), mechanism (converting learned responses to habits), complex overt response (performing complex actions correctly), adaptation, and origination (the ability to develop new skills). The common distinction in religious circles between orthodoxy (right belief or doctrine) and orthopraxy (right behavior, both ethical and liturgical) underscores the value of a taxonomy that addresses the latter.

These taxonomies are helpful in determining the kind of learning activities that are appropriate for learning outcomes focused on the affective and psychomotor domains. But in an open-enrollment institution, in which there is no requirement for students to be professing Christians, it seems unreasonable to expect all students to demonstrate Christian attitudes (e.g., faith, mercy, love) or perform Christian acts (e.g., pray, witness). If a student does not profess to be Christian the most one could expect is that they are able to engage with a Christian worldview at a cognitive level. If an institution restricts admissions to those who are professing Christians, then perhaps learning outcomes related to a Christian worldview in the affective and psychomotor domains would be appropriate.

---

10. Krathwohl et al., *Taxonomy of Educational Objectives*. See also Krathwohl, "Revision of Bloom's Taxonomy"; and The Peak Performance Center, "Affective Domain of Learning."

11. Simpson, *Classification of Educational Objectives*.

FAITH, LIFE, AND LEARNING BEYOND THE CURRICULUM

The discussion thus far has focused on the assessment of faith, life, and learning as it relates to the formal curriculum: the academic programs, courses, and assignments that result in formative or summative assessment of a student's achievement of faith-related learning outcomes. But most Christian institutions also typically seek to guide students' spiritual formation through an informal curriculum, those ways in which an institution seeks to promote faith, life, and learning outside the classroom. In a traditional campus setting the informal curriculum often includes chapel services, discipleship groups, service opportunities, and a variety of other activities designed to promote spiritual growth. In an online higher education institution designed primarily for post-traditional students (i.e., working, financially independent, with dependents, etc.), such traditional spiritual formation activities do not fit well.

This, however, does not diminish the need for or possibility of meaningful spiritual formation activities in the online Christian higher education environment. David Stark has made a convincing case for this by arguing that in both on-ground and online Christian institutions, spiritual formation is mediated by "presence" and "community," both of which are established primarily through exchanges of communication, but not necessarily through physical proximity. Stark suggests that spiritual formation should be viewed through the metaphor of game, using "game" to refer to a definite relationship between players and the game they are playing. When spiritual formation is viewed as a language game, it refers to the way in which faculty, staff, and administrators "bring *themselves* authentically and immersively 'into play' as they seek to care for students whom they may never meet face-to-face."[12] By mentioning staff and administrators in addition to faculty, Stark highlights the fact that spiritual formation extends beyond the formal curriculum to include many forms of communication between institutional personnel and students.

One of the key players in this regard at LAPU is the success coach, whose role is explained further in chapter 10. For the purpose of this chapter and the focus on assessment, it is sufficient to note that one of the key roles played by the success coaches is engaging students in conversations about faith, life, and learning. While these conversations take many forms (e.g., telephone, email, and text messages) and cover a wide range of topics related to faith, life, and learning, there are several specific questions that

---

12. Stark, "Gaming the System," 51.

coaches are encouraged to ask students that provide an opportunity for assessment. These include the following (questions are modified depending on whether they are asked initially or as a follow-up):

- Have you thought about how what you are learning in class connects to your faith? In what ways do you expect your learning in this class to impact your faith or beliefs?
- How do you think the Christian worldview presented in this class will inform your life and work outside of class?
- Have you had any conversations with others (e.g., significant others, spouse, friend, children, etc.) about what you are learning in class and your Christian worldview?
- Do you feel that you are or will be living your life differently at home or work because of the faith-oriented discussions and activities in class? How so?

Currently, no effort is made at LAPU to track the answers to these questions. However, the questions provide a foundation for assessing the effectiveness of spiritual formation activities at a deeper level.

An evaluation model that may provide practical guidance regarding how such assessment can be accomplished is Donald and James Kirkpatrick's four-level evaluation model for training programs. The four levels—reaction, learning, behavior, and results—are sequential levels that measure increasing depth of program effectiveness. The Kirkpatricks demonstrate that as one progresses through these four levels the assessment process is more extensive, but also has the potential to provide better quality feedback.[13] Reaction, which primarily measures customer satisfaction, is typically captured in end-of-course surveys. LAPU includes two statements in end-of-course surveys that focus on a Christian worldview:

- This course helped me better understand the relationship of a Christian worldview to the content area of the course.
- This course helped me better understand the relationship of a Christian worldview to my life and work in the world.

Generally, students respond positively to both these statements, rating them 4.3 on a five-point scale. Interestingly, during the eight-week session

---

13. Kirkpatrick and Kirkpatrick (*Evaluating Training Programs,* 21–26) explain what is involved in evaluation at each of the levels and then state, "Reaction is easy to do, and we should measure it for every program. Trainers should proceed to the other three levels as staff, time, and money are available" (26).

that included the rise of the coronavirus pandemic (March through April 2020), the scores for both of these statements averaged 4.4. This may merely indicate that students were giving more thought to a Christian worldview during this time period, but the overall strong rating shows that students are largely satisfied with LAPU's efforts to incorporate a Christian worldview into its curricula.

Assessing the second level of the Kirkpatricks' model, learning, takes place within the assessment activities related to the formal curriculum as discussed above. This process includes not only the instructor's grading of the assignments students submit but the annual program learning outcome assessment process as well. As noted above, in order to be effective the assessment of learning requires a close correspondence among the PLOs, CLOs, assignments, and assignment rubrics. Provided the PLOs and CLOs are clearly stated and appropriately address faith, life, and learning—and the assignment authentically assesses these learning outcomes—assessing whether students have learned what is expected should be straightforward.

The Kirkpatricks' third level of assessment, behavior, is reflected in the coaches' questions noted above. This level of assessment seeks to discover whether that which has been learned has impacted a person's behavior. The four coaching questions all focus on the extent to which a student may have applied what they learned about a Christian worldview, both in their personal lives and in their workplace. While the Kirkpatricks' model focuses on evaluating training programs in the workplace, higher education institutions attempting to promote spiritual formation are concerned with the application of what has been learned more holistically. The authors note that success at this level is often influenced by four conditions that are necessary for change to occur: (1) the person must have a desire to change; (2) the person must know what to do and how to do it; (3) the person must work in the right climate; (4) the person must be rewarded for changing.[14] While the first two conditions can be influenced by the training itself (in the case of higher education, the curriculum and the instructors), the third and fourth conditions lie largely outside the scope of the institution's influence. The Kirkpatricks identify five types of climates that hinder or promote change: preventing, discouraging, neutral, encouraging, and requiring. The reward for change can also be intrinsic or extrinsic, neither of which lie within the institution's power to change once students complete their studies. This is simply a recognition that while it may be desirable for institutions to assess behavioral changes related to faith, life, and learning, they may have limited ability to influence some of the conditions necessary for such changes.

14. Kirkpatrick and Kirkpatrick, *Evaluating Training Programs*, 23.

Despite the limitations of higher education institutions being able to assess the behavior of graduates who may or may not remain connected to the institution, there does appear to be merit in attempting to assess the four coaching questions noted above. The Kirkpatricks suggest behavior change can be assessed using either interviews or well-designed survey questionnaires.[15] Whichever type of instrument is used, it is important to ensure it focuses on the respondent's perception of their behavior before and after the learning experience. Two possible opportunities for conducting such assessments would be via an exit interview, just prior to the student's graduation, and via an alumni survey questionnaire, administered at a set interval (e.g., six months or twelve months) following the completion of their program. Hopefully, such assessments would provide insight into the extent to which students are achieving the institutional learning outcome related to faith, life, and learning.

The fourth level of the Kirkpatricks' evaluation model focuses on results, which in corporate training is often tied to improvements in customer service, revenue, profit, or other such goals. Higher education institutions can measure some of the results of the education they provide by assessing the employment and career advances of their graduates, average earnings of graduates, and preparedness of their graduates for postgraduate studies. However, measuring the results of faith, life, and learning is much more difficult. While faith, life, and learning results could be conceived as students thinking and behaving in manners influenced by a Christian worldview or developing greater intimacy with God, measuring such results would require extensive observation of the student's life, which lies outside the scope of most higher education institutions' missions.

CONCLUSION

This brief discussion of LAPU's experience of reviewing learning outcomes related to faith, life, and learning has highlighted several important principles. First, faith, life, and learning outcomes are a core component of the mission of most Christian higher education institutions. Second, faith, life, and learning outcomes must permeate all levels of an institution's learning objectives, including ILOs, PLOs, CLOs, assignments, and assignment rubrics. Next, the effectiveness of such learning outcomes depends largely on the degree of alignment throughout these various levels. This means a robust assessment process is necessary to ensure outcomes are being achieved and to correct any misalignments that occur. Further, while faith, life, and

---

15. Kirkpatrick and Kirkpatrick, *Evaluating Training Programs*, 56.

learning may be assessed in the cognitive, affective, and/or psychomotor domains, the appropriateness of such assessments will depend largely on whether the institution accepts only Christian students or has an open admission policy. Finally, assessment of behavior changes related to faith, life, and learning outcomes may be achieved through exit interviews or alumni survey questionnaires. As challenging as it may be to assess faith, life, and learning across the university, online institutions have both the responsibility and opportunity to use the assessment process to develop and engage students toward holistic faith formation. Chapter 5, the final chapter of Part 1, takes a step back from assessment and explores the larger context of how faith, life, and learning fit into broader statements of institutional identity, purpose, and ethos.

Chapter 5

Faith, Life, Learning, and Institutional Identity

JOHN W. WASHATKA

JOHN WASHATKA, *Associate Professor at Los Angeles Pacific University, describes and develops aspects of institutional identity that inform the university's faith formation mission. The chapter addresses the key question: How does institutional identity impact specific commitments, practices, and resources for faith formation?*

THE UNIVERSITY'S IDENTITY

A university's identity provides the philosophical foundation for its existence, mission, and purpose. Identity shapes curriculum, culture, reputation, and engagement in community and campus life. Universities rely on their identities to set themselves apart and to offer students unique opportunities and experiences for their educational journey. At Los Angeles Pacific University (LAPU), identity provides an important context for understanding the role of the university's core organizational principles as they relate to faith, life, and learning. LAPU's statements of identity, vision, purpose, core values, and Christian worldview work together to describe the unique environment and institutional culture that foster a commitment to holistic faith formation. Identity statements are not abstract aspirations. Universities craft and refine them in order to define their purpose and to set the guardrails for how they will (and will not) operate.

Exploring aspects of LAPU's institutional identity throughout this chapter is an exercise in how universities can look to their own statements of identity and purpose to foster mission-centric initiatives, such as the integration of faith, life, and learning. For LAPU, the institution's identity is the key driver for virtually all aspects of faith, life, and learning development, and acts as a central guide and filter for content development and the direction in which it goes. This means activities and materials should be prioritized as they relate to an institution's identity.

To start, the chapter explores LAPU's identity, statement of vision, statement of purpose, and core values.[1] In addition, LAPU's Christian worldview statement is considered—given that the university's identity, vision, purpose, and core values, are also part of its worldview—along with its core operating principles. This concept of a worldview is understood to be essentially a set of beliefs about reality.[2] By way of application, university administrators and faculty may find it helpful to reflect systematically on their own identity statements when considering ideas for innovation and growth.

Identity

LAPU's identity has been shaped both collectively and collaboratively by a number of different influences: its Wesleyan heritage, its ongoing relationship with Azusa Pacific University, its Christian worldview, and its community (including its board of trustees, senior leadership, employees, and students). The statement asserts the university's commitment to quality, faith-based online learning that is focused on the needs of students:

> Los Angeles Pacific University is an accredited, online, Christ-centered learning community that creates new hope for the future by offering convenient and affordable associate, bachelor's, and master's degrees to students of all backgrounds.[3]

Fostering this identity is a matter of stewardship. Identity drift is prevented by the university's adherence to its worldview and by ongoing vigilance of

1. Los Angeles Pacific University, "About Us."
2. Sire, *Universe Next Door*, 20.
3. Los Angeles Pacific University, "About Us."

its community, particularly the board of trustees and senior leadership, to preserve its substance and integrity even as its identity continues to develop in the midst of a broader culture of continuous change.

Vision and Purpose

LAPU's vision and purpose statements expand on the identity statement by providing "the direction and task to which the university applies its resources and effort, with the understanding that the integrative nature of faith cannot be fulfilled apart from a mission of transformation consistent with a Christian commitment."[4] The vision and purpose statements, then, set out how the university's identity translates to organizational mission:

> *Vision*
> Los Angeles Pacific University exists to serve people around the world who desire education delivered in the context of faith, excellence, and flexibility, removing the barriers to affordability and accessibility.
>
> *Purpose*
> We create for people a new hope for the future, by investing in lives through learning pathways that are Christ-centered, flexible, and accessible.[5]

Essentially, while the university does not use explicit "missional" language, its vision and purpose serve as its mission, which is focused on service in the context of hope-filled faith. Interestingly, the university's regional accrediting agency recognizes a university's mission in terms of its stated purpose. According to the agency, the terms *mission* and *purpose* are interchangeable. Consequently, the terms are meant to be interchangeable in this chapter.[6]

---

4. Los Angeles Pacific University, "University's Christian Worldview."
5. Los Angeles Pacific University, "University's Christian Worldview."
6. See WASC Senior College and University Commission, "Standard 1." Criteria for Review (CFR) 1.1 states: "The institution's formally approved statements of purpose are appropriate for an institution of higher education and clearly define its essential values and character and ways in which it contributes to the public good. Guidelines: The institution has a published mission statement that clearly describes its purposes. The institution's purposes fall within recognized academic areas and/or disciplines."

Core Values

LAPU's core values "serve as a strategic guide to focus the efforts needed to fulfill the university's mission. They reflect the strategic emphases of implementation."[7] If identity statements describe what a university is about, and vision and purpose statements describe why a university exists, then core values describe how a university will function. LAPU is committed to three core values:

- Exemplary: We honor God in our actions, attitudes, and aspirations.
- Caring: We serve with grace the needs of our colleagues and students.
- Learning: We continually nurture new thinking that generates and contributes to ongoing learning opportunities for all.[8]

These values serve as self-checks on the university's direction and culture and create an expectation for how the university will engage in its own growth and development.

The University's Christian Worldview[9]

Four documents express the university's worldview: The Statement of Faith, Vision and Purpose Statements, Core Organizational Principles, and Core Values. Two of the four documents, Vision and Purpose and Core Values, have dual roles as they are part of both the university's identity (see above) and its Christian worldview. A third document, Statement of Faith, "is the central statement of the university in matters of identity and nature. It provides a Christian declaration of the theological underpinnings on which the university is built. It contains a clear description of faith and living as a reflection of the institution's heritage of integration of right belief and right living."[10]

The statement of faith, core to the university's worldview, is also central to the university's identity. It is in part understood through the university's core organizational principles, which "describe the nature of the university

---

7. Los Angeles Pacific University, "University's Christian Worldview."
8. Los Angeles Pacific University, "About Us."
9. Los Angeles Pacific University, "University's Christian Worldview." LAPU's Statement of Faith, inherited from Azusa Pacific University, is most similar to statements of faith by the Free Methodist Church of America. The FMCA is largely the source of LAPU's particular theological tradition. See Free Methodist Church of America, "We Believe."
10. Los Angeles Pacific University, "University's Christian Worldview."

in living out core values in the pursuit of its mission."[11] Practically speaking then, when it comes to faith, life, and learning, the university's Christian worldview is best carried out through its core organizational principles.

Summary

The question "Who is Los Angeles Pacific University?" is answered by the aggregation of its identity, vision, purpose, core values, and worldview. The university's identity provides the foundation for its vision, purpose, and values. Additionally, the university's vision, purpose, and values can be regarded as a further explication of its identity. The university's identity is separate from, but related to, its worldview, given the overlapping appearance of the university's vision, purpose, and core organizational values. The next section is devoted to further exploring the university's core organizational principles, and how they inform the university's commitment to faith, life, and learning.

THE UNIVERSITY'S CORE ORGANIZATIONAL PRINCIPLES

LAPU's core organizational principles help illuminate a response to the chapter's key question: how does institutional identity impact specific commitments, practices, and resources for faith formation? Preliminarily, the key question can be answered by extrapolating how the university's identity (as described above) serves as the foundation for its core organizational principles. These principles can then be applied directly to the university's commitment to faith, life, and learning. LAPU has identified five core organizational principles: Christ-centered, academic excellence, accessibility, market relevance, and organizational sustainability. Each principle carries distinct implications for the integration of faith, life, and learning.

The five core principles are part of the university's worldview and "describe the nature of the university in living out core values in the pursuit of its mission."[12] They begin to operationalize the university's worldview which, in this context, is work related to faith, life, and learning. Now, it should be obvious the principles are not unique to LAPU. Other faith-based universities could easily adopt these principles, more or less, as their own. (In fact, any institution could utilize these principles, less the principle

11. Los Angeles Pacific University, "University's Christian Worldview."
12. Los Angeles Pacific University, "University's Christian Worldview."

of being Christ-centered.) The university's uniqueness, when compared with other faith-based universities, is the nature of its work, and how the principles inform and provide practical guidance in that work. So, when it comes to faith, life, and learning, the five core operating principles serve as five practical commitments the university has to the cultivation of holistic faith. What follows, then, is not a general introduction to the principles, but a consideration of their relevance as commitments, and their related practices, resources, and applications to faith, life, and learning.

Christ-centered

Commitment: We are believers who teach and serve from a Christian worldview.

Generally, how LAPU is "Christ-centered" is drawn from its historical and theological roots. Its statement of faith is introduced by the comment, "As an educational institution with a Wesleyan tradition at its core, it seems natural to us to embrace a statement of faith that is common among many Christian traditions."[13] While it is not explicitly stated, the statement of faith commits those who work at LAPU to a common understanding of Christ, particularly the section, "We believe in the deity of our Lord Jesus Christ, in His virgin birth, in His sinless life, in His miracles, in His vicarious and atoning death through His shed blood, in His bodily resurrection, and in His ascension to the right hand of the Father, and in His personal return to power and glory." Based on the statement of faith, a related aspirational expectation is that employees will "model a Christian lifestyle as outlined in the Word of God." Such an aspirational expectation allows room for a variety of lifestyles and behaviors. Seeking common ground in the midst of theological diversity tends to be characteristic of Wesleyan-grounded institutions, institutions that focus on shared beliefs and not on exclusivity and an absolute theology. As part of the Azusa Pacific University System, LAPU remains grounded in a Wesleyan heritage.

University-wide practices that arise out of the commitment to be Christ-centered include all employees signing a statement of faith, all employees able to attend weekly, university-wide devotions, and a regular institutional focus on faith, life, and learning for students and employees through announcements, activities, and discussion questions posted within each class. Resources that provide guidance and direction for the community include the university's statement of faith and various positional statements.[14] In addition, as it is related to faith, life, and learning, the university

13. Los Angeles Pacific University, "What We Believe."
14. Los Angeles Pacific University, "What We Believe."

provides a website that expands on various related, relevant topics.[15] The website is regularly updated with new resources and content.

Two groups of individuals serve as the primary human resource for the university's students: success coaches and instructors. The university's success coach model is fully explored in chapter 10. The purpose is to support students from enrollment through graduation, providing opportunities for academic and spiritual growth.[16] Instructors are the other group that facilitates faith conversations with students. Since the majority of instructors are adjuncts, training materials are provided for guidance and direction on how to approach the topic of faith in their classes. More importantly, qualities such as student-centeredness, empathy, and personableness are looked for during the adjunct interviewing and hiring process, so a "high-touch" habit is cultivated in a "high-tech" environment.[17]

When it comes to applying Christ-centeredness to faith, life, and learning, the university uses a whole-person, whole-institution approach. As part of this endeavor, for example, employees and instructors are encouraged to share with students how their story connects with God's story. Each individual has a unique story to tell, and in the telling and hearing of those personal stories students begin to get a sense of what it means to be Christian. Suffice to say, being Christ-centered is the critical ingredient for LAPU's holistic commitment to the cultivation of faith, life, and learning among all students, staff, and faculty. This commitment then filters through the other four organizational principles to provide additional direction and context for the university's endeavors.

Academic Excellence

Commitment: We are committed to educational excellence and quality certificates for professional skills and continuing education.

As described by its own documents, the university defines academic excellence as educational quality that encompasses four areas: is student-centered, not teaching- or content-centered; concerns learning experiences, which encompass certificates, degrees, continuing education, non-credit-bearing programs and courses, and other forms of lifelong learning; must be measured through the assessment of learning outcomes; and must be relevant to the academic and career goals of students.

---

15. Los Angeles Pacific University, "Faith, Life, and Learning."
16. Los Angeles Pacific University, "Student Success."
17. For related discussion, see Naisbitt, *High Touch High Tech*.

Practices for achieving and maintaining academic excellence include using a post-traditional, student-centered approach to learning experiences (immediately applicable, professionally oriented, and lifelong) and using an andragogical approach to curriculum design. Adherence to both practices is achieved through using a centralized course development process. The process takes into consideration the inherent complexity of creating material suitable for the online environment. The process also acknowledges the centrality of the online modality for content delivery, and that curriculum developed for the traditional classroom is generally unsuitable for online use. A reason for recent failures in online learning during the coronavirus pandemic could be the difficulty of adapting material designed to be delivered in a classroom, face-to-face setting for delivery in an online setting.[18] Rather than trying to replicate the face-to-face experience via distance learning, the creation of online courses involves a team of content and curriculum development experts who work together to create material suitable for post-traditional students learning in an online environment. The team uses standardized templates for same-look familiarity regardless of class (or program) and submit developed material through an approval process for consistent quality control and with a view to future, continuous improvement.

Resources that provide guidance and direction for the university's curriculum development practices include work by Jane Vella, Malcolm Knowles, Ernest Boyer, Angela Duckworth, and Carol Dweck.[19] Additional resources that guide appropriate complexity of course content are learning taxonomies. Such taxonomies help ensure cognitive, psychomotor, and affective development is relevant to the learning level and outcomes of the class. Chapter 4 of this book explores cognitive, psychomotor, and affective taxonomies in the context of assessment.

When it comes to curriculum development, perhaps the main resource of the university is the eLearning group specifically dedicated to designing and creating active learning experiences and courses with the adult learner in mind. The group works collaboratively with faculty and other members of the LAPU community to produce and deliver "rich, immersive content that captures and holds the learner's attention, as well as educates."[20] Such content is created by the curriculum development team using educational and scholarly principles developed by Vella, Knowles, Boyer, Duckworth, and Dweck.

18. See, for example, Hobbs and Hawkins, "Results Are In."

19. Vella, *Learning to Listen*; Knowles, *Modern Practice of Adult Education*; Boyer, *Scholarship Reconsidered*; Duckworth, *Grit*; and Dweck, *Mindset*.

20. Los Angeles Pacific University, "University Wins 2020 Omni Awards for Instructional Media Design."

A culminating practice for achieving and maintaining academic excellence is having regional accreditation through the WASC Senior College and University Commission (WSCUC). Such accreditation serves as a standard for academic quality control that assures the university achieves a level of academic quality suitable for a postsecondary institution. One of the expectations of LAPU's regional accrediting agency is that programs must be aligned with LAPU's mission. Given the Christ-centered nature of the university's vision and purpose noted above, LAPU must show how new program proposals help achieve its stated purpose and how existing programs are helping students achieve the program learning outcomes related to faith, life, and learning. As such, the university's commitment to academic excellence as it is applied to faith, life, and learning occurs through the development and delivery of high quality, relevant course materials. Instructors are then empowered to apply Boyer's ideas of the scholarship of teaching to all elements of teaching, including those that inform and support the holistic development of faith, life, and learning among students.

Accessibility

Commitment: We are committed to economic affordability, global delivery, and wherever feasible, open admission.

The university has a broad commitment to accessibility in a number of ways. When individuals in higher education think of "accessibility," most likely they have equal access for individuals with disabilities in mind, along with compliance with the American Disabilities Act (ADA) of 1990. LAPU shares that commitment, and has a department dedicated to supporting those with disabilities.[21] Relatedly, courses are designed to meet ADA standards.

However, as stated by the commitment, other kinds of accessibility include overcoming economic and enrollment hurdles. Simply stated, "economic affordability" means the university indexes total program tuition cost to be lower than the annual national median household income. The low-cost tuition is administered as an alternative to the practice of discount pricing followed by other universities. Other practices related to program tuition costs include using open educational resources for class use wherever possible, and keeping the total cost of class resources under 10 percent of the course tuition, with few exceptions.

The university's commitment to overcoming enrollment hurdles begins with having an open admission/enrollment policy. The idea behind the policy is to give individuals who would otherwise not have one,

---

21. Los Angeles Pacific University, "Accessibility."

an opportunity for an education. (In informal conversations, the university president has stated that "LAPU is the university of second, third, and fourth chances and can be so without sacrificing academic integrity.") An open enrollment policy has two broad implications. First, the university is not selective when it comes to applicant academic qualifications. Academic support services are available for those students who may need them.

Second, the university does not require students to provide or sign a statement of faith—students are admitted with no regard for religious beliefs. In fact, information related to student religious preferences is not collected. As a result, curriculum and other materials, activities and events, and conversations related to faith, life, and learning take into account a broad spectrum of student perspectives and ideas as they are related to religious topics, with no assumptions made about a student's religious background or beliefs. Such information may be volunteered by students in the application and enrollment process, and in response to questions posed by success coaches, instructors, and the curriculum. Students are able to be as evasive or forthcoming as they want about what they actually believe, since assignment rubrics do not grade them on their beliefs.

The university's commitment to accessibility as it is applied to faith, life, and learning occurs through the availability of materials. Resources and materials are posted on the university website, accessible to all, including the viewing public. In addition, faith, life, and learning materials are integrated into courses and programs across the university. Finally, student access to faith, life, and learning is achieved through instructors, coaches, and other community members who model Christian faith in their various interactions. Admittedly, the university does not always get things right, but mistakes provide opportunities for the university to demonstrate Christian humility as it seeks to make things right (whole) for the student.

Market Relevance

Commitment: We are responsive to market demand, employer needs, and professional occupations.

The academic programs the university offers are developed in response to market demands, with the term *market* here generally understood to mean programs students are interested in and skills employers require. Broadly, the kinds of educational programs the university attempts to offer, and the format in which it attempts to deliver them, are the ones most appealing to the kind of student the university is most likely to attract. Understanding the unique demographics of LAPU's student profile helps the university determine market relevance. At LAPU, 43 percent of students are between twenty-five and thirty-four years old, while less than 17 percent are twenty-four or younger. Seventy-nine percent of students are female, over 28 percent are single parents, 43 percent are Hispanics of any race, and 75 percent are enrolled part-time.[22] Additionally, employment profile data collected by the university show 63 percent of LAPU students work thirty or more hours per week, 12 percent do not work, and 45 percent "see their jobs affecting their school work."

The LAPU student profile is consistent with those characteristics of nontraditional students as described by Susan Choy. Choy's research shows the nontraditional college student typically delays enrollment (does not enter postsecondary education in the same calendar year that he or she finished high school); attends part time for at least part of the academic year; works full time (thirty-five hours or more per week) while enrolled; is considered financially independent for purposes of determining eligibility for financial aid; has dependents other than a spouse (usually children, but sometimes others); is a single parent (either not married or married but separated and has dependents); and does not have a high school diploma (completed high school with a GED or other high school completion certificate or did not finish high school).[23] For Choy, to the degree an individual has those characteristics is the degree to which they are considered nontraditional.

More recent conversation has suggested replacing the term *nontraditional* with *post-traditional*. In his manifesto, Louis Soares gives three reasons for changing:

> The first . . . is that terms currently used for data and statistical purposes—nontraditional, employees who study, independent, at-risk—frankly describe these learners as aberrations to the postsecondary education system rather than the courageous learners they are. Second, statistically speaking, these categories are becoming increasingly irrelevant. . . . Third, we believe that post-traditional learners and their need for customized education experiences is actually mirrored by millennial generation students now enrolling in postsecondary education who show a deep desire to integrate experience and education and tailor their learning.[24]

Later in his essay, Soares states that 85 percent of the current undergraduate student population is comprised of post-traditional learners, individuals

---

22. Los Angeles Pacific University, "Fast Facts."
23. Choy, *Nontraditional Undergraduates*, 3.
24. Soares, "Post-traditional Learners," 5.

not interested in attending college in a traditional classroom setting, and individuals interested in pursuing further education for either professional or personal reasons.[25] However, a different analysis of the data suggests the population of post-traditional learners is closer to 74 percent.[26] Differences in percentages may be explained by how the data was tracked and analyzed. While percentages of post-traditional learners may vary, the point that the majority of college students are no longer traditional remains.

Soares also takes the view that a holistic approach to a college education takes into consideration the development of skills demanded by employers, skills developed by both liberal arts and professional programs.[27] While the university's curriculum is undergirded by a liberal arts core, its focus is similar to Soares's view by offering development of those professional skills students most attracted to the university want, and employers require. The university uses two main resources to guide its development of educational programs. The first is industry-expert advisory councils composed of individuals who have experience within a particular industry. (For example, the university has a Public Administration Advisory Council for its criminal justice and public administration programs that includes active or former local city officials, police chiefs, lawyers, judges, and parole officers who support the university's core values and program goals.) Councils provide guidance and direction for a particular program so it stays professionally relevant and applicable. The second resource used by the university is course instructors who are scholar-practitioners in the discipline of the academic program. Most instructors are terminally degreed and active in the field of their expertise. As practitioners, instructors lend relevance, applicability, and currency to the subject matter they teach.

The university's commitment to market relevance as it is applied to faith, life, and learning is demonstrated by addressing how holistic faith formation is relevant to a student's professional development as it is related to their employment and career. Both success coaches and instructors raise focused, open-ended questions, and have meaningful conversations, designed to help students think about applications and implications of faith, life, and learning in their career and in their workplace.

---

25. Soares, "Post-traditional Learners," 6.
26. Radford et al., "Demographic and Enrollment Characteristics."
27. Soares, "Post-traditional Learners," 9.

Organizationally Sustainable

Commitment: We are economically viable and scalable, valuing the gifts, talents, and resources of the university.

The university recognizes key practices associated with upholding the core operating principle of organizational sustainability. These include operating within a shared governance framework committed to data-driven decisions, developing non-tuition-related revenue streams, keeping labor costs to less than 60 percent of the annual operating budget, and monitoring and improving security policies and procedures to safeguard confidentiality and security of data. Sustainability is intentionally addressed on an annual basis as part of the university's management goals.

The shared governance framework in which the university operates is addressed in chapter 3. The framework cultivates a culture of collaboration across various university groups and departments, providing greater consistency in the university's processes and products that lead to more understanding and less conflict and confusion among the university employees and students than if there was less collaboration. This culture of collaboration is supported by a commitment to data-driven decision-making. Examples of data-driven decisions include: constructing an annual operating budget based on historic enrollment trends and enrollment projections; staffing throughout the organization; selecting academic programs and course development based on research regarding student inquiries, competitive intensity, and job demand; developing and launching a "mobile university initiative" with the goal of creating student accessibility to the university on a mobile device; conducting program learning outcomes assessment and program review process; and managing continuous improvement university-wide.[28] As the above examples indicate, intentional and thoughtful data-driven decision-making occurs throughout the university. Collaboration allows for thoughtful and efficient implementation of decisions and initiatives for the health and sustainability of the organization.

Resources associated with organizational sustainability include the university's zero-based budget model and a relatively flat organizational structure. The flat organizational structure shortens the time and minimizes the number of individuals needed for the organization to make decisions. Having a flat structure results in quicker development time and time to market of services and products. Another university resource is the university's

---

28. Examples of university-wide continuous improvement initiatives include student classroom support protocols and processes, refining the academic petition process, selecting supply vendors, and administering professional development of university employees.

board of trustees. The board is composed of individuals with complementary experiences and competencies in order to provide broad guidance as it relates to organizational sustainability.

As it applies to faith, life, and learning, organizational sustainability ensures the continuation of the university's vision and purpose. Faith, life, and learning is intrinsic to the university's identity such that being continually sustainable means being continually committed to cultivating holistic faith. The sustainable organization is then able and empowered to offer a Christ-centered hope to its entire community.

CONCLUSION

Taken together, the university's five core organizational principles can be regarded as central commitments, with related practices, resources, and applications. The principles demonstrate the centrality of faith, life, and learning to the identity and work of the university. This identity—described by a number of statements related to LAPU's worldview, vision, purpose, core values, and operating principles—is seen as the foundation for the engagement and cultivation of holistic faith formation, with such engagement regarded as an outworking of the university's identity.

In sum, the university is Wesleyan in its theological perspective, which lends itself to the practices of being inclusive and addressing the whole person. It places the person and work of Jesus Christ at the core of all that it does. The university is post-traditional in that it blurs traditional roles and organizational structures found in traditional universities. It also is primarily online, which requires establishing specific methodologies to meet the needs of its learners. The university is student-centric, with its learners the focus of its work. Its learners are post-traditional and are not required to make a statement of faith, which provides a context for determining not only course content but the direction of the work of faith, life, and learning. The end goal of a commitment to faith, life, and learning is the development of a Christ-centered hope in each member of the institution's community.

PART 2

Faith, Life, and Learning in the Curriculum

PART 2 *explores how faith formation concepts can be integrated into the online classroom, organized according to the four themes from Los Angeles Pacific University's Statement of Faith, Life, and Learning: Christian worldview (chapter 6), God's story (chapter 7), diverse faith perspectives (chapter 8), and faith through academic disciplines (chapter 9). These chapters provide concrete examples of how concepts and practices of faith formation can be included in a variety of online courses.*

Chapter 6

Christian Worldview

JOHN W. WASHATKA

JOHN WASHATKA, *Associate Professor at Los Angeles Pacific University, presents both concepts and examples of how online students learn to apply a Christian worldview to their life and work in the world. The chapter explores the key question: What does it mean to hold to a Christian perspective in a culture of contested worldviews?*

Christian colleges and universities distinguish themselves among the thousands of other public and private institutions of higher education by their robust commitment to integrate a Christian worldview into their organizations. Online Christian universities are no different; they seek to infuse Christian worldview principles into their operations and, especially, into their diverse program and course offerings. As introduced in chapter 2, Los Angeles Pacific University (LAPU) uses the four points from their Statement of Faith, Life, and Learning to guide their work towards holistic faith integration across the curriculum.[1] The first of these commitments,

---

1. Students will be able to: (1) apply a Christian worldview to their life and work in the world; (2) articulate how and in what ways their life journeys connect to God's story; (3) engage with diverse faith perspectives within the learning community at LAPU; and, (4) recognize God's work in the world through all academic disciplines. See Los Angeles Pacific University, "Commitment to Faith, Life, and Learning."

that students will learn "to apply a Christian worldview to their life and work in the world," is in many ways foundational to the pursuit of holistic faith integration. As students discover what it means to think and work Christianly, they are more prepared to study and apply the Bible to their lives, grow in their understanding and appreciation of diverse faith perspectives, and discern God's call for their lives in relation to their academic discipline and career trajectory. To be sure, the four commitments work together to form a holistic framework for the integration of faith, life, and learning; one need not precede another in a linear progression. However, of the four commitments, the application of a Christian worldview permeates each of the others as a grounding principle. This chapter, then, begins Part 2 of the book by considering the concept of a Christian worldview in relation to course content, the andragogy the university uses to engage online students with a Christian worldview, and examples of how students learn to apply such a worldview to their life and work in the world. The chapter concludes with addressing the key question: What does it mean to hold a Christian perspective in a culture of contested worldviews?

THE CONCEPT OF CHRISTIAN WORLDVIEW

How an institution interprets and teaches a Christian worldview is in many ways a question of its own heritage, theological tradition, and contemporary commitments. Indeed, the literature on Christian worldview comes from a variety of traditions and covers a broad range of topics, themes, and applications. As such, this section of the chapter is content with briefly introducing various themes and patterns related to Christian worldview. The authors and texts considered here are not exhaustive, but rather illustrative of how the topic is often addressed. In addition, themes addressed vary from text to text due to the intent and focus of the authors when writing their books.

Some texts begin with *a general definition of a worldview*. This is a theme addressed by various authors in their work, including James Anderson's *What's Your Worldview*;[2] Tawa Anderson, Michael Clark, and David Naugle's *An Introduction to Christian Worldview*;[3] Deane Downey and Stanley Porter's *Christian Worldview and the Academic Disciplines*;[4] Michael

---

2. Anderson, *What's Your Worldview?* Anderson uses an interactive approach with readers answering yes/no questions to determine one's worldview.

3. Anderson et al., *Introduction to Christian Worldview*.

4. Downey and Porter, *Christian Worldview and the Academic Disciplines*. Topics included in the book, but not highlighted above, include the state of the Christian university in current culture and the development of a Christian mind.

Goheen and Craig Bartholomew's *Living at the Crossroads*;[5] Ronald Nash's *Life's Ultimate Questions*;[6] Philip Ryken's *Christian Worldview*;[7] James Sire's *The Universe Next Door*;[8] and Brian Walsh and Richard Middleton's *The Transforming Vision*.[9] Some of these authors focus more on a *definition/description of a Christian worldview*. They include Anderson, Clark, and Naugle; Downey and Porter; Goheen and Bartholomew; Ryken; Sire; and Walsh and Middleton.

Still others consider *tests of a worldview* as a means of determining coherence and sustainability. Anderson, Clark, and Naugle take this approach; as do J. P. Moreland and William Craig in *Philosophical Foundations for a Christian Worldview*;[10] Nash; Sire; and Walsh and Middleton. Others, like Goheen and Bartholomew; David Naugle in *Worldview*;[11] Sire; and Walsh and Middleton, offer a story of the concept through either a *history of worldviews,* or *worldviews through a historical perspective.*

Alternative worldviews are considered by Anderson, Clark, and Naugle; Sire; and Walsh and Middleton; while the relationship between *Christian worldviews and academic disciplines* is explored by Downey and Porter; Moreland and Craig; and Walsh and Middleton. In addition, the practical outcome and application of *living in view of embracing a Christian worldview* is examined by Anderson, Clark, and Naugle; Goheen and Bartholomew; Sire; and Walsh and Middleton.

Finally, various authors explore *the content or components of any individual's particular worldview*. Anderson, Clark, and Naugle identify four components of a worldview, and form them as questions: What is our nature? What is our world? What is our problem? What is our end?[12] Similarly, Walsh and Middleton see a faith commitment as the basis of a worldview, formed by the way four questions are answered: Who am I? Where am I? What's wrong? What is the remedy?[13] Nash explores the philosophical side

---

5. Goheen and Bartholomew, *Living at the Crossroads*.
6. Nash, *Life's Ultimate Questions*.
7. Ryken, *Christian Worldview*.
8. Sire, *Universe Next Door*.
9. Walsh and Middleton, *Transforming Vision*.
10. Moreland and Craig, *Philosophical Foundations*. The authors focus on presenting Christian philosophy that would inform and provide presuppositional foundations for the development of a Christian worldview. Their book is not about worldviews, *per se*.
11. Naugle, *Worldview*. The book is a comprehensive history of the concept of worldview, including tracing its development from theological, philological, philosophical, and disciplinary perspectives.
12. Naugle, *Worldview*, 19–21.
13. Naugle, *Worldview*, 35.

of "five central worldview beliefs:" God, metaphysics, epistemology, ethics, and anthropology.[14] And Sire explores the components of worldview as they relate to eight core questions: What is prime reality—the really real? What is the nature of external reality, that is, the world around us? What is a human being? What happens to a person at death? Why is it possible to know anything at all? How do we know what is right and wrong? What is the meaning of human history? What personal, life-orienting core commitments are consistent with this worldview?[15]

While all of the above books—and many more not listed—are written with the Christian college classroom in mind, it is difficult to find any college-level text that is written for an audience of post-traditional students in post-traditional, online classroom settings. Developing curriculum for a course on worldviews designed for post-traditional students is thus challenging in view of the absence of practical guidance from the texts listed above. All are, at the very least, adequate when it comes to content ("*what* am I going to teach?"). None, though, is very helpful when it comes to methodology ("*How* am I going to teach content?"). Developing curriculum requires knowledge of the learner, the subject matter, and the learning context. Knowledge of the post-traditional learner and learning context is largely absent in the texts.

The post-traditional learner and the context of online learning is discussed in Stephen and Mary Lowe's *Ecologies of Faith in a Digital Age*, which focuses on spiritual growth.[16] Mark Maddix, James Estep, and Mary Lowe's *Best Practices in Online Education* explores practices related to online education and theoretical pedagogy at Christian universities.[17] However, neither presents practical ways of developing course content or methodology to teach worldview in an online environment to post-traditional learners.

Consideration for the post-traditional student or post-traditional learning environment appears to be lacking in more than just texts on worldviews. As an example, in their texts on the pedagogy of teaching and faith formation in the context of a Christian university, James K. A. Smith's *Desiring the Kingdom*,[18] David Smith's *On Christian Teaching*,[19] as well as their co-authored volume *Teaching and Christian Practice*,[20] do not include

14. Naugle, *Worldview*, 14–17.
15. Naugle, *Worldview*, 22–23.
16. Lowe and Lowe, *Ecologies of Faith*.
17. Maddix et al., *Best Practices of Online Education*.
18. Smith, *Desiring the Kingdom*.
19. Smith, *On Christian Teaching*.
20. Smith and Smith, *Teaching and Christian Practice*.

consideration of post-traditional learners in an online or post-traditional environment.

The challenge, then, is to develop worldview curricula for the post-traditional learner in an online classroom given the relative lack of curriculum guidance as summarized from the above literature review. Chapter 2 offers a summary of LAPU's course design process, a process that is adopted and adapted from Jane Vella's Dialogue Education approach that uses eight questions to guide course development.[21]

DEVELOPMENT OF WORLDVIEW CURRICULUM

This portion of the chapter, then, explores part of the process for developing an online course on Christian worldview for post-traditional students. Examining a few of the eight course development questions for LAPU's PHIL 205: Introduction to Philosophy provides further context and practical insight into how and why curriculum development must be adapted for the post-traditional student in the online environment. As the chapter will show, resources developed for traditional classroom use—like those discussed above—can readily be incorporated into the online, post-traditional environment when filtered through an andragogical, adult-learner curricular design approach.

The course design process starts with the question of who: who are the participants involved in this course? In this context of developing the PHIL 205 class on worldview, the "who" question has to do with discerning a worldview profile for LAPU students. Any worldview class being developed should anticipate what the expected worldview might be of students who enroll in such a class. LAPU students are not required to have a profession of faith, so a wide range of worldviews among students is possible and, in fact, present. Informally and anecdotally, the worldview of newly or recently enrolled LAPU students generally consists of the following loosely held beliefs, in no particular order: everything happens for a reason (with the implicit assumption that the reason is related to the action of some generally benevolent higher being); what is true for you is not necessarily true for me; what is moral for you is not necessarily moral for me; we are not to judge ("Who am I to judge?"); we are all God's children; everyone is entitled to their opinion; and as long as we do not hurt anyone, it is okay.[22]

---

21. Vella, *On Teaching and Learning*. See also Global Learning Partners.

22. As encountered, observed, and cataloged through countless class conversations with students and their written assignments.

More cohesively and coherently, the list above basically reflects Sire's description of deism, particularly "moralistic therapeutic deism."[23] However, LAPU students appear to have a view of God not nearly as well-developed and described by Sire. It also doesn't seem to make much of a difference if the student professes to be a Christian. In general, many students are at a similar stage of worldview development—at best only a nominal understanding of a Christian worldview. A related perspective is shared by one of the university's instructors:

> In my teaching, I usually have the opportunity of interacting with students having their first exposure to the Christian ethos of LAPU. I have found that they broadly fall into three categories: (1) those for whom faith and a relationship with God is already normative in their lives; (2) those who were raised in some kind of Christian (frequently Catholic) environment and so are vaguely comfortable, even if they have drifted quite far from it in practice; and (3) those who are frankly antagonistic at being "forced" to study the Bible when all they really want is a degree. I have been gratified to see how, in just eight weeks, many of those in the third category have moved to accept that there may just be some value in a Christian worldview, since obviously there are some good principles here that the world could benefit from.[24]

The starting point, then, for the development of a worldview class is the working assumption that students have generally deistic beliefs.

A second question in the course design process is the issue of why: why is this course being offered? How does it fit into the curriculum, both in the major and across the university? At LAPU, the simple reason for offering a worldview class is that it is an outworking of the university's identity, vision, and purpose, and is a reflection of its commitment to faith, life, and learning.[25] More practical reasons include first, as an introduction to philosophy class, the class would be able to fulfill a general education requirement. And second, it would introduce to students philosophical ideas used in the development of worldview.[26] According to Malcolm Knowles, adult learners look for immediate relevance and application of the material they learn.[27] Since philosophy by nature tends to be abstract, students could use

---

23. Sire, *Universe Next Door*, 63–64.
24. Reg Codrington, interview by author, November 20, 2020
25. See chapter 5.
26. For example, see Moreland and Craig, *Philosophical Foundations*.
27. Knowles, *Modern Practice of Adult Education*.

the material presented in the class to further the development of their own worldview to address the question, "How, then, should I live?" with immediate application to their professional and personal lives.

Another question for curriculum development concerns the course content: what is the content of the course, including the knowledge, skills, and attitudes students will acquire? Course content then, is provided by worldview content. The brief literature review above provides some insight into various worldview topics for which philosophy could provide answers. The depth with which each topic is covered is in part determined by the number of topics covered and the duration of the course. In PHIL 205, Sire's eight questions were chosen because of the relative (but admittedly, unequal) attention they gave to three out of the four classical subdivisions of philosophy: ontology (questions one, two, three, four, and seven); epistemology (question five); and ethics (question six). The subdivision of logic is not addressed in any structured manner, but is employed in the class as a test for worldviews, similar to Anderson, Clark, and Naugle.[28]

Simply put, a worldview is a set of beliefs about reality.[29] Sire's text, *The Universe Next Door*, was chosen as required reading for the class for three reasons. First, Sire's answers to his own questions provided an exemplar of a prototypical Christian worldview without getting into denominational differences and distinctions.[30] Students are able to see how a Christian might answer the questions. They are free to disagree with Sire's answers, and some of the more thoughtful students do. Second, the content he provides keeps the class primarily, but not exclusively, grounded in Christian philosophy of religion. Answers to the questions can, but need not, be influenced by either religion or theology. Third, the practical consideration of how Sire's eight worldview questions neatly fit into an eight-week class (one question each week) cannot be ignored.

What, then, can be hoped to be achieved in a worldview class—what are the course learning outcomes? What is the takeaway for students? If the long-term institutional goal is for students to develop a Christian worldview, how far along in the development process can students be expected to shift as a result of taking this class? Or a series of classes? The development of an individual's worldview in PHIL 205 is guided by course learning outcomes. As a result of their learning in the course, students will: apply key philosophical concepts toward the development of a worldview; recognize various philosophical theories within popular culture; articulate their

---

28. Anderson et al., *Introduction to Christian Worldview*.
29. Sire, *Universe Next Door*, 15.
30. Sire, *Universe Next Door*, 25–46.

worldview using the concepts, categories, and terminology of philosophy; reflect on the impact of their worldview in their personal lives; and compare their worldview with a Christian worldview.

PHIL 205 is an introductory course to worldviews and is one of several classes the university offers that address worldviews. While this class focuses primarily on the concept of worldview, other classes discuss worldview in the context of a student's major or their career. For example, currently four undergraduate programs and one graduate program have a Program Learning Outcome related to some aspect of Christian worldview development.[31] The university conducts periodic program reviews as part of its commitment to continuous academic improvement. As programs are reviewed and as new programs are developed, learning outcomes are revised to include integration of worldview formation where it is absent. The goal is to ensure that students wrestle with the implications of a Christian worldview throughout their entire academic journey.

LAPU faculty member Robert Carter's description of the rationale for including a Christian worldview in the Master of Public Health program is illustrative of the imperative to integrate worldview across the curriculum:

> The Christian worldview is fully integrated into the Master of Public Health Program. Some individuals argue we must separate our Christian worldview from the public aspects of our lives. However, this does not make sense from the Christian worldview, in particular in public health. In 1999, former U.S. Surgeon General Dr. David Satcher stated, "Through a partnership with faith organizations and the use of health promotion and disease prevention sciences, we can form a mighty alliance to build strong, healthy, and productive communities."[32]

For many students, the Christian worldview finds practical application in how they approach their careers and professions. As Carter's comments show, in public health for example, integrating the Christian worldview is a catalyst for the kind of excellence, creativity, compassion, and collaboration that is needed in the field.

It is not difficult to browse the LAPU course catalog and compile a list of courses that integrate Christian worldview into the curriculum. Depending on the level and type of course, discussion and assignment topics around

---

31. The following list is of those programs that have Program Learning Outcomes addressing the development of a Christian worldview: Associate of Arts in Humanities PLO 1; Associate of Science in Health Sciences PLO 1; Bachelor of Science in Organizational Leadership PLO 1; Master of Public Administration: PLO 5.

32. Robert Carter, interview by author, October 6, 2020.

worldview range from business, history, writing, information systems, leadership, nursing, and ethics, to name a few. A common thread throughout the diversity of topics is offering students the opportunity for reflection. As one instructor said, "A reflective student is one that will think deeply about their ultimate purpose in life—what they believe and why they believe what they believe."[33] No matter their academic or professional context, questions of Christian worldview application find meaning and relevance when students are given opportunities for reflection and integration. A variety of assignments can aid in this process of integrative learning, including guided discussions, case studies, reflection papers, capstone projects, and research papers. In sum, when worldview development is present across academic programs and is embedded in program learning outcomes, different levels of course content, and a variety of course assignments, students experience a regular rhythm of opportunities for the holistic integration of the Christian faith.

How effective the institution actually is in student worldview development is an ongoing assessment task, part of the larger effort to assess faith, life, and learning as described in chapter 4. Data from such assessment processes rely less on surveys and other indirect measures and feedback and more on direct, immediate artifacts and samples of learning. How well the university is doing is connected more directly to the results of its assessments and less to any sort of individual perception or bias. However, staff and instructor interviews provide firsthand accounts of how students are learning to apply a Christian worldview in their life and work in the world. For example, one success coach recognizes the importance of "thought-provoking and real-life-relevance questions that cause students to consider how their worldview (Christian or otherwise) resonates with the teachings found in Christian Scriptures."[34] Another instructor follows up with this insight:

> I have the benefit of seeing students articulate and answer key life questions which forces them to stop and reflect on what their faith or virtues are. Many students have said they have never had to answer these questions before in their life until they take my class. And many are appreciative of doing so (after the fact). Several students are able to answer the question "Who Am I?" beyond the academic context of solely being a college student by voicing what their faith identity is and why they pursue learning at all. It then becomes a much bigger take on life that goes beyond the grade and is instead a way for the student to see what their priorities really are in their life. These students begin to see

---

33. Sara Admiraal, interview by author, October 3, 2020.
34. Andrew Lindstrom, interview by author, October 5, 2020.

learning through a more holistic lens, and I as the instructor facilitate that discovery and holistic learning.[35]

Another instructor reflects on the importance of diversity in the formation of a Christian worldview: "Students learn from a variety of perspectives, just as their faith is often drawn from such diversity. A Christian worldview is expansive, inclusive, and practical. As an LAPU instructor, it has been my privilege to encourage multicultural Christian practices and beliefs in the online classroom."[36] Staff and instructors alike take on the joy and responsibility of walking with students as they discover more and more what it means to integrate a Christian worldview into all aspects of their life and learning.

HOLDING TO A CHRISTIAN PERSPECTIVE IN A CULTURE OF CONTESTED WORLDVIEWS

Students attending Christian colleges and universities today wrestle with worldview questions in the context of global pluralism. The worldview texts described earlier in the chapter generally are all responses to a predominant global pluralism which is primarily relativistic; a relativism that permits a broad marketplace of diverse perspectives and ideas, all of which are regarded as being equally valid, sound, and truthful. A Christian perspective would be only one among many perspectives in a globally pluralistic culture, competing as it were for predominance. In this regard, Gene Veith makes the point that the contemporary dominant global worldview has slid past a postmodern framework to a "post" postmodernism he calls "post-Christian."[37] His book includes a broad description of a post-Christian culture, its rise, and its shortcomings. Veith's claim of the dawning of a post-Christian era appears to be borne out, at least in America, by research done by the Pew Foundation.[38] This research describes the continued "decline of Christianity" in the United States.

As such, LAPU students are learning to reflect on the place of their Christian worldview in this context of a post-Christian culture and increasing religious diversity. Two recent graduates offer insights into what it means for them to hold to a Christian perspective in a post-Christian culture. The first student highlights the importance of the Bible: "As an LAPU graduate, one of the ways I will navigate Christian worldview challenges is by asking

---

35. Belen McDaniel, interview by author, September 16, 2020.
36. Lora Erickson, interview by author, October 2, 2020.
37. Veith, *Post-Christian*.
38. Pew Research Center, "Decline of Christianity Continues."

myself if my thinking and actions are consistent with biblical teachings."[39] The Bible is the ultimate authority and guide when it comes to a holistic understanding and application of faith, life, and learning. The student is illustrating the central role of the Bible when it comes to determining appropriate beliefs and lifestyles in the context of global culture. The student also points out the role of reason and reasoning when it comes to determining those appropriate beliefs and lifestyles. Whether the inconsistency is logical or behavioral, critical thinking and reasoning are required to aid interpretation and application of the Bible to life. The second student reinforces this idea of critical thinking: "LAPU has helped me apply a Christian worldview to my life and work by challenging me to define what those Christian views are and how they were formed. In a culture of contested worldviews, my Christian perspective is vital because it defines who I am. As a graduate of LAPU I will navigate challenges to my Christian worldview with answers that I can substantiate with scholarly resources."[40] Students recognize the importance of their values, critical thinking, study, and reasoning as they discern what it means to apply their faith in the world today.

Even with a strong commitment to a Christian worldview, scholars point out the cultural challenges many Christians face. Anderson, Clark, and Naugle suggest Christians are susceptible to consciously or subconsciously embracing "worldly views," including scientism, technicism, individualism, and functional atheism. They call on readers to "respectfully embrace a scripturally vibrant, Christ-centered, and faith-integrated worldview—one that places the work of salvation on Christ's shoulders, deposits the grace of the Father into our hearts, and liberally pours the anointing of the Spirit of God all over us."[41] To experience this, Goheen and Bartholomew propose Christians are to be "critical participants" in culture, willing to live in the tension created by living out the biblical story in cultures that misdirect and pervert it. Christians are to be communal, merciful, tolerant and suffering, and faithful witnesses.[42] Finally, Sire contends individuals adopt a worldview that has, as a characteristic, "inner intellectual coherence."[43] Intellectual coherence would include recognizing how the three laws of logic—identity, noncontradiction, and excluded middle—act as a standard by which worldviews are measured. He concludes that Christian theism is the most reasonable. Sire and other authors also mention living a life of

---

39. La Quenta Gross, interview by author, November 14, 2020.
40. Denise Schweinfurth, interview by author, November 19, 2020.
41. Anderson et al., *Introduction to Christian Worldview*, 323–30.
42. Goheen and Bartholomew, *Living at the Crossroads*, 132–45.
43. Sire, *Universe Next Door*, 281–86.

consistency that goes beyond logic, to include a consistency between beliefs and behavior, and an existential consistency related to the sustainability of an adopted worldview.[44]

The charge to live within an existential consistency is a high calling, and many Christians seem willing to ignore consistency for the sake of their cultural context. For example, LAPU students who have taken PHIL 205 typically are not aware of inconsistencies in their worldview, or between their beliefs and behavior. They participate in a simple two-question quiz designed to raise the idea of consistency between their beliefs and behavior. The first question is, "Do you believe people are basically good?" (beliefs), and the second question is, "Do you lock your car?" (behavior). Invariably, the most popular answer is "yes" to both questions. Implicit in that combination of answers is the question why they would lock their car if they thought people were basically good. Explanations for their answers include criticism of the exercise and rationalization for their answers, usually related to their living circumstances. Many students also recognize the inconsistency, but disregard the importance of consistency. Most rare are those responses that recognize the inconsistency between their belief and behavior, and the importance of being consistent. This exercise reveals the challenges some students can have in articulating and living within a principle of consistency between beliefs and behaviors.

As students journey through their academic program, they develop a deeper and more holistic understanding and practice of their faith, life, and learning. As seen above, by graduation, students can step back and reflect on the knowledge, skills, and attitudes they have gained and can continue to cultivate in their lives and careers. Developing and applying a Christian worldview is a lifelong commitment, and Christian universities play a significant role in equipping their students for a Christ-centered life in the midst of a culture of contested worldviews.

CONCLUSION

Christian colleges and universities have a unique opportunity to help students learn to apply a Christian worldview to their life and work in the world. While there is no shortage of relevant literature and resources on the topic, adapting these to an online, post-traditional learning environment requires focused knowledge of the context and background of the learners themselves. In a pluralistic culture that is more and more defined by personal feeling and experience, many post-traditional students find a

---

44. See, for example, Anderson et al., *Introduction to Christian Worldview*, 76–90.

biblically informed Christian worldview to be both novel and relevant to their lives. When presented with consistency across the curriculum, students journey towards ever greater understanding and appreciation of how a Christian worldview is a vital aspect of their own faith, life, and learning. As will be explored in coming chapters, when combined with learning about how God's story connects to their lives, diverse faith perspectives, and connecting their faith across all academic disciplines, students experience a robust and meaningful journey toward holistic faith formation.

Chapter 7

God's Story

BRANT M. HIMES

BRANT HIMES, Associate Professor at Los Angeles Pacific University, presents both concepts and examples of how online students learn to articulate how and in what ways their life journeys connect to God's story. The chapter explores the key question: How does the Bible connect to contemporary life?

The journey of the Christian life is an invitation to participate in God's grand narrative of redemption. Throughout history, Christians have looked to the Old and New Testaments for the foundational beliefs and practices that form their communities and guide their faith. Today is no different. Christians learn about the content, meaning, and purpose of God's narrative by immersing themselves in the Bible. But how should one understand the complexities of meaning and application from an ancient collection of disparate books, written in different languages in differing forms to people in very different historical contexts? It helps to see the Bible as connected by the overarching themes of creation, fall, and redemption. When Christians realize these seemingly distinct stories are connected by the arc of God's work through creation, fall, and redemption, they can begin to place themselves into the story as well.

Scholars have different ways of describing the connected themes of the biblical narrative. Many parse out "creation, fall, and redemption" into four, five, or six movements in order to explain the important historical and theological developments of God's work in the world. For example, Ed Stetzer includes the culminating theme "restoration" in the list of creation, fall, and redemption.[1] In *The Blue Parakeet*, Scot McKnight describes the development of five biblical themes: oneness, otherness, otherness expands, one in Christ, and perfectly one.[2] In their book *The Drama of Scripture*, Craig Bartholomew and Michael Goheen outline the Bible in six acts: creation, fall, redemption initiated, redemption accomplished, the mission of the church, and redemption completed. They further focus each act around the theme of God's kingdom and kingship.[3] N. T. Wright, Tremper Longman III, Richard Middleton, Robert Wall and David Nienhuis, and others provide similar thematic frameworks for understanding the story of the Bible.[4]

More recently, in *Reading While Black*, Esau McCaulley emphasizes how the African American ecclesial tradition "has a distinct message of hope arising from its reading of the biblical texts. This message of hope is not simply a thing of the past; it is living and active, having the ability to provide a way forward for Black believers who continue to turn to the Scriptures for guidance."[5] This hermeneutic is important in how it helps readers to recognize "the great truths of God as creator, liberator, savior, and judge."[6] Christians of all backgrounds would do well to consider how the universal truths of God's work and character apply to the distinct experiences of God's people throughout history and into today. To be sure, "God as redeemer" is a universal, biblical truth. How that truth is realized and experienced—particularly in the lives of the historically marginalized—is just as important as the truth itself.

This living hope of the Scriptures, then, is experienced as a story in which all of creation is engaged. C. Christopher Smith and John Pattison write in *Slow Church*, "The biblical narrative is the story of the whole creation, from the beginning through the present to the end—and yet it's not so much a script that we mechanically act out but rather a story that serves to form us into the people we need to be."[7] What is more, participation in this

---

1. Stetzer, "Big Story of Scripture." In this blog post, Stetzer is referring to David Nelson's chapter on "The Story of Mission: The Grand Biblical Narrative," in Bruce Ashford's *Theology and Practice of Mission*.

2. McKnight, *Blue Parakeet*, 67.

3. Bartholomew and Goheen, *Drama of Scripture*, 22–23.

4. See, for example, Wright, *Scripture and the Authority of God*; Longman, *Genesis*; Middleton, *New Heaven*; and Wall and Nienhuis, *Compact Guide*.

5. McCaulley, *Reading While Black*, 23.

6. McCaulley, *Reading While Black*, 123.

7. Smith and Pattison, *Slow Church*, 19.

drama is not about following a script but about engaging in improvisation. Improvisation involves responding to the people and characters of the situation, and then adding and contributing layers of unique experiences and meanings. For Christians, Smith and Pattison explain: "The enactment of Scripture has astonishing formative power. The deeper our engagement with the story, the better our improvisation will be."[8] The Christian life is an invitation to experience the Scriptures through God's redemptive work, and then to participate in the continuing story.

PARTICIPATING IN GOD'S STORY

On a traditional university campus, students are invited to participate in God's story in a variety of ways. The campus ministry office employs a professional staff and organizes regular chapel services, guest speakers, Bible studies, small groups, service teams, and many other opportunities and activities designed to facilitate the faith formation process. In an online learning environment, the strategy must be different. The online classroom itself becomes the main avenue for faith formation. While other extracurricular opportunities exist throughout the online university, degree programs and individual courses must be designed and facilitated intentionally toward holistic faith formation. Otherwise, students could largely miss out on the unique process of character and faith development so critical to the mission of Christian higher education institutions.

In the online learning environment, it is not uncommon for students to stumble a bit into the process of growing their faith. Whereas a traditional campus university attracts students to the unique experience of living in a distinctly Christian community, most students who choose to attend an online university do so for its accessibility and affordability. Online students simply may not be in a season of life that allows them to move onto a traditional campus, especially since many of them already have families and full-time jobs. So, students attending a Christian university online are not sure what to expect in regards to faith formation. Since faith formation has largely been experienced as an in-person or on-campus phenomenon, there may not be much expectation for their online classes to play a part in the cultivation of faith. It is up to online learning practitioners to change this perception.

As has been argued throughout this book, with intentional course design and engaging faculty presence, online courses can facilitate dramatic and meaningful changes in students' understanding and experience

---

8. Smith and Pattison, *Slow Church*, 20.

of their faith. For example, in *Ecologies of Faith in a Digital Age: Spiritual Growth Through Online Education,* Stephen and Mary Lowe set out a biblical theology of ecology as a framework for engaging online students in God's story.[9] They see great potential in spiritual formation through digital ecologies, by which they mean a series of networks and opportunities that serve to facilitate connectedness among online communities. Of particular importance is their contention that "spiritual formation is not a magical occurrence resulting from the presence of Christians gathered together in the same place, whether online or on campus. There must also be intentionality, reflection, engagement, and interaction between and among those gathered."[10] A campus learning environment in and of itself does not guarantee student engagement and interaction. Students have to make intentional efforts to connect with the community around them whether they are bustling around campus or logging into their online courses. Crafting an overarching framework for biblical engagement and community formation, as the Lowes have done, provides a common vision and theme for students and faculty to pursue together. While Los Angeles Pacific University (LAPU) employs the hermeneutic of "God's story" as a connective theme, this example of a theology of ecology shows there are multiple ways to move toward the shared goals of community and faith formation in the various learning modalities.

GOD'S STORY ACROSS THE CURRICULUM

Universities that establish a commitment to faith formation at the institutional level can then work to align and carry through their vision into individual programs and courses.[11] For example, LAPU crafted a Commitment to Faith, Life, and Learning and stated that its students will be able to "articulate how and in what ways their life journeys connect to God's story."[12] This theme is carried through the program and course development processes, and then discipline-specific assignments are created that align with the broader institutional learning goal.[13] A brief tour through several LAPU courses illustrates how the theme of "God's story" is reinforced throughout a variety of programs and courses. The goal here is to encourage a

9. Lowe and Lowe, *Ecologies of Faith*.
10. Lowe and Lowe, *Ecologies of Faith*, 87.
11. See chapter 4.
12. Los Angeles Pacific University, "Commitment to Faith, Life, and Learning."
13. See chapters 2, 4, and 6 for explanations of the course development process at LAPU.

comprehensive and strategic approach towards holistic faith formation across the university's curriculum.

Faith-based universities can use their unique course offerings to introduce and develop key institutional commitments to faith formation. At LAPU, two required Introduction to Biblical Literature classes serve as the backbone to the concept of "God's story." BIBL 100: Exodus/Deuteronomy introduces course learning outcomes and assignments that will enable students to "articulate how and in what ways their life journeys connect to God's story." BIBL 230: Luke/Acts then reinforces these same course learning outcomes, so students can continue to practice and deepen their developing skills. In both of these courses, the course learning outcomes are virtually the same. Through the various course readings, videos, lectures, discussions, and assignments, students will be able to: identify the themes of creation, fall, and redemption within the drama of Scripture; employ basic tools of biblical scholarship by investigating aspects of the historical, literary, and theological contexts of biblical texts; evaluate various attributes of God, as expressed in biblical texts, from multiple perspectives and interpretive lenses; apply interpretive insights from biblical texts to relevant questions of personal faith formation and development; and propose a way for themselves and/or others to view, understand, and apply key themes and insights from biblical texts into their personal, professional, and vocational contexts.

By reinforcing these learning outcomes across both biblical literature courses, students have the opportunity to immerse themselves in the knowledge, skills, and attitudes needed to understand God's story and how it applies to their life and living. Once these foundational skills are established, they can recognize where and how to apply their learning about God's story in other courses and programs.

Crafting deliberate course learning outcomes related to biblical integration is essential to carrying a holistic notion of faith, life, and learning across the curriculum. When students encounter repeated expectations for biblically focused personal reflection in their various courses and degree programs, they learn to apply the foundational skills of biblical interpretation and application to a broad context of situations and subject matter. If students are indeed going to connect their own life journey to God's story, they need to practice making those connections in as many different courses and learning environments as possible.

Again, course learning outcomes provide a window into opportunities for reinforcing the concept of connecting one's life to the story of the Bible across the disciplines. The following sample of courses and learning outcomes highlights the possibilities for creative and meaningful learning and application. Since students generally take at least BIBL 100 at the very beginning of their studies at LAPU, they have some foundational skills to apply in other courses and contexts. So, for example, in CRJU 105 Introduction to Criminology, students are asked to demonstrate clear knowledge of the basic themes and truths of the Old and New Testaments through critical thinking and personal and professional application. In ACCT 220 Managerial Accounting, students are likewise expected to integrate and apply knowledge through the lens of Scripture when evaluating ethical concerns related to accounting. In both cases, students are given opportunities to deepen their understanding of the scriptural story and its relevance to their respective fields of study. Each course is an invitation to introduce students to additional resources and perspectives on the integration of their faith, life, and learning.

Additional courses across the curriculum emphasize the connection between God's story and issues of ethics. In EDUC 310 Human Growth and Development for Educators, students are expected to describe the biblical and ethical implications of teaching to the whole child, while in LIBS 404 Liberal Studies and Ethics and Worldview, students work to identify pedagogical styles that integrate an awareness of the different worldviews and the vital role the Bible can play in developing an ethical vision for human behavior. These future teachers are not only learning how to connect their story to God's story, but they are also considering how God's story impacts the children they will be engaging in their own elementary school classrooms.

In other courses, the connection between God's story and ethics is extended to worldview considerations. So, in HMGT 410 Healthcare Ethics and Quality Control, students demonstrate an ability to apply biblical worldview thinking to healthcare ethics. In SCHM 420 Consumer Value Ecosystem students recommend global sourcing solutions, based on assessment of opportunities and challenges, within the context of a Christian worldview. One way they accomplish this is by explaining how decisions were, or were not, consistent with Christian core values and biblical ethical standards. Even at the graduate level, students are asked to reflect on these connections. PSYC 600 Industrial and Organizational Psychology asks students to evaluate the importance of organizational ethics, based on a biblically shaped worldview. Students then make connections among organizational values, a faith-based worldview, and organizational ethics.

The thread of connecting one's story to God's story runs deliberately throughout these courses—and many others. One of the main points of emphasis here is that these connections are *deliberate*. Because collaboration is a defining characteristic of the online university, there is an infrastructure of course development that facilitates the deliberate integration of these faith, life, and learning principles into each degree program and course. This culture of collaboration allows for a shared vision and understanding of core principles. The goal is for students to receive a unified and robust experience of making connections between their own life and the overarching story of God's work in the world. As explored in other places in this book, clear principles and practices of course development go a long way toward making this goal a reality.[14]

THE ROLE OF FACULTY

Courses in and of themselves do not make for a robust and holistic learning experience. The real transformative learning takes place in the dynamic that students experience between the course material, their own experiences, the learning community, and the unique contributions of their instructors. Courses come to life through faculty presence and engagement. A caring, knowledgeable, and engaging instructor connects with students and helps them connect with each other, opening new opportunities of learning and application. Similar to how holistic faith formation is a matter of mission not modality, a commitment to faculty engagement and presence is not dependent on whether one is teaching face-to-face or online. While the delivery and modality may be different, the fact remains: faculty play a critical role in growth and development of students. The challenge for faculty is not allowing a face-to-face paradigm of instruction to limit their commitment to engagement in the online environment. Clearly, online engagement looks and feels different from face-to-face engagement. But passionate, dedicated faculty members will find ways to channel their gifts for instruction across any modality as they cultivate thriving learning communities.[15]

Students are also aware that online learning looks and feels different from face-to-face learning. They know they are not in a traditional classroom, and so they do not expect a traditional classroom experience. This means they are open to new ways of learning and engagement, both with their instructor and with their colleagues. With this openness, faculty have the opportunity to explore new avenues of communication and support. Whether through video recordings, phone calls, video chats, emails, text messages, forum posts, or anything else, trust is established when students experience a personal connection with their instructor and with each other. With trust comes a vulnerability and an excitement to embark on a whole new level of learning and growth. This personal connection is important in

---

14. See chapters 2, 4, and 6.
15. See chapters 1 and 11.

both face-to-face and online classes, and the reality is that students connect with instructors on different levels. Not every student will make the same level of connection, and that is not the expectation. What is important is that the invitation for deeper engagement is extended to everyone, and all students experience the genuine care and unique expertise of their instructors.

GOD'S STORY: FACULTY AND STAFF INSIGHTS

Authentic connections with faculty and staff are key to helping students continually wrestle with faith formation concepts, like what it means to connect their life journeys to God's story. When the entire university takes on the responsibility for the care and formation of its students, staff and faculty alike can work together to reinforce the centrality of the biblical narrative. Frank Rojas, LAPU Executive Vice President and Chief Operations Officer, explains:

> Students learn to articulate how to connect their life to God's story through their interaction with faculty and staff. We each have our own testimony to share. Our students can learn through them. God created us uniquely in his image to share the good news. Each one of us has the opportunity to witness to students and staff in a way that is meaningful to them. The Bible should be central in the lives of those of us at LAPU. It gives hope in a new life being saved through Christ's blood. The Bible is God's divine word that inspires us and keeps us girded in his ways in a world that may feel differently.[16]

Faculty and staff can use their unique positions and personalities to bear witness to God's work in their lives. Everyone at the university—faculty, administrators, and both student-facing and non-student-facing staff—recognize their role in building an institutional culture centered on the redemptive work of Jesus Christ. Peggy Cooney, LAPU Executive Assistant, explains the importance of participating in the shared biblical narrative:

> LAPU community members acknowledge the work of the Lord Jesus Christ on the cross and his risen body on the third day. They profess the forgiveness of sin and the saving grace and mercy of Jesus in their lives. Each LAPU member has their own journey to share and story to tell of how God is working in their life. They also connect with the Bible at different points. As their knowledge and understanding of the Bible increases, their faith

---

16. Frank Rojas, interview by author, September 16, 2020.

matures, and they learn to apply biblical truths and principles in their life. In essence, they live their daily journey connecting their story to God's story.[17]

Cooney reminds us that the journey of faith formation is not limited to the student experience. When the university as a whole embraces and lives into the mission of connecting daily life with God's story, a strong bond and network of support is created among the entire faculty, staff, and student community. When staff and faculty are supported internally, those who have student-facing positions are better equipped to demonstrate God's redemptive story both to students in their classes and to those seeking university support.

As those in primarily student-facing roles, faculty use the course subject matter to provide context for reflection on the nature of faith, life, and learning, and in these contexts, students often make profound and life-altering connections. Reg Codrington reflects on the paradigm shifts that can occur when students in his classes first encounter the concept of connecting their life to God's story:

> In the early stages of the BIBL 100 course, I find that some students rather boldly insist that their life journeys do not connect to God's story in any way, and they don't really understand the question! However, it has been enlightening to see how, especially through the discussion forums, students point each other to ways in which the learning material is relevant to contemporary life. The pandemic has provided rather amazing opportunities for showing how the truths of the Bible in fact do apply to real life, even thousands of years after they were written. The usual, "Why does God allow it?" question is often deflected by fellow-students pointing out that there's not much point in living as if God doesn't exist, but then blaming this "non-existent" God for everything that goes wrong. Even those within the Christian tradition have found the concept of the Bible being an unfolding of "God's story" to be enlightening and refreshing.[18]

When faculty set the table in their courses for genuine questions and engagement, students can open up to new opportunities for learning and engagement. Reflective assignments and exercises can be a key strategy for helping students make the connection between God's story and their life journey. Irene Kao explains how reflection assignments in her courses can help students focus and sift through the seemingly endless amount of

17. Peggy Cooney, interview by author, October 5, 2020.
18. Reg Codrington, interview by author, September 17, 2020.

information that confronts them in their daily lives. "On the one hand," she explains, "there is so much benefit to being able to access resources, speakers, and the written word so easily. However, I think with this access comes a difficulty to focus on what is being spoken and heard." Reflection helps students not only to process content, but to slow down and dive deeper into the implications for personal application. Especially when making the bridge between course content and faith formation, personal reflection allows students to ask themselves the hard questions of meaning and application. Kao helps her students connect with God's story by emphasizing the idea of journey: "I like to imagine the Bible in the metaphor of a road sign which helps us follow the path and move forward even if there are detours in life. I think the Bible means movement forward even if it is not according to our plan."[19] When students see the Bible as part of their journey, they can discover an ever-unfolding invitation to participate in the life of Christ.

GOD'S STORY: STUDENT EXPERIENCES

It is rewarding to see such aspirations for helping students to connect their life to God's story actually take shape in the life of graduates. All of this is just rhetoric if students' lives are not changed. LAPU students and recent graduates have taken some time to reflect back on their learning experiences and provide some context for what connecting their life journeys to God's story has meant. Students often say it best:

> LAPU has helped me with being able to express my Christian views in a manner that others can understand. My life journey connects to God's story by recounting my trials and tribulations and heavily depending on various passages in the Bible to get me through those difficult times. The Bible connects to my contemporary life because I can take those same principles and apply them to my life today. As an LAPU graduate, I can continue to participate in God's story by showing grace, forgiveness, and living the life he has instructed me to live.[20]

> LAPU has helped me articulate the connection of my life's journey to God's story of redemption by having me thoughtfully search areas of my life that have been redeemed. The Bible connects to my life because it reaches into the deep recesses of my mind and heart and helps me bring calm into a chaotic world.

19. Irene Kao, interview by author, September 16, 2020.
20. La Quenta Gross, interview by author, November 14, 2020.

As an LAPU graduate I will continue to participate in God's story by being a blessing to my community.[21]

LAPU has become a part of my life journey. The more time I spend dwelling on godly things the better I am able to articulate what God's story means in my life. Having said that, I am in my second year here and I can honestly say that every single class I have taken is somehow interwoven into a Christian worldview. Having an academic education that is viewed through a Christian lens has helped shape me and distinguish myself.[22]

LAPU has helped me articulate how God is tied into the work that I did at the university. My life journey connects to God's story in the way that I had been living in darkness and God called me to the light to follow him and what he has in store for me. I accepted his calling as I knew I couldn't do it without him in my life. I will continue God's story in my life by sharing my testimony of how God has guided me to stay on his path so that I can continue to serve him and others that are in need of my help.[23]

I am a recent graduate of the MLOS [Master of Arts in Leadership and Organizational Studies] program. It has been a wonderful learning experience. After over a thirty-year career in federal law enforcement, I retired a couple of years ago and now serve as the senior pastor of a church in Compton. I do not doubt that God led me to LAPU. Since I am an African American retired law enforcement officer assigned to minister in Compton, I have a unique opportunity to bridge the gap between the police and our community. Compton is predominately comprised of Black and Brown people. The MLOS program energized and refocused my attention toward making changes in our community. I have joined the Police Clergy association and work with city and county leaders to resolve the homeless situation and other issues in our community, such as violence and drug problems. I am working with the local hospital and serve as a member of the mental health board in our community. My church actively engages in outreach efforts and reinvests in our members and community to better our environment.[24]

21. Denise Schweinfurth, interview by author, November 19, 2020.
22. Emerson Medrano, interview by author, November 20, 2020.
23. Nahivic Echenique, interview by author, November 22, 2020.
24. Kalvin Cressel, interview by author, November 24, 2020.

Attending LAPU has been a life-changing experience in many ways. One of the most valuable lessons that I've learned and will carry with me in future endeavors, is that biblical Scripture has presence and commonality which can be applied to all areas of our lives. Even through my science courses, there was value connected to our lessons, including those that were mathematical and factual in nature. LAPU has provided a well-rounded educational opportunity, inclusive of the foundation of God's word. I've learned to be open and free in ways that I did not previously think were possible. I've been given invaluable tools for life and have a much better understanding of purpose, reason, and how each of us is provided countless opportunities for the betterment of humankind each day.[25]

These students show us that the holistic integration of faith, life, and learning is not only possible in the online university, but can become a central and defining aspect of the student experience. God's Spirit is changing lives, and Christian universities can join in and participate by committing to giving their all in helping students—and indeed the entire university—recognize and live into the reality of God's work of redemption in and through all areas of life.

---

25. Jennifer Holly Pruitt, interview by author, November 28, 2020.

Chapter 8

Diverse Faith Perspectives

LISA D. PHILLIPS

LISA PHILLIPS, *Assistant Dean at Los Angeles Pacific University, presents both concepts and examples of how online students learn to engage with diverse faith perspectives within the learning community. The chapter addresses the key question: How can a learning community foster diversity, understanding, and acceptance?*

More and more, colleges and universities are exploring how their learning communities can foster diversity, understanding, and acceptance. Two primary areas of research can help address this question. The first is campus climate research and the spiritual dimensions of climate, focusing on their application to religion, spirituality, and worldview. The second body of research is interfaith studies and intergroup relations. Intergroup relations include an examination of how learning communities can create opportunities for engagement and facilitate quality interaction between students. It includes teaching students to engage in difficult dialogue about controversial subjects related to race, politics, and religion.[1] Engagement

---

1. See Smith, *Diversity's Promise for Higher Education*.

is also an important element of interfaith studies, but includes as a goal fostering an orientation towards pluralism.[2]

This chapter begins with a background discussion that establishes the importance and relevance of engaging diverse faith perspectives in higher education due to shifting demographics and an increasingly pluralistic national and global landscape. A discussion of religion as a diverse dimension within the framework for inclusive excellence follows. This framework establishes an approach for measuring effectiveness around efforts related to diversity, equity, and inclusion. Then, a literature review examines campus climate as a critical factor for assessing a university's plans for creating an inclusive environment. The climate research examines the link between religion, spirituality, campus climate, and student outcomes. Finally, an exploration of diverse faith perspectives in the curriculum includes how faith-based universities can maintain their religious identity in the context of increasing religious diversity. Christian universities must hold in tension a commitment to theological traditions that reflect the university's identity while simultaneously building an environment of belonging and acceptance. The last section includes specific examples of how faculty and staff engage with diverse faith perspectives in an online setting at Los Angeles Pacific University (LAPU).

BACKGROUND

For many colleges and universities, a commitment to diversity, equity, and inclusion is a strategic, economic, and moral imperative and is vital for continued relevance, viability, and sustainability. Universities have responded to changing demographics by creating centers and committees for Diversity, Equity, and Inclusion (DEI) or appointing senior leaders to manage DEI strategy and initiatives. LAPU established the Imago Dei Committee to promote and support the university's commitment to God-honoring diversity in a multiethnic, professional community. This commitment to diversity extends to ethnic and individual differences, age, class, gender, sexual orientation, ability, and religious affiliation. This commitment also reflects the university's Christ-centered mission, which is based on respect and value for each individual, created in the image of God.

For many years, a diverse, multiethnic student population has been the norm in accessible, online educational environments. Even among many Christian universities, there has been a significant shift in student demographics. According to the CCCU, diverse populations among Christian

---

2. See Patel, "Preparing Interfaith Leaders."

universities have grown significantly over the past fifteen years. Overall student diversity among CCCU colleges has increased from 17 percent in 2004 to 31 percent in 2019.[3] For the past few decades, many universities have been committed to creating an ethnically diverse, equitable, and inclusive environment. However, recently, the *Chronicle of Higher Education* has described faith as both the diversity issue colleges have ignored, and as Christian "evangelical colleges' diversity problem."[4] As the US becomes more religiously and ethnically diverse, it is also becoming more polarized. Christian colleges and universities must be prepared to provide students with the skills and tools to engage in diverse communities and build bridges for reconciliation and partnerships for addressing societal issues.

Colleges and universities can no longer ignore the religious dimension of diversity. Based on Pew Research statistics, 32 percent of the worldwide population is Christian, 23 percent Muslim, 16 percent unaffiliated, 15 percent Hindu, 7 percent Buddhist, and 0.2 percent Jewish.[5] Within the United States, which has historically been a religiously homogeneous nation, the religious landscape is rapidly changing with significant differences across generations. In the US (as of 2018/2019), 65 percent of adults identify as Christians compared to 77 percent in 2009. Among millennials, only 49 percent identify as Christians, compared to 67 percent of Generation Xers and 76 percent of baby boomers. Twenty-six percent identify as agnostic for the same period compared to 17 percent in 2009. The adult population that identifies with non-Christian faiths has increased slightly, from 5 percent in 2009 to 7 percent in 2018/2019.[6] Given this increasingly religiously diverse population, any approach to engaging with students of diverse faith perspectives must be holistic. A holistic approach considers the diverse characteristics of the entire person—ethnicity, age, gender, sexual orientation, ability, socioeconomic status, religion—as these characteristics intersect to create a unique, complex identity.[7]

---

3. See Council for Christian Colleges & Universities, "2021 CCCU Campus Diversity Stats."

4. See Patel, "Faith is the Diversity Issue Ignored by Colleges"; and McMurtrie, "Evangelical Colleges' Diversity Problem."

5. Pew Research Center, "Global and Religious Landscape."

6. Pew Research Center, "Decline of Christianity Continues."

7. The concept of intersectionality was conceived by Kimberlé Crenshaw, professor of law, and has been applied across all disciplines including politics, psychology, social studies, education, healthcare, economics, and law. See Crenshaw, "Demarginalizing the Intersection of Race and Sex."

RELIGION AS A DIVERSE DIMENSION IN HIGHER EDUCATION

The Association of American Colleges and Universities (AAC&U) has provided a model for Inclusive Excellence and Change designed to support university efforts to connect diversity, equity, inclusion, and educational quality in a comprehensive, unified, and sustainable manner.[8] Many universities have adopted this model, a holistic, integrated approach to strategically aligning the university culture and resources to foster positive, long-term change for a more diverse, equitable, and inclusive campus climate.

The framework includes four components: *Access and Equity, Campus Climate, Diversity in the Curriculum, and Learning and Development.*[9] Access and equity represent the structural diversity component. Most online universities have removed all barriers to admission by providing open access to education, resulting in a diverse student population across all demographics, including ethnicity, age, religion, and other diverse characteristics. The second component, campus climate, is the measure for inclusion and encompasses the surface-level elements of an organization's culture and the more profound elements, including long-held values, beliefs, and norms. Campus climate will be central to the discussion of how a learning community can foster diversity, understanding, and acceptance when engaging with those of diverse faiths.

Campus climate is the barometer for measuring how students feel when entering a campus space, whether it is a physical or a virtual environment. It "includes people's attitudes and behaviors, and is more malleable than culture. Further, climate interacts with organizational policies and practices."[10] Students engage with faculty, staff, peers, and the curriculum, and the interplay of these factors creates the student experience. Interaction with instructors has a more significant influence because they establish and monitor the classroom climate by setting the tone in their communication to students, whether verbally or in writing, facilitate positive peer-to-peer interactions, and develop and deliver the curriculum. Fostering a culture that supports a climate for inclusion is the responsibility of university leaders, staff, and faculty.

Diverse faith perspectives include a spectrum of beliefs, from those within the Christian community, to those of a different religious affiliation, and the nonreligious. Religious and nonreligious students choose to

8. Association of American Colleges & Universities, "Making Excellence Inclusive."

9. Williams et al., "Toward a Model of Inclusive Excellence."

10. Association of American Colleges and Universities, "Creating and Assessing Campus Climates."

attend Christian universities like LAPU with the expectation that they will learn to apply a biblically based, Christian worldview to their life and work. Perceptions held by nonreligious and religious minority groups can inform university approaches to creating a more inclusive spiritual climate.

For learning and development, productive engagement with individuals of diverse backgrounds and perspectives is one of the primary purposes of a college education and is a highly desired workplace skill.[11] A few of the desired outcomes from engaging with those of diverse faith perspectives include greater awareness and knowledge of differences, greater empathy towards those who espouse a different perspective, and the ability to think critically about theological differences.[12] The following section includes a review of the literature related to religion and faith as a diverse dimension and how spiritual climate affects student satisfaction, student identity, and belonging.

REVIEW OF THE LITERATURE

An increasingly diverse student population on dimensions of culture and faith has led to an emerging body of research related to religion, spirituality, and campus climate. According to the research findings, for those students who do engage with those of different cultures and faiths, there are long-term, mutual benefits that accrue to the student, the university, and ultimately society.[13] One of the recurring themes across all diversity and climate research is the need for creating a sense of belonging during the student's entire academic experience. Those colleges and universities that create an inclusive climate, allowing for a full expression of students' spiritual identity, may improve their psychological well-being.[14] Research has proven this to be true for those who hold a Christian worldview. According to Bowman and Small's longitudinal sample of 15,527 students at 136 educational

---

11. See Rockenbach and Mayhew, "Campus Spiritual Climate"; Bowman et al., "Religious/Worldview Identification and Student Success"; Bowman and Smedley, "Forgotten Minority"; Bowman and Small, "Exploring a Hidden Form of Minority Status"; Fosnacht and Broderick, "An Overlooked Factor?"; Rockenbach et al., "Fostering the Pluralism Orientation of College Students"; and Rockenbach and Mayhew, "How the Collegiate Religious and Spiritual Climate Shapes."

12. Dey et al., *Engaging Diverse Viewpoints*.

13. See Patel, "Faith is the Diversity Issue Ignored by Colleges"; Patel and Giess, "Engaging Religious Diversity on Campus"; and Patel and Meyer, "Religious Education for Interfaith Leadership."

14. See Paredes-Collins, "Campus Climate for Diversity"; and Paredes-Collins, "Cultivating Diversity and Spirituality."

institutions, students who attended a university with an inclusive religious climate and who actively embraced their Christian faith, experienced enhanced well-being. And for nontraditional students, the gains in sense of well-being and purpose were even more significant than for traditional students.[15] The findings suggest that universities should provide resources that support the student's spiritual development, including counseling and other coping mechanisms for facing life's challenges.

Another line of research examining the relationship between student satisfaction and campus climate builds upon an understanding of how students' religious affiliation might positively influence their ability to persist to graduation. Alyssa Bryant Rockenbach and Matthew Mayhew's research examined how spiritual climate dimensions predict student satisfaction based on four dimensions of spiritual climate: student characteristics, diversity of worldviews among the student population, psychological climate, and the behavioral climate.[16] The instrument used was the Campus Religious and Spiritual Climate Survey developed for higher education to assess multiple spiritual climate dimensions concerning religious and worldview diversity.[17] The most relevant finding to an understanding of inclusivity for diverse faith perspectives is that spiritual climate did not have a differential effect on satisfaction across religious worldviews. However, there were negative perceptions and dissatisfaction among Asian and African American students, with students of color perceiving the climate more negatively than white students. The most pronounced dissatisfaction was among African American students.[18] Climate also plays a vital role in spiritual development for students of color. A sense of belonging is the most crucial climate dimension and predictor of satisfaction for students of color.[19] Positive cross-racial interaction is a critical factor for establishing a sense of belonging for students of color. Given the potential for intrafaith conflict along racial lines, creating opportunities for positive cross-racial interaction is essential. Sense of belonging was not a significant factor for white students; instead, overall satisfaction was the most key determinant for spiritual development.[20]

Psychological well-being and student satisfaction have direct and mediating effects on academic performance, persistence, and graduation and are evidence of the benefits of providing resources, such as counseling

15. Bowman and Small, "Exploring a Hidden Form of Minority Status."
16. Rockenbach and Mayhew, "Campus Spiritual Climate," 45.
17. Bryant et al., "Developing an Assessment."
18. Bryant et al., "Developing an Assessment"; and Mayhew et al., "Silencing Whom?"
19. Paredes-Collins, "Campus Climate for Diversity."
20. Paredes-Collins, "Campus Climate for Diversity."

and other support mechanisms that encourage students' spiritual development.[21] Those students who take advantage of these resources to develop and fortify their faith have a greater sense of purpose and more positive interpersonal relationships, leading to persistence and graduation. These studies support prior climate and ethnic diversity research and reinforce the need for addressing inclusion holistically by considering the intersecting identities such as religion, ethnicity, gender, and social location.[22] Christian colleges that focus on spiritual formation as a central institutional goal must work diligently to create a climate for inclusion for all students while addressing systemic issues and unique barriers for students of color. Religion can be a bridge for facilitating more significant cross-racial interaction for students of color, and engaging with others of diverse worldviews can be a tool for transformational learning.[23]

DIVERSE FAITH PERSPECTIVES IN THE CURRICULUM

The curricula at Christian universities are typically oriented exclusively towards integrating and teaching a Christian worldview across disciplines. An increasingly pluralistic campus environment and adherence to a Christian worldview requires a careful balance between preserving theological traditions foundational to the faith while finding common ground for meaningful engagement and dialogue with individuals with diverse faith perspectives. Leaders of Christian universities must work to maintain the university's core identity while removing barriers and building bridges for creating a more inclusive climate.

A university's philosophical stance concerning pluralism and how to engage with students of diverse faiths will have a significant and defining effect on the curriculum. Furthermore, curriculum design and the pedagogical approach will significantly influence how students perceive the climate and whether they experience a sense of acceptance and belonging. Heterogeneity is necessary as it provides an opportunity to develop interpersonal relationships with diverse others, and intentionally creating opportunities for meaningful engagement in curriculum design and cocurricular activities is the next essential step. It provides students with a chance to develop

---

21. Li and Murphy, "Religious Affiliation, Religiosity, and Academic Performance"; and Bowman et al., "Religious/Worldview Identification and Student Success."

22. Baldwin, "Culturally Responsive Pedagogy"; and Samuel, "Re-viewing Christian Theologies of Religious Diversity."

23. Park and Bowman, "Religion as Bridging or Bonding Social Capital"; and Mayhew et al., "Association Between Worldview Climate Dimensions."

an intellectual understanding and appreciation for cultural and religious differences and to build positive relationships through engagement with the curriculum, instructors, and peers.

DIVERSE FAITH PERSPECTIVES: INTERFAITH ENGAGEMENT

Intergroup dialogue is an innovative pedagogical approach associated with intergroup research (IGR), which was formally launched in 1988 as a university initiative for developing students' understanding and appreciation for diversity, a way of building competencies related to resolving intergroup conflict, and a means for building bridges across racial, ethnic, and religious differences.[24] Interfaith research provides a framework for fostering pluralism, facilitating a more inclusive spiritual climate, and achieving learning outcomes related to interfaith leadership skills and competencies as well as personal and spiritual development.[25] The theoretical framework for pluralism based on Diana Eck's seminal research is defined as "Engagement with diversity rather than the sheer fact of diversity alone; migration from tolerance to acceptance of others; commitment as developmentally distinctive and possible within a relativistic society; and an understanding and appreciation of worldview differences (not merely commonalities)."[26] Eck is concerned with living harmoniously in an increasingly religious and culturally diverse society. She proposes interfaith dialogue as a method for resolving conflict by confronting ingrained assumptions, engaging in difficult conversations, and developing greater self-awareness regarding how worldview shapes one's view of religious others.[27] Dialogue must be authentic and allow individuals to bring their whole selves to the process. It is an emotionally laborious process that involves "discourse, disagreement, and disputation," moving beyond tolerance to understanding and acceptance.[28]

Eboo Patel is a leading scholar and practitioner for interfaith leadership and cooperation who founded the Interfaith Youth Core (IYC) in

24. Maxwell and Thompson, "Breaking Ground Through Intergroup Education."

25. See Poppinga et al., "Building Bridges Across Faith Lines"; Campbell and Lane, "Better Together"; Patel, "Preparing Interfaith Leaders"; Patel and Giess, "Engaging Religious Diversity on Campus"; and Patel and Meyer, "Religious Education for Interfaith Leadership."

26. Rockenbach et al., "Fostering the Pluralism Orientation of College Students," 28. See Eck, *Encountering God*.

27. Eck, "Religious Pluralism."

28. Azaransky, "Religious Pluralism and American Democracy." See Eck, "Religious Pluralism."

response to an increasingly religiously diverse nation with a goal of promoting interfaith cooperation through service and dialogue.[29] While significant research on multiculturalism was advancing, Patel saw a substantial gap in the research on religious diversity. Building upon Eck's pluralism framework, Patel proposed a three-part framework that includes "respect for diverse identities; nurturing relationships between different communities; and cultivating commitment to the common good."[30] According to Patel this framework can be a catalyst for positive societal outcomes through the removal of barriers that hinder understanding among individuals of diverse identities. Patel's approach establishes common ground for those of different religions to combine resources and work collaboratively to alleviate and address societal issues, such as poverty, social and economic justice, and other goals related to the common good.[31]

Interfaith research is an emerging field that provides helpful insights for how Christian universities can promote acceptance and belonging for those of diverse faiths. But the research does not address how a biblical perspective should inform one's approach to creating a sense of acceptance and belonging. The power of Christ to transform lives is in his acceptance of all people. Therefore, how should a Christ-centered institution embrace those of diverse faiths in a way that is compatible with loving one's neighbor and the unique calling to witness Christ to others? In *The Gospel in a Pluralist Society*, British theologian and former general secretary of the International Missionary Council (IMC), Lesslie Newbigin, provides a way of thinking about the typical classifications of religious perspectives concerning Christianity that is compatible with a commitment to grace and truth. He describes his position as:

> Exclusivist in the sense that it affirms the unique truth of the revelation in Jesus Christ, but it is not exclusivist in the sense of denying the possibility of salvation of the non-Christian. It is inclusivist in the sense that it refuses to limit the saving grace of God to the members of the Christian Church, but it rejects inclusivism which regards the non-Christian religions as vehicles of salvation. It is pluralist in the sense of acknowledging the gracious work of God in the lives of all human beings, but it rejects a pluralism which denies the uniqueness and decisiveness of what God has done in Jesus Christ.[32]

29. Interfaith Youth Core, "Building Interfaith America."
30. Patel, "Preparing Interfaith Leaders," 77.
31. Patel, "Preparing Interfaith Leaders."
32. Newbigin, *Gospel in a Pluralist Society*, 182–83.

Building upon the emerging interfaith research while maintaining a philosophical stance similar to Newbigin, Amy Poppinga and colleagues ground their research in a Christ-centered approach based on the command to love one's neighbor.[33] Avoiding misconceptions, the blurring of lines of distinction between religious differences, and pluralism that denies the uniqueness of Christianity and the centrality of God's work through Christ, Poppinga and colleagues propose a different model for interfaith engagement. Integrating both Patel's and Eck's perspectives as essential to an understanding of pluralism, Poppinga and colleagues redefine Patel's and Eck's framework, aligning it with civic pluralism and distinguishing it from theological pluralism. Interfaith engagement as a call to love one's neighbor establishes a higher standard than simple tolerance of those of diverse faiths, requiring intentional effort, active involvement, ongoing dialogue, relationship building, and valuing and learning from those of different philosophical and religious viewpoints.[34] This method aligns well with a Christian institution's commitment to spiritual formation and its mission and values. A well-executed plan for interfaith dialogue can provide students with essential skills and attitudes for navigating diverse relationships in their local and global communities. Research substantiates pluralism as a method for engaging diverse faith perspectives in the curriculum and the long-term benefits that accrue to the student, the university, and ultimately society when students authentically engage with those of different cultures and faiths.

DIVERSE FAITH PERSPECTIVES: INTRAFAITH ENGAGEMENT

Creating a climate for inclusion is a dynamic, arduous process that is further complicated by intersecting faith and culture dimensions. Culture and religion are closely intertwined, and one's social location affects how one perceives the campus climate.[35] While Christian universities are committed to spiritual formation as a central institutional outcome, some may fail to recognize the link between spiritual formation and cultural or ethnic heritage, ignoring how racial inequality and the social and historical context in which people live influence this process. This oversight can lead to misunderstanding, conflict, and division. Efforts to create an inclusive climate cannot be one dimensional. Universities must take a holistic approach to creating an inclusive climate.

33. Poppinga et al., "Building Bridges Across Faith Lines."
34. Poppinga et al., "Building Bridges Across Faith Lines."
35. Bryant and Craft, "Challenge and Promise of Pluralism."

The intersection of race and culture is relevant to all religions and ethnicities, however, the racial divide among Blacks and whites (particularly in the US, although the issue is not uniquely a US problem) provides the most significant opportunity for positive impact. Educational institutions have historically been a catalyst for social change and play an essential role in preparing the next generation of leaders. As churches struggle to address racial conflict and move toward racial reconciliation, Christian universities must take the lead in identifying ways for bridging this divide, beginning with specific changes to the curriculum. Higher learning institutions must understand how Eurocentric approaches have dominated curriculum design, measurement, and assessment. They must find ways to dismantle systemic issues that hinder change while expanding curriculum design options with a mindset for inclusion.[36] LAPU uses a collaborative approach to curriculum design that begins with developing a course vision. This occurs before the course design process begins. The purpose of the course vision process is to establish a clear purpose and vision for the course. This process also allows for integration of multiple perspectives with input from the academic dean, members of the instructional design team, and the faculty or subject matter expert.

As a part of the course design process, George Hanshaw, Director of eLearning Operations at LAPU, has adopted a more inclusive curriculum design strategy based on a few key practices from Harvard University and the Bok Center for Teaching and Learning:

1. Provide multiple ways for students to demonstrate mastery of competencies. A traditional approach that depends exclusively on written assignments is not inclusive.

2. Assess early and often to provide opportunities for students to receive feedback that can help them succeed on future assignments.

3. Diversify resources to include videos, articles, textbooks, and a multiplicity of voices.

These key practices highlight how a student-centered, inclusive model combined with culturally competent faculty who can vary teaching styles to accommodate multiple ways of learning establishes a strong foundation for building a more inclusive online learning experience.

---

36. See Andraos, "Engaging Diversity in Teaching Religion and Theology."

DIVERSE FAITH PERSPECTIVES: FACULTY AND STAFF INSIGHTS

LAPU has created curricular and cocurricular activities that allow students to engage with those of diverse cultures and faith traditions. The role of instructors and their ability to engage with diverse populations and the ability to facilitate positive engagement between students is an essential skill for creating an inclusive classroom experience. Irene Kao, a faculty member on the LAPU Imago Dei Committee, shared her perspective on how to foster acceptance and belonging for those of diverse faiths. She highlights the importance of exposure to others of diverse faiths. She emphasizes understanding others' cultural practices, values, and faith-based traditions rather than arguing facts. It involves having an intellectual conversation about the other person's religious perspective; she states:

> A learning community can foster diversity, understanding, and acceptance through exposure and experience. Students learn to engage with diverse faith perspectives through exposure, but I think we could do a better job with this as well. I often tell my students in my cultural diversity course that my hope would be that they would be able to have an intelligent conversation about the culture/religion they are studying with a person from that culture and religion. Not as an expert, but with at least enough of a foundational knowledge that the conversation is not spent arguing the facts, but more discussing the application and larger implications of some of the cultural practices and values that are known to be believed within a certain culture or faith-based tradition.[37]

Kao also partners with other psychology instructors to facilitate an online community forum for psychology students. This cocurricular activity provides an opportunity for students to engage on a more personal level outside of the formal online classroom. LAPU's success coach team interacts weekly and informally with students, crossing boundaries of race, ethnicity, and religion. De'Onna Hampton, a success coach and member of the LAPU Imago Dei Committee, states the following regarding how students engage with one another:

> Students may learn how to engage with diverse faith perspectives within the LAPU learning community by approaching others with dignity, love, and respect. Also, in taking a humble approach by understanding they do not know everything. An

---

37. Irene Kao, interview by author, September 16, 2020.

online learning community can foster more acceptance and diversity regarding faith by educating students/faculty/staff on various faith perspectives that align with the demographic of its student body (e.g., agnosticism, atheism, Catholicism, Hinduism, Islam, etc.).[38]

LAPU instructors across multiple disciplines shared their past experiences engaging and dialoguing with others of diverse faith perspectives. Many emphasized the importance of acceptance and embracing those of different faiths, noting that acceptance aligns with LAPU's Christ-centered mission based on respect and value for each individual as a child of God, created in his image. Reg Codrington provided his perspective acknowledging students' willingness and openness to such dialogue:

> One thing that surprised me when I began teaching online some eight years ago was the almost brutal honesty that came from students, which I had never experienced in face-to-face teaching. It is almost as if their anonymity provides a protection for them, and they are willing to let down their guard to share often deep secrets from their past or present situations. I note this because what I have experienced is an almost total lack of criticism and rebuke of others' stories, lifestyles, or comments. I'm not quite sure how to account for it, but in all my years of online teaching, I can only recall one comment that I would call divisive in terms of diversity.[39]

Robert Waltz talked about the discomfort associated with engaging in difficult conversations, the importance and value of raising students' awareness of their misconceptions and preconceptions, and some of the positive learning outcomes he has observed over his many years of teaching adult students:

> Religious diversity is a big part of who we are as Americans. It ought to be impossible, bordering on negligent, to embrace diversity, equity, and inclusion only to the extent that it's comfortable or convenient. Students can learn more about the power of perception and stereotypes. They can learn about managing and resolving conflict. They can learn about the value of reflecting upon meaningful learning that comes from student colleagues of a different faith, and then putting that meaningful learning to practice. They can learn about diverse religious tenets, and how those tenets inform personal and professional structures

38. De'Onna Hampton, interview by author, September 16, 2020.
39. Reg Codrington, interview by author, September 17, 2020.

and values. In turn, they might find reason to celebrate that we are all seeking a closer relationship with God by being a better human being.[40]

Each of the above examples highlights a few practical approaches that universities can implement for maximizing the benefits and positive outcomes associated with interfaith dialogue and engagement. These include creating specific interfaith learning outcomes within courses across disciplines where there is a precise alignment with course learning outcomes and providing opportunities for informal engagement outside the online classroom. Online communities and similar cocurricular activities can create a safe space for students to share more openly and authentically by reducing power asymmetries. These power asymmetries can be more pronounced inside the classroom between instructor/student and/or due to internal and external power structures based on race, ethnicity, and religion.[41]

STUDENT EXPERIENCES WITH DIVERSE FAITH PERSPECTIVES

LAPU emphasizes spiritual formation or whole person development as central to its mission as a Christ-centered university. Interfaith engagement aligns with this university mission by providing students with an opportunity to develop relationships across ethnic, religious, and racial boundaries; to think more critically about their personal faith by examining differences and commonalities with those of diverse faith perspectives; and to deepen their personal convictions as well as develop skills and virtues for managing conflict and working and leading in a diverse global community. LAPU graduates reflected on their experiences while attending LAPU. Just a few examples are included below and represent the learnings and values that resulted from their experiences.

> The discussion posts really helped me to be more accepting of others. Reading and understanding different points of view helped me to have an open heart and mind which is something I have come to use in my daily life.[42]

> Engaging with those of diverse faith perspectives has taught me to have more tolerance and helped show me that despite

---

40. Robert Waltz, interview by author, October 21, 2020.
41. Andraos, "Engaging Diversity in Teaching Religion and Theology."
42. Miranda Browning, interview by author, November 13, 2020.

our differences, we are all very much the same. I am also more understanding and loving towards others. This will benefit me greatly as a teacher and I will be able to share God by showing them his love, through me.[43]

As an LAPU graduate, I will continue to embrace diversity in my life and work and I will continue to stand up for others who are mistreated due to their differences. God would expect no less of me.[44]

I have been more open to learning about other cultures. I have never been one to discuss religion with others, but I am more willing to join the conversation now. Over the past few years, I have learned that we all have our own points of view and we don't see everything the same.[45]

LAPU has not merely facilitated the expression of my biblical foundation. It has created a platform on which an increasingly divisive Christian worldview can be propagated and explored with the proper attention it deserves. This, in turn, has strengthened me and given me the confidence to engage with diverse faiths and perspectives.[46]

The preceding examples represent the value of intergroup exchanges and how this form of engagement can positively influence individual identity and spiritual formation and help prepare students to engage effectively with those of diverse backgrounds while making a positive contribution to their communities.

CONCLUSION

Many universities have renewed commitment to diversity, equity, and inclusion and established new initiatives and strategies to accommodate an increasingly diverse student population. Achieving diversity without equity and inclusion is a failed endeavor. The research demonstrates a significant relationship between an inclusive climate, and student satisfaction, academic performance, retention, and graduation. Furthermore, creating an environment where students of all backgrounds can thrive, grow intellectually,

---

43. Tiffanie Guinane, interview by author, November 14, 2020.
44. La Quenta Gross, interview by author, November 14, 2020.
45. Traia McPherson, interview by author, November 20, 2020.
46. Emerson Medrano, interview by author, November 20, 2020.

emotionally, and spiritually, and persist to graduation is the ultimate goal of every institution of higher learning. Secular universities have led the effort in this complex, arduous work of creating diverse, equitable, and inclusive environments. This is a simple, though not easy task, but it positions Christian universities to glorify God by advancing the cause of Christ. This can only be accomplished within a culture where *imago dei* is not just a slogan, but is reflected in the curriculum, policies, practices, and engagement with students. Christian universities hold the key rooted in the simple command to love one's neighbor as oneself.

Chapter 9

Faith through Academic Disciplines

SHANNON N. HUNT

SHANNON HUNT, *Assistant Professor at Los Angeles Pacific University, presents both concepts and examples of how online students learn to recognize God's work in the world through all academic disciplines. The chapter explores the key question: How do students discover their vocation in their academic discipline and in their careers as disciples of Jesus Christ?*

There is a unique intersection of faith, academic discipline, and professional skill development within the Christian online university. Students from all walks of life sidle up to their computers, their tablets, and phones, with their electronic books showcased in multiple tabs. As they pour themselves into their coursework, they are fueling the drive within them. There is a reason they are pursuing their education. There is a reason for their chosen academic discipline. There is a reason for the profession for which they are training. When students find that reason, they harness a sense of purpose to achieve their goal. As a recent graduate of Los Angeles Pacific University (LAPU) described: "I believe, on a scale of 1 to 10, finding your purpose in your career is extremely important, at a 10! When you know your purpose, it makes you unstoppable, and excited to pursue what you need to do to get there."[1] That is what universities want—students who see themselves as unstoppable! What is more, Christian universities exist to support students in their academic discipline and in their practice of faith through vocation, as they realize their God-given purpose.

While there are many useful resources and frameworks to help students discover and pursue their purpose, LAPU uses Tom Rath's *StrengthsFinder 2.0* to emphasize that each student is created with a unique set of abilities—areas of giftedness, strengths, or talents.[2] The university helps students identify and cultivate these strengths, and then encourages students to move progressively forward towards their purpose within their academic discipline. This may mean helping students realize, in Rath's words, "You cannot be anything you want to be—but you can be a lot more of who you already are."[3] Strengths development helps students connect with "who they already are" so they can see the potential for what they can become. The university then becomes a partner with the student as they grow into their potential.

With a clear-eyed commitment to strengths development, the university follows a strategy to integrate faith with academic disciplines and vocational goals. This strategy requires teamwork and collaboration across various departments. From the first email inquiry or phone call, the university must embrace the opportunity to carefully hear the vision of the prospective student. Does the student already have a passion for an academic discipline? What is the reason behind it? How can the university help the student move towards the realization of their calling, their passion? How do enrollment staff, success coaches, professors, deans, and administrators facilitate a Christian online community that extends beyond academics to student vocation and calling? These are timely questions that must be answered at the various levels and departments of the university.

In order to craft an effective strategy, it is necessary to understand the distinction between commonly used terms. How is a job different from a career, and a career different from a vocation? And what role does God's calling play? There are many works with dueling perspectives on the role of jobs, career, vocation, and calling.[4] Amy Wrzesniewski, a professor at Yale School of Management, provides helpful definitions of job, career,

1. Tiffanie Guinane, interview by author, November 14, 2020.
2. Rath, *StrengthsFinder 2.0*. For example, see the Theology of Work Project for resources for pastors, scholars, and workers.
3. Rath, *StrengthsFinder 2.0*, 9.
4. See, for example, Cahalan, *Stories We Live*; Lemke, "Vocation and Lifelong Spiritual Formation"; Dik and Duffy, *Make Your Job a Calling*; Tisdale, "Job and Vocation"; Placher, ed., *Callings*; and Guinness, *Call*.

and calling. She writes, "A job provides you with pay, benefits, and perhaps some social perks. It's primarily about earning that paycheck. People in this category are typically more invested in their lives outside of the office."[5] Wrzesniewski then differentiates between a job and a career:

> A job you do for others, while a career is what you do for yourself. Career professionals are also working for the paycheck (let's be honest, who isn't?), but they are more driven to seek out opportunities for advancement in the workplace. These individuals tend to strive for the next promotion, look for more training and generally aim to impress. People with a career orientation tend to have a long-term vision for their professional future, set goals and enjoy healthy competition with colleagues.[6]

Finally, Wrzesniewski describes how calling can be connected to one's work:

> Those who experience their work as a calling are most likely to feel a deep alignment between their vocation and who they are as a person. They feel a personal and emotional connection to their work. They are enthusiastic, have a sense of purpose and are willing to work harder and longer to make a contribution. Unsurprisingly, this group is often the most satisfied with their professional situation."[7]

Wrzesniewski's definitions provide a helpful sense of scaffolding as one moves along the rungs of various jobs and careers. However, one's sense of calling certainly does not need to be limited to finding an ideal professional situation. As a deeper exploration of "calling" reveals, there are meaningful connections to be made between one's sense of calling and how one pursues that calling in the context of work and service.[8]

The English word *vocation* derives from the Latin *vocatio*, meaning "summons," and from *vocare*, meaning "to call." While not identical, there is an important association between one's calling and vocation. Becky Horst, a past associate academic dean at Goshen College, explains vocation as "a calling that merges our mission in life with God's mission on earth."[9] Calling is about aligning our work—whatever that may be—with the work that God is already doing in the world. Richard Bolles, author of *What Color Is*

---

5. Wilding, "Do You Have a Job, Career, or Calling?"
6. Wilding, "Do You Have a Job, Career, or Calling?"
7. Wilding, "Do You Have a Job, Career, or Calling?"
8. For a robust theology of how vocation and calling relate to work and worship, see Kaemingk and Willson, *Work and Worship*.
9. Horst, "Job, Career, Vocation."

Your Parachute, provides further insight. "We want to do more than plod through life, going to work, coming home from work," he writes. "We want to find that special joy 'that no one can take from us,' which comes from a sense of mission in our life." Further,

> When used with respect to our life and work, mission has always been a religious concept, from beginning to end. It is defined by Webster's as "a continuing task or responsibility that one is destined or fitted to do or specially called upon to undertake" and historically has had two major synonyms: calling and vocation. These, of course, are the same word and two different languages, English and Latin. Both imply God.[10]

God is the one doing the calling, and as individuals learn to discern the work God is doing in the world, they find a sense of purpose in the work and opportunities for learning and growth set before us.

Clearly, there are important connections between mission, vocation, and calling. For Christian universities, these concepts find their meaning and application with their central focus on God. As students discover their mission and calling to be difference-makers in the world, online universities must take specific, collaborative steps of support. Students' sense of mission must be nurtured within the classroom, within the conversations held between students and the various departments of the university, and especially within the very assignments crafted to engage and guide students. From the first enrollment inquiry to the receipt of a diploma, the university community works collaboratively to support, celebrate, nurture, and train students towards their vocational mission and God-given calling. This is accentuated with the deliberate focus on the holistic integration of each student's faith, life, and learning.

At LAPU, this holistic focus begins with the introductory course ISTU 101: Success in the University. During this class, students complete the StrengthsFinder assessment, an online tool developed by Gallup that helps students identify and develop their top five talents.[11] The assessment and related assignments help success coaches and faculty partner with students in their academic, professional, and personal pursuits. Rather than students beginning an aimless trudge through multiple classes with little direction for the future, the university aims to guide students towards cultivating their areas of strengths and giftedness. This sets up students for success, so that in the future they will both accentuate their talents professionally, and begin

---

10. Bolles, *What Color Is Your Parachute?*, 264.
11. Rath, *StrengthsFinder 2.0*.

to settle within a vocation and mission that leads to deep-seated satisfaction and God-given calling.

The StrengthsFinder research shows that when students become aware of their top five talents, a natural fire builds within them.[12] Call it passion, call it drive, call it calling, call it the Holy Spirit—something moves within students. For many, a recognition and knowledge of their strengths is an awakening of who they truly are, what they can do, and the impact they can make on the future. Students learn never to underestimate the power behind uncovering what one does well. Among toxic cultural tides, where emphasis is on notable failures and inadequacies, a focus on strengths sets a precedent to go against the tide and leave a wake of fulfilled students who are trained, prepared, and ready to lead with their talents and embrace their calling. As Bolles observes, "God has already revealed his will to us concerning our vocation and mission, by causing it to be 'written in our members.' We are to begin deciphering our unique mission *by studying our talents and skills*, and mark more particularly which ones or one we must rejoice to use."[13] Or, in the words of Paul, "For we are God's handiwork, created in Christ Jesus to do good works, which God prepared in advance for us to do."[14] God has already created our students with great purpose; it is the university's responsibility and privilege to help guide them toward their mission and vocation.

The StrengthsFinder assessment provides a window of knowledge into each student's unique set of talents and skills. For Bolles, such knowledge illuminates the pathway to uncovering personal mission and speaks to the importance of "God's guidance of the heart."[15] This is the language of discernment—and such discernment is both personal and corporate. As students ponder their future, they often look to their strengths as they listen for God's guidance. They consider a major by reflecting on their strengths, on their personal experiences, and on conversations with family, friends, success coaches, classmates, and faculty. They envision working in a field where they can apply their talents, make a difference, and find fulfillment participating in God's mission in the world. Kelly Pope, who recently earned LAPU Bachelor's and Master's degrees in applied psychology, states it this way: "I can be trained to do just about anything. However, one thing I have learned over time is that if you are not moving and operating in your gifts and natural abilities, regardless of the amount of money you make, you

---

12. See Rath, *StrengthsFinder 2.0*, 15–28.
13. Bolles, *What Color Is Your Parachute?*, 278–79.
14. Eph 2:10 (NIV).
15. Bolles, *What Color Is Your Parachute?*, 279.

acquire an unsettled and purposeless feeling for your life."[16] A student's commitment of time, finances, energy, and discipline is not without purpose. Rather, students are driven by their calling and mission. Universities, in turn, are called to honor this drive and support the purpose and mission of their students.

FAITH INTEGRATED WITHIN THE ACADEMIC DISCIPLINES

Because of the beautiful craftsmanship of God, each academic discipline can find profound connections to the Bible. Individual academic programs have a role in showcasing how a distinct discipline can be integrated with God's word and a student's personal story. Reg Codrington, LAPU chaplain and instructor, describes it this way:

> The beauty of faith integration, as practiced by LAPU, is that it is not a form of Christianity superimposed on every course, but it grows out of asking how each course fits into God's story for the world. I have found it refreshing, and student after student has commented on how the Bible studies have provided a good, ethical, and moral framework for the careers they are in, or plan to enter.[17]

When students find that their faith can be integrated into their studies and careers, they discover a new lens through which to see and engage with the world around them. They find that God is present and at work, no matter their context, and this provides a new sense of hope and purpose for their classes and for their lives.

Practically speaking, as indicated previously, course content is guided by program learning outcomes (PLOs) and course learning outcomes (CLOs). At the program level, it is critical to incorporate Christian worldview application within the PLOs so that it filters down into the assignments. As a result of PLOs providing a hierarchical precedent, there is a focused effort to keep in step with the expectation to weave faith-based components into the fabric of the curriculum. This, in turn, leads to practical application and integration into the student's story.

An example from the Bachelor of Arts in Applied Psychology (BAAP) program shows this intentional focus on faith integration from the program level, into the course, and through a particular assignment. The first PLO for

16. Kelly Pope, interview by author, May 4, 2017.
17. Reg Codrington, interview by author, September 17, 2020.

the BAAP is "demonstrate the ability to integrate principles of applied psychology and Christian faith." This PLO weaves through each course in the program, eventually leading to the capstone courses—the final archway that leads to graduation for BAAP students. A CLO for these capstone courses is "students will be able to apply integrated principles of applied psychology and Christian worldview." There is an intentional alignment between the program learning outcome and course learning outcome. This alignment, then, filters directly down into assignments. For example, students complete in-field service learning for the capstone experience. While field experience itself is an excellent source for learning and building vocational skill, students are also required to assess their abilities and experiences, and notably to hone in on what God is doing within them and around them while serving. In each report, students reflect on integration questions, such as: "identify and explain two ways in which you saw God at work this week, in this service learning," and "list three specific Scriptures/characters from the Bible that apply to this week's service." Oftentimes students relate "God at work" to their own personal story while serving. Many students begin to have that aha moment, as they see how God is using them now and will continue to use them in the future. Adrianne Newberne, a recent LAPU graduate, describes powerful personal insights related to faith integration:

> Jeremiah 29:11 reminds me, "'For I know the plans I have for you,' declares the Lord, 'plans to prosper you and not to harm you, plans to give you hope and a future.'" I never thought I could accomplish all that I have done. However, when I put my faith in God and finally listened, I accomplished and learned so much about myself. I realized that this is what I should have been doing with my life this whole time. I have continued to see God work through me so that I can help others. Proverbs 3:5–6 also speaks volumes in my reflection of my time at my practicum. "Trust in the Lord with all your heart and lean not on your own understanding; in all your ways submit to him, and he will make your paths straight." There were times when I doubted my abilities to be able to do the job. However, I now see that God has given me a gift to serve and support others. Psalm 119:105 says, "Your word is a lamp for my feet, a light on my path." If I continue to put my faith in God, I know I will be right where I am supposed to be.[18]

As students learn to recognize the connections between their faith, studies, and work, their mission becomes clear, giftedness becomes

---

18. Adrianne Newbern, interview by author, December 12, 2019.

pronounced, and their passion for the future is ignited. Students benefit not only from written reports and discussion that incorporate dialogue about the intersection of their discipline, service, and biblical truths, but also from individual meetings with their professor during each of these capstone courses. Conversations revolve around what the students are learning, questions they have about their service-learning, guidance from the instructor, vocational pathways, and opportunities to pray with students. Xiomoara Ramirez, a student, offered a note of thanks for this personalized, integrated care:

> Thank you for your help, your prayers, and your encouraging words. My journey through these eight weeks was a learning experience for sure, and quite honestly it was emotionally taxing. I can't tell you how many times I wanted to give up, but I didn't because you always popped in at the right time to offer a word of encouragement or a prayer, [and] I appreciate that[19]

Being an online university should not in any way diminish our blueprint for excelling at personalizing experiences for students. Allowing for faith-based conversations, to edify the student but also to highlight application within academic disciplines, should be a norm within the online Christian university environment.

The final service-learning report that students complete for the capstone courses includes additional questions that further promote reflection on how their service-learning shaped them. In the report, students are to "identify four examples of how you were shaped personally by your service-learning" and "identify four examples of how you were shaped professionally by the service-learning." By the end of the capstone experience, students report a profound sense of mission, calling, and integration between their faith and the opportunities before them in their chosen profession. A few examples highlight the impact: "My practicum has confirmed for me that my calling is to help others embark on their academic journey."[20] "Through this practicum, God affirmed my calling to the ministry of marriage and family."[21] "I was able to see myself in a role that suited me professionally. I learned that this is an area I could see myself making a difference to others while at the same time being blessed."[22] "I was able to hone my skills with Scripture and our study of Psychology. It brought the subjects back to life,

---

19. Xiomara Ramirez, interview by author, October 24, 2019.
20. Vanessa Garcia, interview by author, December 8, 2019.
21. Robert Gutierrez, interview by author, August 26, 2018.
22. Elaine Rich, interview by author, December 31, 2019.

and it renewed the part of my mind that seeks answers and wants to delve deeper to provide answers to others who also have questions."[23]

The meaningful integration of students' mission and vocation is evident in these comments. The university should never underestimate its role in guiding students towards understanding how their personal faith intersects with their academic discipline and future vocation. Intentionally crafting opportunities within the curriculum to help students explore these areas has evident powerful outcomes.

UNIVERSITY-WIDE OPPORTUNITIES TO CULTIVATE A STUDENT'S MISSION

It is crucial to acknowledge that each department that interacts with students has the potential to affirm and guide them towards their personal mission or calling. At LAPU, there are four main areas where relationships can be cultivated in service to students: during the enrollment process, with success coaches, with faculty and course instructors, and through peer-to-peer engagement. To start, the LAPU enrollment team works closely with students at the onset of their interactions with the university. Professionals on this team are eager to connect with students, hear their personal stories, and guide them towards a program that aligns with their vision. Recall again Bolles's description about personal mission: "We are to begin deciphering our unique mission *by studying our talents and skills*" and understanding God's "*guidance of our heart*, as to which Talent gives us the greatest pleasure."[24] Re-Admit Specialist and Enrollment Counselor Isabel Monroy describes how these initial conversations can open the door to helping students discover and articulate their motivation, particularly as it relates to their talents, skills, and motivation of the heart. She says,

> When working with re-admits you will always ask, why is now a good time to return? Then you listen and hear what this student is telling you. You show empathy to their situation and what was needed to lift themselves back up. You encourage them by letting them know that they have already taken the first step and that is the hardest one. You let them know God has a plan for them and he is showing the way. You discuss the program and ask what their future looks like? What are they going to do with this degree?[25]

23. Richard Alvarado, interview with author, December 28, 2017.
24. Bolles, *What Color Is Your Parachute?*, 278–79.
25 Isabel Monroy, interview by author, November 20, 2020.

The enrollment team asks simple questions, which allows prospective students to share about their talents, their skills, their experiences, and where they believe they are being led in terms of academic discipline and future vocational path. Effective communication begins with one person who is ready, available, and demonstrating the desire to listen. It is not always easy to share dreams of the future with a stranger. Active listening—utilizing skills such as restatement, summarizing, paraphrasing, and verifying questions—demonstrates to prospective students that the university cares and the enrollment counselors are truly listening. As a result of this authentic interaction, there is a unique opportunity to hear the experiences and goals of each student. Enrollment staff affirm and encourage prospective students, and then help effectively guide them towards a program that encapsulates their desires, their skill set, their talents, and ultimately, their calling. The university starts helping students realize their mission and how God can use them from the very beginning. Enrollment counselors instill confidence within students, resulting in an excitement to jump in and uncover what God can do within their lives through their chosen academic discipline.

Continuity of care is a concept used within the medical and mental health fields. In action, continuity of care allows for a seamless transition from one system of help to another. LAPU's structure of student support aligns with this concept. Students are not dropped between enrollment and the beginning of classes; rather there is a process that has been carefully crafted to support students from one system to the next as they move forward in their education. The enrollment team provides beneficial insights to the success coach team during the virtual hand-off of the student. As part of the continuity of care, the enrollment team updates the identified success coach about each student's vision, experiences, talents, goals, mission, faith, and how this has led to the student's chosen academic discipline. This structured hand-off creates an opportunity for the success coach to have an introductory understanding of the new student in their care. This preparation step allows for success coaches to greet their new students with a robust excitement for what they want to accomplish in their future.

LAPU's success coach team plays an integral part in the life of the student. They are a student's supporter, advisor, liaison, cheerleader, guide, and accountability partner. As LAPU graduate Angela Orozco described, "My success coaches, they were the best! They contributed so much to my education. They took their time. To me, it didn't seem like a job to them because they were so invested in me."[26] Engaging in regular communication, success coaches have an opportunity to create genuine relationships

---

26. Angela Orozco, interview by Los Angeles Pacific University, February 15, 2018.

that enable them to speak into the lives of students. As mentioned earlier, students take ISTU 101: Success at the University at the onset of their time at LAPU. Success coaches play a pivotal role during this class, by connecting with students each week and then helping them uncover their vocational goals and calling. During this class, students not only invest in finding their personal talents through *StrengthsFinder 2.0*, they also write about their "big why" for being in higher education. Success coaches have the opportunity to discuss a student's "why" with them. There is a mutual dialogue fueled by questions and excitement. Coaches collaborate with students in creating a solution-focused approach toward their future vocational goals. During this class, students are also introduced to LAPU's Career and Vocation Center.[27] This is the student's first glimpse at the distinction between vocation versus career. It is also their introduction to uncovering God's purpose and personal calling through the lens of academic discipline and vocation. They see the intersection of God's story and their story and how their education is a pathway to fulfilling their mission. With that fire ignited and vision planted, it is essential for success coaches to remain available and ready to listen. Conversations with coaches are another safe place for students to explore the colliding of their dreams, mission, and their personal story. Clearly, success coaches are key contributors in helping students further uncover their strengths, as well as their vocational dreams and realities. All of this personalized, holistic support can indeed be provided within an online Christian university. A simple click on the computer screen, an online chat, or an email can lead to a world of support for students, geared towards helping them uncover who they were meant to be and equipping them to excel.

While success coaches are an active and present support for students throughout their enrollment at LAPU, the continuity of care also connects to the next system, which is the classroom. As previously detailed, the course curriculum creates opportunities for students to establish the integration of personal faith with their academic discipline and personal calling. However, these opportunities of understanding come to life with the weekly interactions between students and their professors. Angela Orozco, LAPU graduate, recalls, "The amount of the support you get from the professors is indescribable. It's just a testament to the university and how they want you to succeed."[28] Instructors focus on building relationships with students in order to support their learning and growth. Especially within the virtual classroom setting, instructors must be intentional about knowing their students. An electronically submitted assignment does not tell the student's story, and

---

27. Los Angeles Pacific University, "Career and Vocation Center."
28. Angela Orozco, interview by Los Angeles Pacific University, February 15, 2018.

so a professor works to find the balance between caring about the well-being of students, encouraging their personal faith, and providing an excellent education. They help merge God's story with both the field of study and the student's individual story. This is a breathtaking discovery for some students. Enthusiasm and passion can be felt through the computer screen. Instructors have the unique privilege to construct a usable lens through which students can view the intersection of their personal faith and their academic discipline, and in practicality, how that translates to a career and calling. Interactions—whether through discussion forums, assignment feedback, virtual meetings, emails, texts, or phone calls—challenge students to see themselves in their vocation, to apply discipline-related tools and concepts, and to use their faith as the foundation for their work. Deborah St. George, for example, describes the unique opportunities for online instructors:

> Students respond to the culture of LAPU's online format to freely share their Christian perspectives as part of the learning experience. LAPU courses are designed to encourage enriching dialogue, providing deeper insight into our diverse global world. As an instructor, it is very fulfilling to guide discussions for weekly topics to include a principle of faith that is connected to everyday life and the workplace. In the disciplines of business and finance, ideas are freely exchanged about solid leadership and good stewardship of financial resources in business. This process is the face of hope and a better future for us all.[29]

Educators guide those initial dreams that students shared with their enrollment counselor to be translated to mission and vocation within the unique professional field.

Finally, a key system that stems from the classroom and needs to be nurtured is that of students sharpening students. Peer interactions are clearly impactful. Within the online discussion forum alone, there are inquisitive responses that encourage insightful conversation. There is notable influence by student leaders in the forum. With diversity in personal views, challenges from peers lead to critical thinking and introspection. The discussion forum is a prime location to incorporate prompts that require students to contemplate why their faith matters in association to their academic discipline. Envision a whetstone used to sharpen and strengthen a knife. A series of strokes leads to a sharper utensil, soon to be prepared for use. Our students and faculty take a similar role. A series of well-crafted prompts creates interactions between students and professors that lead to sharper, informed students, better prepared for the future.

29. Deborah St. George, interview by author, October 3, 2020.

Online discussion is an evident pathway toward encouraging student interaction in order to enhance faith, life, and learning—but to stop at the obvious would lead to a multitude of missed opportunities for students to sharpen one another. For example, LAPU launched a mobile app that includes a place for students to post insights, ask questions, share encouragement, and create study groups. In addition, LAPU has created discipline-specific online communities in order to provide opportunities for additional student engagement outside the formal classroom. These web pages showcase options for students to introduce themselves, share success stories from alumni, discuss questions about the field, highlight vocation and job options, participate in webinars, ask questions to the assistant deans and instructors, share their personal calling, and the like. The interactions among students are noteworthy. Peering into the communities, the onlooker sees a stream of encouragement. Questions are posed and responses given. A student's story provides motivation. Personal faith applied to vocation is commended. These communities not only emphasize unique opportunities and interactions between students, but they cultivate relationships and skill set development for students.

There are even more inroads to peer interactions within the online university for those who are like-minded in mission and life circumstances. The less obvious alternative are peer groups for unique communities. For example, LAPU has (among others) groups specifically for our military students, as well as moms who are students. Groups such as these create a space for normalcy; students realize they are not alone on their journeys. There are others on this pathway of higher education who experience similar challenges along the way. These groups create another avenue for peer sharpening and discussions of faith, academic discipline, and calling and what this looks like within their unique culture. One other community option for like-minded thinkers is discipline-specific societies. These gatherings create meaningful connections among students with similar ambition and professional goals, providing opportunities for students to grow together and become a thriving network for their college years and beyond. Through it all, students learn how to integrate their faith, live into their calling, and discover how their story merges with God's story.

The online university cannot stop at the ordinary. In and of itself, the concept of the online Christian university is still in its infant stages, still extraordinary in the history of higher education. Now is the time to continue exploring creative options that will serve the unique needs and desires of students today and tomorrow. Some students choose an online Christian university because of its mission and purpose. They identify with the belief system and look forward to integrating their beliefs into their academic discipline and future vocation. Each department of the university must create avenues to generate moments of unfettered faith-in-motion that leads to sustainable vocational impact.

It is time to pause, look ahead to the future, and consider the ripple effects. It begins with a student having a dream, a vision for the future. The student steps into that vision with their first Google search for online universities. With each click of the mouse, there is an opportunity to help the student realize their dream. An email is sent, an online chat is started, a phone call is made. The student applies, is accepted, sacrifices, studies, and grows. Fast forward to months after graduation. Can you see it? Can you see how graduates in every major of every department are changing the world? What started with a dream and a simple inquiry has led to future professionals bringing light into the world—future professionals who are using their gifts and talents to complete their mission through their vocation. It takes just one to affect a multitude. We see that example set forth in the life of Jesus, but we also respond to Jesus' charge: "In the same way, let your light shine before others, that they may see your good deeds and glorify your Father in heaven."[30] And from Peter, "Each of you should use whatever gift you have received to serve others, as faithful stewards of God's grace in its various forms."[31] By creating a curricular and personalized pathway for students that allows them to integrate their personal story with their education, faith, and calling, students become conduits of change in the world, illuminating hope within their sphere of influence and beyond.

---

30. Matt 5:16.
31. 1 Pet 4:10.

PART 3

Faith, Life, and Learning across the University

PART 3 *explores how faith formation is facilitated across the larger university community, outside the classroom. After describing a unique model for student support (chapter 10) and presenting a framework for incarnational practices and additional resources for faith formation (chapter 11), the book concludes (chapter 12) with a call for Christian universities to rely on their institutional identities, resources, and creativity to further develop their own commitment to holistic faith formation in their online learning endeavors.*

Chapter 10

Coaching for Faith Formation

CARRIE M. AKEMANN

CARRIE AKEMANN, *Senior Success Coach at Los Angeles Pacific University, presents a unique student success support model that cultivates holistic faith formation. The chapter explores the key question: How can online universities support the varied needs of their students while also offering resources for individual faith formation?*

Creating a sense of community and connection with their university is not often the priority of post-traditional students, despite that being an integral part to a successful thriving college experience.[1] Many are caring for aging parents, raising children, and working full time. Still, they enter into higher education with the hope to achieve their dreams, advance their careers, and provide for their families. It is in this tension of stress and aspiration that they must incorporate schooling into their already full lives. In these circumstances, becoming overwhelmed and dropping out may be a frequent temptation.[2] An answer to this problem of connection and retention is, in part, implementing the success coach model.

---

1. Schreiner, "Thriving in College," 46–49.
2. Sheffer et al., *Comeback Story*, 10.

THE COACHING MODEL

The coaching model is, at its heart, creating a main point of connection between the student and the university. In congruence with the university's holistic approach, the coach is several things all at once to the student. Although their primary function is an academic advisor, this is only one of their responsibilities. Others include advocating for the student within the institution, orienting the student to the online format, and providing general encouragement. They have access to a student's grades and monitor their performance in their classes and, using that information, provide students with resources and help them strategize ways to improve. In addition, at a Christian institution, coaches encourage students in faith formation, distinguishing their role from their secular university counterparts. This unique role requires coaches to be knowledgeable with academics and be able to engage in faith conversations. A successful coach will be able to balance administrative tasks and relational skills and demonstrate a commitment to spiritual growth and maturity.

Creating a good working relationship between a student and coach is critical as the coach will be the most consistent presence in a student's tenure at the university. Once a student is officially through the admissions process and enrolled in the university, they are assigned a success coach. This coach will work with that student for the duration of their program with the exception of either party leaving or the student changing their major. The coaches work in teams, with each team focusing on specific fields of study. Even though a student will be assigned to a coach and not a team, this model allows for easy substitutions while a student is away or a coach leaves, without negatively impacting the quality of care.

Included in quality of care is the coach's ability to communicate with post-traditional students they are not able to meet in a face-to-face setting. Post-traditional students are, by nature, mobile and busy.[3] This presents its own unique challenge and opportunity: a challenge because the student's ability to participate in conversations may be limited due to their responsibilities to work and family; an opportunity because the mode of communication through phone, emails, and texts makes such a relationship possible. This is especially true for the students identified as particularly vulnerable.[4] Coaches are able to meet students where they are, right in the middle of their lives.

Due to this multichannel style of communication, it is not unusual to have a coach talking with the student while they are on their daily commute

---

3. Klein-Collins, "Strategies for Becoming Adult-Learning-Focused Institutions," 5.
4. See Eisenberg et al., "Promoting Resilience, Retention, and Mental Health."

to work, emailing on a lunch break, or texting while waiting to pick up their children from school. For this reason, it is imperative that the coach, knowing they are competing for the student's attention and have limited time, must ensure their conversations have clearly stated objectives and are deemed helpful by the student themselves. This helps build trust between student and coach, which is critical for building a strong working relationship, where students can get the most benefit.

To help build this foundation between coach and student, Los Angeles Pacific University (LAPU) has embedded the coaching experience into the orientation class that a student typically takes in their first semester at the university. One of the unique features of this class is a requirement for a student and coach to have a weekly conversation. The topics for these weekly conversations range from practical (how to use the library) to aspirational (what are your goals, obstacles, etc.?) and spiritual (how do you see your faith connected to your studies?). Throughout the eight-week course, the conversations create consistent opportunities for the student and coach to build rapport. After the eight weeks are over, communication becomes more personalized and less structured than within a class, but with the expectation that the coach and student will continue to have frequent contact.

This building of rapport and viability between a student and their coach is foundational for the student experience at the university. A recent study focusing on adult students suggests that student relationships with staff at their university supersedes even those of their family members when it comes to their success.[5] Due to the coaching model being integrated into the curriculum and the frequency of communication, relationships formed between coach and student are often substantial. Students will share about their families and jobs along with their struggles in the classroom. By the time a student graduates, a coach and student will have spent hours discussing a myriad of topics including their goals, fears, frustrations, and triumphs. The bond of trust created in this relationship becomes a gateway not only for student success but for their own personal faith exploration and growth.

COACHING PHILOSOPHY FOR ACADEMIC AND FAITH CONVERSATIONS

At LAPU, coaching is, first and foremost, framed by the university's broader mission, vision, and core values.[6] The university's core values, Exemplary, Caring, and Learning, are also the hallmarks of what the coaching

5. Sheffer et al., *Comeback Story*, 7.
6. See chapter 5 for an examination of institutional identity.

department strives to be. The coaching department's mission statement clarifies and further expounds upon these values: "The department exists to provide innovative and effective support services that promote persistence and learning, while encouraging students toward a Christian perspective." This framework of coaching allows the student to be viewed, and therefore cared for, as a whole person, operating under the assumption that a student's academic success is interconnected with their faith formation.[7]

This philosophy of a student being successful in areas beyond the scope of academics stems from the notion of "thriving." In Laurie Schreiner's "The 'Thriving Quotient'" she discusses this holistic approach to student success, defining thriving as being "fully engaged intellectually, socially, and emotionally in the college experience."[8] This thriving principle falls within the context of appreciative education that in part "provides an intentional and positive approach to better educational enterprises by focusing on the strengths and potential of individuals."[9] Appreciative education is derived in part from positive psychology and appreciative advising.[10] Appreciative education's practices include "reciprocal learning" and "holistic engagement"—both being a part of the university's mission, vision, and values and in turn, a hallmark of successful coaching.[11]

A thriving student is also one who is spiritually engaged.[12] A 2011 study conducted by Alexander Astin and colleagues found students who were more engaged spiritually were "more satisfied with college, received higher grades, were more likely to embrace diversity and exhibited higher academic self-esteem."[13] This was confirmed again in another study from a Christian perspective done by Liberty University on enhanced faith formation for online students, which advocated for including faith when considering a successful student. Their findings revealed the following evidence of spiritual formation in online courses: "(a) enhanced spiritual formation as a result of increased knowledge, community development, and personal growth; (b) positively impacted spiritual development in light of peer and faculty relationships; and (c) assimilation of social and spiritual dimensions through course content and practical application."[14]

7. Astin et al., *Cultivating the Spirit*, 7.
8. Schreiner, "'Thriving Quotient,'" 4.
9. Bloom et al., "Appreciative Education," 7.
10. Bloom et al., "Appreciative Education," 8.
11. Bloom et al., "Appreciative Education," 10–12.
12. Schreiner, "Thriving in College," 45–46.
13. Astin et al, *Cultivating the Spirit*, 10.
14. Lowe, "Assessing the Impact of Online Courses," 3.

Coaching at a Christian university addresses a student's spiritual need by focusing on faith formation from a Christian worldview. In the Gospel of Luke, Jesus speaks to the holistic nature of personhood when he gives the greatest commandment, to "love the Lord your God with all your heart, and with all your soul, and with all your strength, and with all your mind."[15] This inherent holistic commandment emphasizes that humans are both one and made of several different parts. This holistic view is easily applied to a post-traditional context in that students are engaging with their studies in the midst of their lives. In this model, a successful coach will address a student's spiritual needs alongside their academic ones.[16] As Patrick Otto and Michael Harrington summarize, "Spiritual formation is not to be viewed as the only important goal of the university, thereby sacrificing intellectual or relational development. Rather, spiritual formation should be seen as the product of all that the Christian college is doing. It is not an either-or phenomenon, but a coordinated commitment that should be engaged holistically."[17]

To provide this holistic care to students, it is important to avoid a uniform approach. When formulating academic advising, coaching draws from the research and insights of Ezekiel Kimball and Susan Campbell:

> In essence, one size does not fit all with regard to academic advising. The field needs, and indeed, requires, multiple strategies so advisors effectively respond to multiple and unique audiences. The field needs flexible, eclectic practitioners able to adapt their advising strategies in accordance with the needs of their students. Being married to a single approach to academic advising, advisors potentially disregard the diverse ways in which students learn and presume a single, linear developmental path that is clearly more idealistic than realistic.[18]

This advising framework relies heavily on the relationship a coach will establish with their student so they can properly assess and address a student's

---

15. Luke 10:27a NRSV.

16. Given that the coach may get to know a student on a very personal level, boundaries and framing the conversation need to be standard practice from the beginning. It is important to distinguish that a coach is neither a pastor nor a therapist. A coach will not approach conversations as being any kind of authority figure when it comes to theology. This is also true for any emotional or mental health issues requiring assistance from a licensed professional. If any of these needs do arise that are outside the scope of coaching, students are referred to resources where they can go to receive additional support.

17. Otto and Harrington, "Spiritual Formation within Christian Higher Education," 260.

18. Kimball and Campbell, "Advising Strategies," 6.

individual needs. This personalized approach places the emphasis on the person and not a narrow end goal of checking certain advising boxes.

Along with being holistic and personalized, successful coaching operates from a place of inclusivity. According to the university's open enrollment policy, a student is not required to profess any type of faith. Thus, there is a vast diversity of thought and belief among the student population. Although many students may consider themselves Christians, there is much room for interpretation on what that means or the degree it impacts the student. Many would be considered nominal or cultural Christians, while some have a deep abiding relationship with Christ, and still others are agnostic or atheistic. Given this diverse population, coaches operate out of the aforementioned appreciative learning practice of reciprocal learning and rely on their relationship to discern where a student is on their faith journey and engage appropriately.[19] The emphasis is on building the relationship instead of trying to convert or proselytize.

Though the emphasis of coaching is on a student's individual journey, this remains a distinctly Christian approach to faith formation. As such, it is appropriate that coaches operate from fundamental guiding Christian principles when approaching any conversation regarding faith. Universal talking points are given to coaches in training, and their use is encouraged when a student is wavering or needs guidance. Simple phrases like, "God loves you," "God is with you," and "God is for you" can bring profound comfort and perspective to students' lives, and they invite further opportunities for listening and meaningful dialogue.[20]

The university's coaching philosophy encourages faith formation and academic thriving by providing care that is holistic, relational, personalized, and inclusive. The hopeful outcome is that any student, regardless of their beliefs entering the university, will leave having formed a deeper understanding of their faith and how it connects with their academic pursuits, and will be encouraged toward a closer relationship with Christ.

BUILDING A SUCCESSFUL COACHING RELATIONSHIP: SKILLS AND RESOURCES

With the theoretical foundation established, a coach has a framework to help students thrive and have enriching faith formation conversations. But, before those conversations can take place, a coach prioritizes their academic

---

19. Bloom et al., "Appreciative Education," 10–12.

20. Lopez, "Guiding Spiritual Formation." See Eph 3:16–19; Zeph 3:17; Ps 46:7; 139; and Rom 8:31–32.

needs, and builds a working relationship. This process takes time, and requires the coach to show competency, care, and trust; but, if done well, the relationship can lead to meaningful and significant conversation.

In coach training, students' needs are presented in a hierarchical form, with each level needing to be satisfied before the next one can be addressed. These needs range from access to technology to a student's calling or purpose.[21] To help both coach and student address these issues, the success and academic departments collaborated to develop the weekly coaching conversations embedded in the ISTU 101: Success in the University class. These loosely scripted talking points are the central focus for the coaching conversations and are designed to address a student's needs and build rapport with their coach. Coaches use their skills and provide resources to provide care for their students at each level of student need, culminating in meaningful conversations about calling and faith. As the weeks progress, students are given both tools and encouragement they need to thrive in their university experience.

At the start, a student's needs are very rudimentary. They need access to adequate technology, a way of financing their education, and a clear timeline of how long their program will take to complete.[22] At this level, the coaches work to display competency and their primary resource will be themselves, using their knowledge of policies, procedures, and university norms to orient the student. Thus, initial communications consist mostly of fielding logistical questions and providing practical information such as purchasing books, course navigation, library resources, and degree requirements. It is crucial at this stage to provide both timely and relevant information for the student, with the hopeful outcome of demonstrating competency and solidifying the benefit of coaching to the student.

At this first level, prayer is introduced to all students as an initial exercise in faith formation.[23] A coach explains to the student they are attending a Christian university and spiritual care can be a part of the coaching relationship. The coach will ask the student if the student has any prayer requests. The coach will assess the student's comfort level based on their tone and response and will either pray for the student directly or let the student know they will pray for them on their own. Unless the student is openly against this practice, prayer will be a part of every conversation with the student going forward. This establishes two important coaching precedents:

---

21. Lopez, "Coaching 101."
22. Lopez, "Coaching 101."
23. Lopez et al., "Active Listening in Spiritual Formation."

the student is asked to share only what they are comfortable disclosing and a consistent faith element is embedded into every conversation.

The second level of meeting students' needs is addressing their academic readiness.[24] Post-traditional students need to plan for strategies when thinking through things like work/life balance, maintaining a healthy support system, and time management. To help guide this process, coaches will help students identify potential obstacles and develop a plan to combat these obstacles if and when they arrive. In addition, SMART goals (Specific, Measurable, Attainable, Relevant, and Time-based) are introduced to provide students with a self-directed resource they can use to help overcome obstacles and challenges.[25] In regards to faith formation, coaches continue to ask students if they have any prayer requests and they inquire about past requests as appropriate.

At this second level, active listening is a primary skill coaches rely on to address student needs. Active listening means being fully present with someone without distractions, where the listener is able to comprehend in full what the speaker is relaying, and then respond in an appropriate manner.[26] Active listening requires a coach to remember specific details about a student, exercising the aforementioned personalized care, and to reflect back to the student what they heard. The coach needs to avoid interjecting their own opinion or deflecting attention away from the student.[27] If done successfully, a student will be comfortable sharing their thoughts, knowing they have a receptive ear that cares about their academic success and personal well-being. This is a crucial building block leading up to faith formation conversations, and it is essential that the student feels cared for and begins to trust their coach.

The third level of meeting students' needs is establishing a relational connection with their university. At this level, a student is successful if they see themselves as seen and feel they are capable of success.[28] The resources used at this level are StrengthsFinder and growth mindset theory. StrengthsFinder is a research-based assessment tool that measures an individual's talents and natural abilities. By focusing on a student's strengths, coaches shift perspective from correcting what are perceived weaknesses to developing what a student does naturally well, resulting in a more productive and

---

24. Lopez, "Coaching 101."
25. Stoltzfus, *Coaching Questions*, 37.
26. Gearhart and Bodie, "Active-Empathic Listening," 86.
27. Lopez et al., "Active Listening in Spiritual Formation."
28. Lopez, "Coaching 101."

satisfying experience.[29] Growth mindset theory is "based on the belief that your basic qualities are things you can cultivate through your efforts, and help from others," and that "everyone can change and grow through application and experience."[30]

Both of these resources draw upon what Schreiner calls "positive perspective," which "represents the ways in which thriving students view life." Students with a positive perspective "view their world and their future with confidence; they expect good things to happen and reframe negative events into learning experiences. As a result, they tend to be more satisfied with their lives and enjoy their college experience to a greater degree."[31] These two combined resources are a way in which coaches can address a student's need for connection and being known while laying the groundwork for future faith formation conversations by affirming that students are wonderfully made and capable of doing good work.[32]

At this third level, a coach relies on their skill of asking open-ended questions that invite substantive conversation. Open-ended questions are pillars of success coaching and become a major part of later faith formation conversations. These questions are easily identified as starting with Who, What, Where, When, or Why, and encourage dialogue while avoiding those types of questions that only require a yes or no answer. (For example: What times have you set aside to work on your schoolwork? vs. Do you have time to do your schoolwork?)[33] The hopeful outcome of this type of inquiry is the continued formation of relationships, with the student being invited to reflect more deeply on their student experiences. At this stage, if a student initiates conversation surrounding faith, a coach can engage with the student by using the same open-ended questions, continuing to allow the student to control where the conversation goes within their comfort level.

FAITH FORMATION CONVERSATIONS

The last level in the student's hierarchy of needs is connecting with their calling, purpose, and faith.[34] Here students are asked to reflect on the deeper meaning of their lives, while coaches, using all of their resources and skills, help a student navigate through these questions. When done well,

29. Rath, *StrengthsFinder 2.0*.
30. Dweck, *Mindset*, 7.
31. Schreiner, "Thriving in College," 43.
32. See Ps 139 and 2 Tim 3:17.
33. Stoltzfus, *Coaching Questions*, 30.
34. Lopez, "Coaching 101."

these conversations "assist students in interpreting their values, beliefs, and experiences so they get somewhere they want to go."[35] Discussions on purpose, calling, and meaning provide a natural fluidity with faith formation questions, as all are leading students to reflect on issues of ultimate meaning and purpose—including, who is God to the student.

Alongside all of the other previously mentioned skills, at this final level coaches need to embody a posture of humility in order to create a safe space to frame these deeply personal conversations. These conversations require intentionality, focus, and discipline. Yet, even with such efforts, it is expected that post-traditional students will display a wide range of comfort and engagement levels. For many students, faith formation conversations are neither a normal nor a frequent occurrence in any setting, let alone their schooling. However, for others, this is a much needed or even a well-versed topic they can readily share. For all students, this is a highly personal exercise that requires trust and vulnerability. But it is in this very place, this sacred space, that fruitful—and ultimately transformational—conversations can occur.

To assume a posture of humility and the creation of a safe space, a coach needs to remember what to refrain from as much as what to do. While in conversation, coaches do not interject their opinion or correct a student's theology. They do not force the conversation to a certain agenda or proselytize. They abstain from dismissing a student's experience, demeaning its significance, or injecting their own thoughts that would steer the focus from the student. A student needs to be able to express themselves with a fully present listener and without the fear of judgement.

The coach thus creates and facilitates conversations that allow a student to express freely their reflections and beliefs about God. This requires a coach to be fully present in the moment, relying on their questions and listening skills, and keeping "one ear to the phone and the other to heaven."[36] Sometimes during a call, a coach may sense a prompting from the Spirit to ask a certain question or offer specific encouragement, such as a timely Bible verse or prayer; but it takes a depth of spiritual maturity, coupled with discipline and humility, to recognize such a prompting and follow where the Spirit is leading.

Prayer in itself is a powerful, near universal way to engage in faith formation. As mentioned earlier, prayer is introduced early, and often not resisted, even among those for whom faith is not readily present. For students, it is still received, at the very least, as a kind, nonthreatening gesture.

---

35. Kimball and Campbell, "Advising Strategies," 6.
36. Lopez et al., "Active Listening in Spiritual Formation."

Coaches report that more than anything prayer is the most impactful practice for students in regards to conversations involving faith, and the primary reason they are able to participate in more in-depth conversations later. Prayer becomes a way for students to feel cared for, and it is a breaker of relational walls. Many students that initially decline prayer will request it later, especially when facing a challenge or hardship.

Sharing a Bible verse or passage can give the student something to anchor themselves to as they navigate questions of faith and calling. For students of faith, coaches can ask what Scriptures they turn to in times of need.[37] For those students less familiar, having Scripture prayed over them can be a meaningful way to expose the student to God's word and its transformative power. As a coach is learning their role, they need feedback and supervision to hone these skills of discernment, but, when done appropriately, incorporating Scripture can be a gateway for breakthrough in a student's awareness of God's working in their lives.

To help with keeping the focus both on the student and to the Spirit, coaches are encouraged to do their own personal prayer before connecting with the student and invite the Holy Spirit into the conversation, asking for discernment and wisdom. Coaches are reminded of the words of James 1:5: "If any of you is lacking in wisdom, ask God, who gives to all generously and ungrudgingly, and it will be given you." This framing puts the coach in the posture of the learner, aligning themselves under God's direction. By praying beforehand, this posture-setting exercise helps quiet the coach's mind, provides focus, and brings the conversation to God, surrendering the outcome to him.

The first time a student and a coach have an intentional conversation about their faith happens several weeks into a student's first class, when the entire university is focused on the theme of faith, life, and learning. The university bifurcates their semesters into two parts, or sessions, each lasting eight weeks. Across the university, week seven is always designated as Faith, Life, and Learning Week, when there are resources and guided conversations related to holistic faith formation. This intentional university-wide focus creates a cultural rhythm that faculty, staff, and students come to know and expect. For new students, the first time they engage in Faith, Life, and Learning Week is during their weekly coaching calls in ISTU 101: Success in the University. By this time in the course, the hope is a coach and a student will have developed good rapport and trust over the weekly conversations beforehand, with the coach displaying care and offering prayer. To guide this initial faith formation conversation, students are given the questions

---

37. Lopez et al., "Active Listening in Spiritual Formation."

a coach will be asking ahead of time. This allows students to plan ahead and anticipate a faith-related conversation with their coach. In ISTU 101, students read:

> Week 7 is Faith, Life and Learning week. Every week 7 LAPU reflects on how faith and learning impact our lives. Engage in a conversation with your success coach. While your coach will tailor the conversation to fit your needs, be prepared to discuss the following questions and topics:
>
> - How does your faith impact your academic experience and how does your academic experience impact your faith?
> - What has been challenging, encouraging, or meaningful in your reflections about your faith?
> - What does it mean to bring your faith into your learning?
> - Reflecting on your life, is there a time that you recall God being really present? Can you share that story?

While exploring these questions with their students, coaches report that students are open to talking about their faith, with many students expressing that they have rarely spoken about these things, if at all. Even some of those who are regular churchgoers express never having reflected deeply on faith formation and how it relates to their lives. Some students across the faith spectrum confide to feeling far from God or express doubt, unsure of their calling, and lay bare wounds inflicted upon them by church or family. Some reveal the belief that God called them to attend school or pursue a certain vocation. Still others lament about a closeness lost with God, but attending the university has reignited a desire to make faith a more prominent part of their lives.

When speaking to students who are agnostic or profess no faith, coaches take a similar but adjusted approach to these conversations. Suggestions include asking about the student experience of being at a Christian university or inquiring if the student has their own non-faith journey. Coaches need to be careful, especially in these instances, not to push any agenda or force an outcome but again, to allow the Holy Spirit to work and the student to drive the conversation. If the conversation is stalled, coaches can always go back to a universal question of asking students to share their story as it relates to faith or lack thereof. In these types of communications, active listening is the most dominant skill. Conversations where a student can have their personal story validated by another can be the beginnings of faith seeds planted, used by God later on in a student's life to draw them nearer to himself.

Once the subject of faith is broached with the student, the coach can return to these conversations at later times, continuing to build the relationship and give space for reflection. Collaboration between coaches and faculty in regards to faith formation becomes more important as the student continues on with their degree. Students will be asked to reflect on faith in their classes and professors will have increased opportunity to engage with students in these reflections. Working together, faculty and coaches can allow the student to explore questions of faith, not just personally, but within their chosen field of study. Coaches can then use these assignments in students' various classes as touchpoints for ongoing conversations about faith. Ideally, a successful coach will approach each conversation with future conversations in mind. Instead of scripted questions, conversations become more organic and personalized, shaped by a student's life, alongside their university experience.

The university's mission is to encourage faith growth and transformation within a student. This, in conjunction with a holistic, individualized approach to care, is a cornerstone of the coaching philosophy. This is done through the building of trusted relationships where a student can explore their questions, doubts, fears, and joys without judgment. There is not a prescribed formula when it comes to faith formation. It requires coaching skills of asking questions, listening, and discernment to allow the work of the Holy Spirit. It means encouraging each student toward a Christian perspective wherever they are on that faith journey, communicating to them the truth that they are deeply loved and uniquely created by their creator for his purposes.

NATALIE'S STORY

Natalie is a student in her twenties.[38] She started off her university experience taking the ISTU 101: Success in the University class and a Bible class focusing on Exodus and Deuteronomy. After she and her success coach formed a good working relationship, she began to share more of her personal story. She grew up in a household where one parent was Pentecostal and the other was Seventh Day Adventist. Despite her religious influences, she came to LAPU not knowing much about the Bible.

As she went on in her class, she began to share with her coach her excitement about the material. She told her coach she loved her class so much that she did not even consider homework work because it was such

---

38. Student stories were collected from success coaches. Student names have been changed for privacy.

a joy for her to learn. As she learned about the Bible, her own beliefs and questions began to take shape. She began talking to her family more about their beliefs and would ask questions about topics like women in ministry, challenging what she had previously learned and experienced through her family of origin.

In one conversation her coach, sensing her growing love and enthusiasm, asked her if she ever considered going into ministry. Natalie said she had never considered it, not ever believing it was possible to do so because of her gender. Her coach encouraged her to consider it given her enthusiasm. Her coach asked Natalie if she was involved in a local church. Natalie said no, so her coach encouraged her to find a local church that supported her newfound passion and would encourage her in her growth and potential future ministry. Natalie is still in school and is looking forward to taking her second Bible class.

SIMON'S STORY

Simon came to LAPU to pursue a business degree. He worked as a janitor and wanted to better his career. According to his coach, initial conversations with Simon seem to indicate that Simon was not very focused on his academic pursuits. His attitude appeared indifferent at best and he did not display much academic ability.

He began his program like many students did, taking the Success in the University class. After a less than stellar start, he and his coach started discussing his assignments every week to help him improve. They eventually expanded to include how the assignments were impacting him on a more personal level. Their conversations became richer, particularly those that dealt with calling and purpose. Simon, through these assignments, began to reflect more on who he was and what that meant for his faith.

Throughout the course, Simon began to talk more and more about his career path. Near the end of the course, he told his coach he believed that God had spoken to him through his class. He said that God had challenged him on who he was and what his motivations in life were. Through this reflection and challenge, Simon decided to make changes. He ended up switching his major from business to psychology because he wanted to help people. He also began to take other areas in his life more seriously; throughout his time at LAPU he got married and he and his wife started a family.

Simon's coach said that he tries not to predict any student's future after working with so many students. Some students who at first do not appear likely to do well, not only graduate, but undergo significant and meaningful transformation. At the conclusion of his degree Simon decided he wanted to be a school counselor and after graduation looked to continue his education through graduate school.

ALICIA'S STORY

Alicia is in her mid-forties with adult children. She is a scientist who converted to Christianity several years ago after seeking first to disprove it. She entered LAPU with a strong faith. Going through the Success in the University class, she was inspired by her learnings related to growth mindset and StrengthsFinder. Alicia started to incorporate things she had learned in her class, expressing to her coach that these lessons changed her. Even though her faith was in a good place when she came, she believed that God had placed her at LAPU and with her coach for a reason.

Alicia's takeaway from her first session was that life is significant, and that regardless of her circumstances she can rely on her faith and positive mindset to get through the tough times. She appreciated the course, especially the faith integration, reminding her she had a purpose. Her coach observed that when students have a strong sense of purpose and faith integration, they are more easily able to persevere and overcome obstacles. This sense of purpose can be enhanced by a strong coaching relationship, allowing the coach to speak into the lives of students through prayer and conversations.

DAN'S STORY

Dan was a single dad around forty who worked retail. He had many hardships in life, having sole custody of his children and having overcome addiction. He had to live with his parents to be able to provide for his family. When he came to LAPU, he did not have much support for his educational pursuits. His father in particular did not understand why he was bothering trying to go to college; no one in the family had attended college. He felt Dan needed to focus solely on working to be able to support his children.

Dan wanted to do social work to help kids that were in trouble or did not have adequate support, so he came to LAPU to pursue a degree in psychology. He loved his classes and really enjoyed the field of study he had chosen. Dan attended a Bible study and services at his local church. He was overjoyed when he discovered what he was learning in his Bible study directly related to what he was learning in class. Excited about this connection, Dan brought it up to his pastor, thinking his pastor would be excited for him, too. Instead, his pastor told Dan that psychology was not a real subject and accused him of not having sufficient faith. Dan left that conversation broken in his faith. He did not feel like his family supported him and his church did not think his chosen profession was valid.

Dan kept going to school to pursue his degree. Occasionally he would pause to take a mental health break for a session, but he would continue to go back and all the while his coach would encourage him. For two years, Dan would cry on the phone with his coach, weary from the stressors of his life, and confiding that his coach was one of the only people he could talk to. Dan also developed a close relationship with his favorite psychology professor, who encouraged him in his chosen field, reassuring him that he was capable of success and a strong student. The faculty and staff became the sole supporters who helped Dan feel supported and that his dreams were valid.

One day, while Dan was near the end of his program, he called his coach to let him know he had been hired as a case manager through his local county government. He was going to help children and families in troubled situations. Both he and his coach celebrated this milestone. Later, at the graduation ceremony, Dan found his coach and professor and thanked them in person for providing him support, saying he would not have made it without them. Dan shared that his dad, having seen him in his new job, told him he finally understood why he went to school, and how proud he was of Dan. He left the university considering graduate school to further advance his career.

These student stories show the positive impact of integrating faith formation with academic pursuits. These life-changing events did not happen quickly, but through intentional, guided conversations with their coaches over time. Although not all student stories will be as dramatic, every student can participate in and benefit from this unique relationship with their coach to enrich their spiritual and academic lives.

CONCLUSION

The success coach model is able to bring together two of the most powerful means of transformation in a person's life, education and Jesus Christ. These two combined lead students to draw nearer to God and toward the purposes for which he created them. A success coach, acting as a guide, can help students navigate through core questions of identity, meaning, and purpose. They give space for students to grow in their faith and academic pursuits, building trust over time through conversations and prayers, showing students they care about them and their futures. This holistic approach to coaching is the gateway for deeper revelation and life-shifting moments. These moments can have a long-term impact, not only for students, but for their families and communities, advancing the kingdom and creating hope for the future.

Chapter 11

Incarnational Practices for Faith Formation

JOHN W. WASHATKA

JOHN WASHATKA, *Associate Professor at Los Angeles Pacific University, presents a framework for incarnational practices and provides additional resources for faith formation in the online university. Resources described include affiliate learning communities and a dynamic website with additional faith formation resources. The chapter begins with a consideration of its key question: How can convening a Faith, Life, and Learning Task Force provide strategic guidance and relevant faith formation resources for the university?*

HISTORY OF FAITH, LIFE, AND LEARNING AT LOS ANGELES PACIFIC UNIVERSITY

Since its founding in 2011, Los Angeles Pacific University (LAPU) has sought to extend the Christian values, history, and traditions of its parent institution, Azusa Pacific University, into a flexible and accessible online learning environment.[1] University documents show that concern for the priority of faith integration existed since the institution's beginning. Early attempts at faith integration occurred under the auspices of academia and were mainly focused on curricular activities, such as discussion forums and assignments. The university's concern for faith integration was also expressed in the commitment to the success coach model, including success coaches having conversations about spiritual matters and praying with students. Impetus for a more formal approach with a related broader focus of faith formation across the institution (not just the curriculum) was provided by the institution's regional accreditation initial site visit recommendations by the WASC Senior College and University Commission in 2017. The commission's recommendations caused the university to think more intentionally and holistically about how faith integration was to be addressed, and encouraged the university to regard faith integration as more than an academic function.

A related outcome of the accreditation visit was the initial formation of a Faith Integration Task Force to oversee the development of faith integration across the university community, with a primary focus on students. Initial membership was exclusively academic and early, broad responsibilities included determining, defining, and quantifying faith integration; considering implementation strategies; and identifying curricular and cocurricular activities. In response to the task force's recognition of its responsibility to be collaborative and inclusive, membership soon changed to include individuals from different departments so it was more representative of the whole institution.

Early work of the task force included introducing the idea of "faith, life, and learning" to replace "faith integration" as a descriptor of the work, and to rename the task force "Faith, Life, and Learning Task Force," in acknowledgment of the approach it wanted to take. Faith, life, and learning work was to be (1) holistic, dialogical, and incarnational; (2) in the curriculum as well as extracurricular; and (3) relevant to the university's student population. Consequently, an early, practical goal was to create Faith, Life, and Learning Outcomes at the program level.

That early practical goal morphed into a larger vision in which the task force identified "four points" as the vision and direction of its work. Students should be able to (1) apply a Christian worldview to their life and

---

1. The university was originally named Azusa Pacific Online University (APOU). For a time, it was referred to as Azusa Pacific University–University College (APU-UC), before coming into its current name of Los Angeles Pacific University (LAPU). See Los Angeles Pacific University, "Our History"; and Azusa Pacific University, "Azusa Pacific University System."

work in the world; (2) articulate how and in what ways their life journeys connect to God's story; (3) engage with diverse faith perspectives within the learning community at LAPU; and (4) recognize God's work in the world through all academic disciplines. Essentially, the task force (now a committee) saw its work as creating those resources to enable students to address those four points. Its work continues today.

The rest of the chapter explores how such an institutional commitment to faith, life, and learning in the online environment is woven throughout the entire university. First, the chapter presents an application of incarnational practices that supports the development of holistic student learning resources. The chapter then introduces a few student resources that illustrate the strategy.

INCARNATIONAL PRACTICES

A criticism common to the online modality is that it minimizes (or ignores) humans as physical bodies. The following quote, in response to Ray Kurzweil's notion that humans can be defined as "spiritual machines,"[2] captures the criticism well:

> The cultural irony is that a hard-nosed, "godless and anti-humanist" cutting-edge physical science yields an anthropology that is a near cousin to hyper-spiritual second-century gnostic anthropological dualism. If what makes me a person is that I am a center of consciousness, then my personhood is different in principle from my organic body and can be transferred without loss of personal identity in a kind of resurrection to another, silicon-chip body. Such an anthropology seems to be widely influential in the culture of a large percentage of our students.[3]

While the background of the quote is theological education in the context of mediated technology (to include the online modality), it is an example of a sentiment that is critical to online teaching and learning in general. Critics see online education as somehow deficient because there is no unmediated face-to-face interaction that takes into consideration a physical body.

A principle that best describes the approach the university takes to meet the challenge of faith integration in an online environment (including the providing of resources for students) is the principle of incarnation. Some proponents of online education, in response to the criticism, have suggested

---

2. Kurzweil, *Age of Spiritual Machines.*
3. Kelsey, "Spiritual Machines, Personal Bodies, and God," 8.

"incarnational teaching" as a means to acknowledge students as embodied learners, and to minimize the influence of a modern day hyper-spiritual gnostic dualism. What follows is a brief overview of incarnational teaching drawn from writing by Robert Wingard, Kevin Miller, Darren Iselin and John Meteyard, and John Gresham.[4]

Note the overview here is not meant to be exhaustive in its treatment of incarnational teaching, nor does it respond to criticisms. Rather, it is meant to be an introduction of a strategy that takes into account the modality (online) a university can use to fulfill its mission. Incarnational teaching recognizes that what works in a traditional setting, on a traditional campus, may not work in an online environment. It is offered as a means of performing traditional campus functions otherwise seen to be not "translatable" to an online environment. Second, the concept of incarnational teaching is expanded to go beyond theological education (the specific context of some of the authors listed above) to include all undergraduate programs at an online institution like LAPU. Last, the concept is also broadened to include noninstructional resources and activities. As the chapter later points out, some of the nonacademic faith, life, and learning resources listed below illustrate the concept in their approach.

INCARNATIONAL TEACHING

As a strategy, incarnational teaching includes seven principles that can guide implementation of faith, life, and learning resources in an online environment. While what follows is not meant to be an exhaustive literature review or address criticisms of incarnational teaching, even a cursory introduction to the concept reveals a promising strategy for authentic and holistic teaching and learning in the online modality.

I. *Incarnational teaching promotes learning that is integrative and holistic* (Col 1:18).[5] It avoids a sacred vs. secular, head vs. heart, belief vs. behavior dualism along with the compartmentalization and isolation of fields of study. Using the incarnation of Christ (John 1:14; Phil 2) as a model of integration and holism, Iselin and Meteyard observe, "the motif of incarnation . . . seeks to transcend the commonly experienced problems of current higher education: compartmentalization, competition, isolation,

---

4. See Wingard, "Incarnational Model"; Miller, "Reframing the Faith-Learning Relationship"; Iselin and Meteyard, "'Beyond in the Midst'"; and Gresham, "Divine Pedagogy."

5. Iselin and Meteyard, "'Beyond in the Midst,'" 38.

and individualism."[6] Holism and integration also include the idea of the relational along with the propositional. For example, Miller makes the point that incarnational scholarship defines truth as relational (John 14:6), rather than solely as propositional, and that communication of truth is a process that not only has content, but is dependent on relationship.[7]

II. *Incarnational teaching is one of adaptation.* According to Gresham, "the central element of the divine pedagogy is the idea of adaptation."[8] Gresham points out that in the same way God accommodated himself to the human condition by translating divine truths into human language, educators can adapt traditional educational practices to the online environment. In addition, in the same way that the incarnate Christ adapted himself to his hearers, instructors are to adapt themselves to their students. Gresham notes, "while such adaptation to individual students is difficult in the classroom, the modular nature of digital tools provides resources for modifying content to accommodate diverse learning styles and needs."[9]

III. *Incarnational teaching is not merely physical bodily presence.*[10] Gresham writes that a face-to-face classroom is not inherently more incarnational than online instruction if the instructor has an aloof teaching style. Likewise, an online instructor who does not "personally communicate with students" fails to be incarnational.[11] Adapting a point made by Gresham, incarnational pedagogy does not require the physical bodily presence of an instructor, since the pedagogy of the incarnation points to the realm of the student's life experience. It is in the life of the learner that incarnational learning takes place, not in the physical presence of the instructor. This does not mean that a bodily presence is never required, or "unessential to other areas of a Christian life."[12] Gresham points out that participating in faith rituals like the sacraments requires bodily participation. He concludes his comments on bodily presence by writing, "while physical presence is crucial

---

6. Iselin and Meteyard, "'Beyond in the Midst,'" 39.
7. Miller, "Reframing the Faith-Learning Relationship," 137.
8. Gresham, "Divine Pedagogy," 26.
9. Gresham, "Divine Pedagogy," 26.
10. The idea of "social distancing" that gained popularity during the COVID-19 pandemic may have been a misconstrual of what was actually intended. It seems what was actually intended was observing "physical distance" while managing some sort of continued social closeness or familiarity. See, for example, the use of "physical distancing" language used by Mount Vernon Nazarene University, "COVID-19 Policies."
11. Gresham, "Divine Pedagogy," 26.
12. Gresham, "Divine Pedagogy," 27.

to certain aspects of an incarnational faith, it does not seem to be an essential factor in an incarnational pedagogy."[13]

Two other, more personal observations can be made here. First, John 1:14 is key in the biblical assertion that Christ was God incarnate. As theologians have pointed out, the incarnation of Christ is central to a biblical concept of salvation. The importance of the incarnation of Christ cannot be overstated. However, Christ no longer makes "his dwelling among us." Christ is still God incarnate, and work related to his incarnation continues, but he is absent in the sense of not being bodily present. The now bodily absence of the incarnate Christ bears out the idea that bodily presence is not required for incarnational work to occur. Perhaps simplistically, this sort of argument from analogy can be applied to online education. The bodily presence of either instructor or student may not actually be required for learning to occur.

Second, the concept of bodily presence in a traditional classroom also warrants some scrutiny. Students and instructors who have experienced a traditional classroom can both testify that the bodily presence of either does not guarantee engagement, or any sort of active presence (as pointed out by Gresham earlier). One may also wonder why bodily presence is required, in a traditional classroom on Monday-Wednesday-Friday from eight to nine in the morning, or on Tuesday-Thursday from one to two-thirty in the afternoon, but not any other time. Does not learning go on outside of attending class, without requisite attendance requirements, or the presence of the instructor or other classmates? A natural (but most likely absurd, and never intended) conclusion drawn from the idea of bodily presence is that instructors should continually be with their students, and students with each other. It seems the role of bodily presence in a classroom, traditional or otherwise, requires articulation and greater clarity.

IV. *Incarnational teaching requires embodied content.* When it comes to incarnational teaching, it is not the bodily presence of the instructor that is required, but rather that the instructor comes to embody the course content. This idea is an adaptation from Wingard, who writes about theological education, and who calls for teachers "to embody the tradition, to be what he or she teaches, at least for purposes of the role-playing dynamics of the learning process. It is difficult for a person to respond to an abstract idea or an unembodied concept of a static record of revelation. The most meaningful interaction, and therefore the greatest potential for learning, takes place between person and person."[14]

---

13. Gresham, "Divine Pedagogy," 27.
14. Wingard, "Incarnational Model," 47.

Iselin and Meteyard appeal to John 1:14 as the "heart of the incarnational approach" and the foundation for instructors to be "an authentic embodiment of subject matter."[15] Teaching is ultimately relational, and Jesus becoming flesh is a "cornerstone for the Christian educator who desires to connect self, student, and subject."[16]

In addition, incarnational teaching calls for instructors not only to be relational, but to exemplify humility (Phil 2:5–8). For Iselin and Meteyard, this means to commit to servant leadership and to be willing to "admit honestly the limits and imperfections of his or her own knowledge."[17] Relatedly, for Miller, incarnational scholarship includes meekness (Phil 2) related to education: "it is not the forced imposition of the delivery of knowledge but the skillful drawing out and maturing of knowledge in the student."[18] The principle of humility is recognizable in the clichéd characterization of degree-completion and online faculty that they are a "guide on the side, and not the sage on the stage."

Not only does incarnational teaching require humility on the part of the instructor, for Iselin and Meteyard it also calls for instructors to engage paradox and mystery.[19] Such engagement acknowledges not only gaps in the instructor's knowledge, but gaps in academic scholarship. Engaging in paradox and mystery helps avoid easy, neat, and tidy answers in favor of "re-imagining and re-conceptualizing our 'answers.'"[20]

Humility linked with relationship provides a paradigm by which instructors engage students. The instructor is seen not as an ultimate authority that dispenses propositional knowledge, but rather as a mediator between the subject matter and the student.[21] Such an approach invites "the seeker to embrace a process of discovery mediated through relationship to the source of all truth" and emphasizes learning that "unfolds and develops over time and in relationship to the learner."[22]

V. *Incarnational teaching requires "active participation of the student."*[23] Gresham notes that online learning cultivates an active role for students,

---

15. Iselin and Meteyard, "'Beyond in the Midst,'" 37.
16. Iselin and Meteyard, "'Beyond in the Midst,'" 38.
17. Iselin and Meteyard, "'Beyond in the Midst,'" 41.
18. Miller, "Reframing the Faith-Learning Relationship," 133.
19. Iselin and Meteyard, "'Beyond in the Midst,'" 42.
20. Iselin and Meteyard, "'Beyond in the Midst,'" 43.
21. See Freire, *Pedagogy of the Oppressed,* for a critique of a similar model of pedagogy.
22. Iselin and Meteyard, "'Beyond in the Midst,'" 44.
23. Gresham, "Divine Pedagogy," 27.

one which includes the idea students are responsible for their own learning.[24] Particularly, an active role includes regular and meaningful participation in discussions and forums. Taking an active role, or engaging in active learning, complements the teaching approach that the learner embarks on a process of discovery, rather than being handed propositional knowledge (regardless of discipline). A related idea considered by Wingard is the "personhood of students."[25] He sees personhood (as it relates to discovering the presence of God) related to "the experiences and happenings of their own lives."[26] In addition, "the feelings and thoughts of the students are part of the curriculum."[27] While Wingard writes about theological education, more broadly, active learning acknowledges the experiences the student brings into the learning process, regardless of discipline.

A comment or two can be made about *where* student learning actually takes place. Incarnational teaching recognizes that learning does not solely take place in the classroom, but rather in the lives of the students. Or rather, the life of the student is their classroom—the "sphere outside the classroom"—to borrow a phrase from Gresham.[28] Learning occurs in the workplace, at home, at social gatherings, wherever the student engages in active learning. Incarnational teaching does not emphasize the place of learning so much as it does the person who learns.

VI. *Incarnational teaching emphasizes learning communities and collaborative processes* (Rom 12:4).[29] Iselin and Meteyard's point here is that "knowing and learning within this context are essentially relational and interactive, participatory rather than accumulative, shared rather than merely personalized" to avoid "the prevailing arrogance and presumption that can grip contemporary education, in both Christian and non-Christian contexts."[30] Gresham sees it a bit more practically when he recognizes the "ecclesial or communitarian dimension."[31] He writes, "online education provides many communications tools that can facilitate group discussion and cooperative learning through interpersonal dialogue among students.

---

24. It is not emphasized by Gresham, but the notion of students being responsible can be extended to being willing to be held accountable for activities that require meeting deadlines, taking the initiative, and perseverance.
25. Wingard, "Incarnational Model," 53.
26. Wingard, "Incarnational Model," 55.
27. Wingard, "Incarnational Model," 53.
28. Gresham, "Divine Pedagogy," 27.
29. Iselin and Meteyard, "'Beyond in the Midst,'" 43.
30. Iselin and Meteyard, "'Beyond in the Midst,'" 43.
31. Gresham, "Divine Pedagogy," 27.

Such dialogue can be quite difficult in a traditional face-to face classroom."[32] In either case, incarnational teaching in an online environment invites instructors and students to learn in community, as a community, rather than as separate individuals.

VII. *The goal of incarnational teaching is hope.*[33] Wingard makes the simple point that "the presence of the incarnate God means the presence of love and hope in human life" and that God is hope.[34] Recognizing God as hope does not deny present reality, but believes in a future governed by God. Believing God as hope is believing nothing less than the creator of the universe has, at the very least, nothing less than good intentions for his creation.

Practically speaking, LAPU has identified the goal of cultivating hope in the lives of students through an education, to culminate in the ultimate hope that is in Jesus Christ. For a more comprehensive treatment of how the university regards the goal of hope, see chapter 2.

STUDENT RESOURCES

This section broadens the principle of incarnational teaching beyond the classroom curriculum to include noninstructional resources and activities. Some of the nonacademic faith, life, and learning resources listed below illustrate the concept of an incarnational approach to bringing to an online environment those resources and activities related to faith, life, and learning. It may very well be the case there is no matching department, resource, or activity in a traditional setting, if for no other reason than mission (not modality) dictates what the work of the university looks like, and how it is accomplished. Mission is not dependent on modality, and an incarnational approach helps achieve mission in the context of modality.

To begin this section, when it comes to faith, life, and learning, the university recognizes that it is not a church, nor a replacement for a local church. Indeed, the greatest resource any student has in their faith development is their local church. Participation and involvement in their local church is the simplest and most effective way students have of deepening their faith (here Gresham notes that bodily presence is essential to worship). In that regard, LAPU ultimately provides resources to students in support of the work of local churches.

---

32. Gresham, "Divine Pedagogy," 27.
33. Wingard, "Incarnational Model," 52.
34. Wingard, "Incarnational Model," 50.

The Faith, Life, and Learning Website

After initial vision casting was completed and the direction of the work established, the Faith, Life, and Learning Task Force identified a list of tasks to be completed, the most important of which was the construction of a faith, life, and learning website that addressed the vision of the task force. The initial structure and content of the website took two years to complete, with new resources added six times a year, once every eight-week session during a newly introduced "Faith, Life, and Learning Week." The content focused on the four points in the form of essays, stories, interviews, and videos by university employees and students. The website also includes links to other resources. Current work on the website includes revisiting content for timeliness and relevance. The website is "public-facing," in that any individual who has access to the internet has access to the website. It is designed so visitors gain a clear understanding of the university's worldview, and so students are able to develop their faith in the context of their relationship with the university, by taking in website content and, where possible, putting the content into practice. The website is an example of embodied content in the lives of its contributors, as well as an example of establishing relationships.

In addition, the task force is not the lone driver for, or creator of, resources linked with faith, life, and learning. In part, it acts as a clearinghouse, identifying resources and determining suitability of those resources for use by the university, including whether it has a role in supporting and coordinating those resources. The following are resources created by other individuals or groups at LAPU, with the task force having a minimal role. The resources illustrate the collaborative and inclusive nature of work related to faith, life, and learning, and that the work is larger than any individual or single group.[35]

Faith, Life, and Learning Community Group

The university established a Faith, Life, and Learning Community Group as part of its larger initiative of launching an app to provide virtual access to all of LAPU (for example classes, accounts, announcements, forms, transcripts, and events) through mobile devices regardless of location. Developed with students in mind, the myLAPU app is a platform to provide them with access to crucial resources they need through their academic journey. Relatedly, the app also creates a sense of belonging and community

---

35. Note the application of the incarnational concept of "collaborative processes" articulated by Iselin and Meteyard earlier.

the students might otherwise not have. Benefits of the app also include the students being able to connect with each other socially, outside the context of an academic setting like a classroom. Overall, there is at least one claim retention is improved when online students use an app, as compared to when they do not.[36]

Along with the app, several Community Groups were formed, to be accessible from within the app. They are: LAPU Mom's Group; LAPU Strengths Community; Psychology Learning Community; Nursing and Health Sciences Community Group; Liberal Studies and General Studies Community Group; Criminal Justice and Public Administration Community Group; Business and Leadership Community Group; and Faith, Life and Learning Community Group.

The main goal of all of the community groups is to give students the opportunity to build social, personal connections with other students, take in content, and share thoughts and ideas. The groups provide both a platform and opportunity for students to sound off and to engage with each other. All of the groups are facilitated by a moderator (which is university staff), and the tone is meant to be informal and casual.

The Faith, Life, and Learning Community Group, then, is a platform in the university app that provides students an opportunity to engage with each other in an informal, social way (that is to say, nonacademic) as they respond to app and website content. While topics are mainly related to faith, life, and learning, students are also able to interact with each other on other subjects, ideas, or themes.

Chaplain

The idea of a university chaplain was a response by the university president to an expressed interest by university employees in having one. Originally conceived of as a staff chaplain, the role was expanded to include students. Staff responsibilities of the chaplain include participating in one-on-one conversations to informal counseling and prayer requests (for example, illness, encouragement, family situations). The chaplain is also responsible for occasionally presenting at weekly staff devotionals. Student responsibilities of the chaplain include providing content for virtual student chapels in the form of a fifteen-minute video, posting a weekly verse in the app, and

---

36. See READY Education, "Student Retention Research Report." Also, note the application of the incarnational concept of "learning communities" articulated by Iselin and Meteyard earlier.

participating in one-on-one conversations with students to include informal counseling and prayer requests.[37]

The role of the chaplain is to be a facilitator, helping faculty, staff, and students to integrate their own faith into their studies and everyday lives. This inevitably raises questions about how the Christian faith works in an increasingly post-Christian culture, and the chaplain serves as a guide to offer answers to "Bible problems" that satisfy a student, academically oriented mind. The chaplain helps to equip graduates with a Christian worldview that can respond to challenges which inevitably come their way, in whatever field they find themselves. The chaplain also manages a web page, "Chaplain's Corner," devoted to three main themes: addressing student questions related to the interpretation and application of various biblical passages; posting prayer requests related to the global church; and providing resources to the students, including books and other websites.

Career and Vocation Center

As mentioned in chapter 9 (regarding the connection of faith to academic disciplines), LAPU's Career and Vocation Center serves as a faith, life, and learning resource for students as it links the notion of holistic faith with career and vocation through the idea of calling and a theology of work.[38] Ideally, professional career and employment should be integrated with a student's sense of calling and vocation, resulting in holistic development and growth of the individual.

Additional Activities

Diversity, Equity, and Inclusion (DEI) activities implemented by the university are the result of what the university president sees as a biblical mandate associated with the *imago dei* (image of God). Faith, life, and learning among students is strengthened as they participate in, and experience the results of, such activities. Student-focused activities include the development of a Community Group for first-generation students. Other university activities include incorporating a DEI speaker during university devotions; reading and discussing relevant DEI texts in university devotions; and developing an expanded university-wide program for inclusion and belonging

37. Note the application of the incarnational concept of "embodied content" articulated by Wingard, and Iselin and Meteyard, earlier.

38. For example, see the Theology of Work Project for resources for pastors, scholars, and workers. See also Los Angeles Pacific University. "Career and Vocation Center."

of both training and other engagement/development opportunities for all employees at every level of the university.[39]

Two other activities students can participate in are asking for prayer and participating in commencement. Students are not required to, but can participate in prayer, ask for prayer, and submit prayer requests through a number of different individuals and the university website. Students express how appreciative they are to be able to have opportunities to engage in prayer, and see it as part of the ethos and culture of the university. Students are also encouraged to participate in commencement, either online or in person, to mark the ending of their lives as undergraduates and the beginning of their lives as graduates. Such a demarcation indicates a level of academic achievement and maturity that has significance across many facets of their lives, including family, professional, and spiritual. Commencement is a symbol that students are equipped to pursue lifelong learning and engagement in faith, life, and learning. Participating in commencement reinforces the significance of that ability.

Aspirational Ideas

What follows is a list of aspirational ideas relating to the development of faith, life, and learning the university is considering. In recognition of the principle of continuous improvement, these ideas reflect a "work-in-progress" mentality, and depend on other university goals and strategic projects. It should be noted that what makes sense for LAPU to implement is related to context and feasibility, and may or may not be applicable to other universities.

Perhaps the simplest idea to implement would be to ensure comprehensive resources related to faith, life, and learning are available to students. Such resources would be made available on the university website and could include a list of churches for students to consider for a home church; links to various Bible study resources; and a virtual library which includes a recommended reading list by various faculty.[40]

While LAPU is primarily asynchronous in its work with students, it is possible the university could also host synchronous webinars on matters related to faith, life, and learning. Such webinars could be recorded and archived as additional resources. Lastly, the university may be able to create

---

39. Note the application of the concept of "promoting learning that is integrative and holistic" articulated by Iselin and Meteyard earlier.

40. This would require "active participation of the student" articulated by Iselin and Meteyard, Gresham, and Wingard earlier.

opportunities for staff and students to become involved in their communities through partnering with local churches in service projects. A "boots-on-the-ground" experience would model for students an incarnational approach to humanitarian work similar to how Christ "dwelt among us" (John 1:14).

Conclusion

By creating and facilitating a culture of collaboration around the goals of faith, life, and learning, the university provides strategic guidance and relevant faith formation resources for its students and staff. The Faith, Life, and Learning Task Force fostered a sense of vision and direction for holistic faith formation; participated in creating resources for students; and acted as a coordinator and clearing house for other activities and resources associated with faith, life, and learning. Recognizing that the task force accomplished its primary purpose but that faith, life, and learning are core to the mission of the university, university leadership has transitioned this function from a temporary task force to a permanent committee. This body is charged with the ongoing work of ensuring that university-wide resources and activities are designed to cultivate a student's spiritual development in a manner that reflects the university's regard for the whole person and the importance of integrating faith through the entire life of the student. The work of faith, life, and learning is dynamic, continuous, and must remain responsive to the goals of the university and the needs of the community.

Chapter 12

A Call to Cultivate Mission across Modalities

WAYNE R. HERMAN

WAYNE HERMAN, *Chief Academic Officer at Los Angeles Pacific University, challenges readers to think creatively about next steps in integrating faith, life, and learning into their own courses, departments, and institutions in this concluding chapter. The chapter reminds readers that institutional mission must translate across all learning modalities, and that different modalities will call for different experiences and resources. Finally, the chapter offers a call for collaboration—both within colleges and universities and across higher education institutions—as we explore together the unique challenges and opportunities of fostering faith formation in any and all learning environments.*

The previous chapters of this book have explored the journey of Los Angeles Pacific University (LAPU), a Christian online university serving primarily post-traditional students in California, as it has navigated the challenges of living out its commitment to faith, life, and learning. Along the way we have reflected on what spiritual formation looks like in the online space; discussed the merits of a holistic approach to faith, life, and learning; described a collaborative approach to faith formation; examined the role of assessment in assuring that faith, life, and learning outcomes are achieved; and considered how institutional identity impacts specific commitments, practices, and resources that are conducive to faith formation. We have also explored ways in which four specific themes—a Christian worldview, connecting one's story to God's story, engaging with diverse faith perspectives, and recognizing Christian faith through all academic disciplines—allow students access to the journey of faith, life, and learning from multiple starting points and perspectives. Finally, we have underscored that the journey is not only for students and instructors, but success coaches also serve as key guides along the journey and the institution as a whole creates a supportive community that helps keep students moving toward a hope-filled future.

The focus thus far has largely been on one online Christian higher education institution (HEI), LAPU. However, although LAPU is one of very few Christian HEIs that are 100 percent online, the data show that in recent years there has been a marked increase in students studying online at Christian HEIs. This is supported by data reported in the Integrated Postsecondary Education Data System (IPEDS) for fall enrollment among HEIs that affiliate themselves with the Christian tradition.[1] An analysis of fall enrollment data from 2019 compared to the same data from 2014 shows that among the 878 Christian HEIs, overall enrollment had declined by 0.6 percent (10,856 students) to 1.88 million students. This downward enrollment reflects a 3.4 percent decline of undergraduate enrollment offset by a 7.8 percent increase in graduate enrollment. During this same period, however, those students enrolled in some or only distance education courses increased by 38.4 percent, from 22.5 percent of total enrollments to 31.2 percent of total enrollments. This increase was largely due to a 33.8 percent increase in undergraduate students enrolled in some distance education courses. Of the 878 institutions, 704 (80 percent) of them enrolled students in distance education courses in fall 2019. Fall enrollment data for 2020, which was significantly impacted by the coronavirus pandemic, showed 65.1 percent of all students at Christian HEIs enrolled in at least some distant education courses. While the 2021 fall enrollment data will likely show

---

1. This data is based on those institutions that report to IPEDS (The Integrated Postsecondary Education Data System within the US Department of Education) a religious affiliation that is clearly within the Christian tradition (as opposed to Jewish or Muslim, for example). One particularly large online and campus-based institution, Grand Canyon University, which identifies itself as a Christian university on its website, reports "Not applicable" to IPEDS under religious affiliation and, therefore, is excluded from this analysis. See US Department of Education, "Fall Enrollment Surveys."

a decline in distant education enrollment, these data establish an increasing need for Christian HEIs to consider what an education informed by a Christian faith commitment means in the online modality. The authors and editors of this book hope that the chapters herein will help stimulate conversations among the faculty, administrators, and support staff of Christian HEIs as they develop online educational programs and courses.

Of course, the vast majority of students (75 percent of undergraduate students and 53 percent of graduate students) at Christian HEIs as of fall 2019 were not enrolled in any distance education courses. The question of how a Christian HEI reflects its Christian identity and mission in the face-to-face modality is just as pertinent as how it does this in the online modality. The primary difference is that most Christian HEIs have developed their thinking, approaches, and strategies related to faith development in the traditional campus environment for decades, if not centuries. While such approaches have no doubt evolved over time, there are fundamental differences in the way an HEI interacts with students in the traditional campus environment and in the distance education environment.

As has been suggested earlier in this book, one of the key differences is that the students themselves are different. Strategies for faith formation that work with eighteen- to twenty-four-year-old campus-based students are not likely to work with older post-traditional students who are working, are financially independent, and have dependents. Gathering daily or weekly for a midmorning chapel session is simply not an option for the latter type of student. While this example of a cocurricular faith formation strategy perhaps seems patently obvious, what may not be as clear is that curricular faith formation strategies also need to vary based on the modality and needs of the students. Even something as simple as beginning class with a prayer may not have the same meaning for students in an asynchronous learning environment.

Inasmuch as the desire to promote faith formation among students has been identified as a common institutional *learning* outcome among Christian HEIs, every attempt by a Christian HEI to achieve this outcome must be approached not merely as a programming issue but as a curricular issue. That is, the development of faith formation activities is not an end in itself. Rather, faith formation activities—whether on campus or online—provide a learning opportunity for students and, applying a learner-centered design approach, institutions must consider who their learners are, their location in a spiritual development process, what their needs are, and what methods will be most effective in helping them advance on their faith journey. Various studies examining religious identification among American adults help inform the current religious composition of segments of the US population.[2] While such studies provide helpful insights at the macro level, there is no substitute for engaging in meaningful relationships with students and getting to know their stories. Such stories need to inform the curriculum design process as institutions identify effective ways to connect with students and help them connect with God in their lives and studies.

Mary Lowe has highlighted the important finding from her own research and that of others that learning about matters of faith typically takes place in the context of significant relationships.[3] Christian HEIs must consider how they leverage their greatest asset—Christian staff and faculty—to engage in meaningful relationships with students and help them achieve faith-related learning outcomes. As noted above, at LAPU instructors and success coaches play primary roles in this endeavor, but all LAPU staff share the commitment and the responsibility to help students "relate a Christian worldview to academic disciplines, life, and work; articulating ways life journeys connect to God's story in the Bible." As I reflect on my own academic career—including several public undergraduate institutions and two seminaries for master's and doctoral degrees—my own spiritual formation was most positively impacted by the significant relationships I built with faculty and others. Their guidance regarding vocation and support during times of personal crisis helped me grow in my relationship with God and understanding of his purpose for my life.

While faculty and support staff have opportunities to facilitate the faith formation of students, it must also be recognized that the modality of teaching significantly influences the roles that instructors play. This point was highlighted in a research report by Ní Shé and colleagues. The authors conducted an impressive survey of the literature about online teaching and provided a critical analysis of the many roles of an online educator: managerial, pedagogical, social, technical, assessor, facilitator, content expert, instructional designer, researcher, and evaluator.[4] Most, if not all, of these roles are also exercised by face-to-face instructors but the time spent on each role often differs in the two modalities.[5] Christian universities typically add the role of spiritual guide to the list of instructor expectations and the

---

2. See, for example, Kosmin and Navarro-Rivera, "Transformation of Generation X."
3. Lowe, "Assessing the Impact of Online Courses."
4. Ní Shé et al., eds., "Teaching Online is Different," 32.
5. For example, a face-to-face instructor who delivers classroom lectures spends considerable time in the content expert role whereas an online instructor is likely to spend much more time facilitating discussions. Ní Shé and colleagues note that the last three roles—instructional designer, researcher, and evaluator—may be provided by other personnel in the online institution.

asynchronous online modality often encourages students to discuss personal and spiritual matters that they would be unwilling to discuss in the context of a face-to-face classroom. Instructors at LAPU have reported they have enjoyed more opportunities to discuss spiritual matters with students in the online setting than they had previously experienced when teaching face-to-face courses.[6]

The above analysis of enrollment data, based on the most recently available IPEDS data, shows some of the impacts of the coronavirus pandemic in fall 2020 and the resulting switch to a remote teaching model for many traditional campus-based HEIs. As has been argued in this book, based on statements by the Department of Education and various accrediting agencies, this switch to teaching via videoconferencing is not a change of modality, but a temporary allowance so that traditional HEIs could continue to educate students in the midst of the pandemic. When one considers the speed with which most institutions had to begin teaching remotely there was little time to consider how best to address faith, life, and learning in this teaching change necessitated by the pandemic. It will be interesting to see once the effects of the pandemic lessen whether the increase in movement to online educational programs accelerates or continues at the same pace.

The purpose of this book has not been to suggest that LAPU has worked out all the answers for promoting faith, life, and learning in the online education environment. Rather, it has been to share our journey of exploring the meaning of faith, life, and learning in this modality. We recognize that others have similarly wrestled with such issues and have developed alternative solutions. We are eager to learn from the collective wisdom of colleagues who are on the same journey. We also see the need for further research regarding faith, life, and learning initiatives. Several possibilities have emerged from the discussion thus far:

1. What faith, life, and learning initiatives have value across different learning modalities?
2. Which faith, life, and learning initiatives are more effective with either an online or face-to-face modality?
3. What curricular strategies are most effective with the different modalities?
4. What practices are effective in helping faculty promote faith, life, and learning among their students?

---

6. Also, the Inside Higher Ed Student Voice survey found that fully online college students are twice as likely to say that they are "comfortable sharing their opinions in class" compared to fully in-person students. See Busteed, "This May Be the Biggest Lesson Learned."

5. How do instructors' roles in regard to promoting faith, life, and learning differ across the different modalities?
6. To what extent are faculty able to negotiate the differing requirements of the two modalities?
7. How can support staff (e.g., success coaches) best collaborate with instructors in promoting faith formation among students?

Such research initiatives provide opportunities for collaboration across different departments within institutions as well as across various HEIs. The common commitment to fostering a Christian worldview and offering Christ-centered educational programs should enable Christian HEIs to work together for the common good of their students and society at large. However, the major disruption in higher education caused by the coronavirus pandemic means such collaborative research is likely not high on the agenda of many Christian HEIs, particularly those that are struggling to survive. But given the recent trend among such institutions toward increasing online enrollments, it is certainly in the best interests of Christian HEIs to engage in such collaborative research efforts.

Given LAPU's demonstrated interest in such research, evidenced by the publication of this book, the Academic Affairs department at LAPU would like to explore the level of interest among like-minded institutions regarding the formation of a Center for Faith, Life, and Learning to further the conversation with researchers at Christian HEIs regarding faith, life, and learning research initiatives. Those interested are invited to share their research ideas and projects by emailing academicaffairs@lapu.edu and LAPU is happy to facilitate networking opportunities among faculty interested in similar research topics. LAPU also envisions the development of a platform for sharing resources for the common good in light of our common desire to promote spiritual formation among students. It is the firm belief of the authors of this book that Christian HEIs partnering with one another is vital to the achievement of our common goals and the spiritual formation of our students. We welcome your collaboration.

Bibliography

Anderson, James N. *What's Your Worldview? An Interactive Approach to Life's Big Questions*. Wheaton, IL: Crossway, 2014.

Anderson, Tawa J., et al. *An Introduction to Christian Worldview: Pursuing God's Perspective in a Pluralistic World*. Downers Grove, IL: IVP Academic, 2017.

Andraos, Michel Elias. "Engaging Diversity in Teaching Religion and Theology: An Intercultural, De-colonial Epistemic Perspective." *Teaching Theology and Religion* 15 (2012) 3–15.

Association of American Colleges and Universities. "Creating and Assessing Campus Climates." https://www.aacu.org/publications-research/periodicals/creating-and-assessing-campus-climates-support-personal-and-social.

———. "Making Excellence Inclusive." https://www.aacu.org/making-excellence-inclusive.

Astin, Alexander W., et al. *Cultivating the Spirit: How College Can Enhance Students' Inner Lives*. San Francisco: Jossey-Bass, 2011.

Azaransky, Sarah. "Religious Pluralism and American Democracy: How the World Religions Classroom Can Become a Site of Struggle." *Journal of Feminist Studies in Religion* 28 (2012) 157–64.

Azusa Pacific University. "Azusa Pacific University System." https://www.apu.edu/about/university-system/.

———. "A Faith and Learning Community." https://www.apu.edu/about/faithandlearning/.

Bailey, Kendra L., et al. "Spirituality at a Crossroads: A Grounded Theory of Christian Emerging Adults." *Psychology of Religion and Spirituality* 8 (2016) 99–109.

Baldwin, Timothy A. "Culturally Responsive Pedagogy: A Transformative Tool for CCCU Educators in Multicultural Classrooms." *Christian Education Journal* 12 (2015) 97–117.

Balzer, Cary, and Rod Reed, eds. *Building a Culture of Faith: University-Wide Partnerships for Spiritual Formation*. Abilene, TX: Abilene Christian University Press, 2012.

Bartholomew, Craig G., and Michael W. Goheen. *The Drama of Scripture: Finding Our Place in the Biblical Story*. Grand Rapids: Baker Academic, 2014.

Bergquist, William H., et al. *Engaging the Six Cultures of the Academy: Revised and Expanded Edition of The Four Cultures of the Academy.* San Francisco: Jossey-Bass, 2008.

Biola University. "Mission, Vision and Values." https://www.biola.edu/about/mission.

Bloom, Jennifer, et al. "Appreciative Education." In *Positive Psychology and Appreciative Inquiry in Higher Education,* edited by Peter C. Mather and Eileen Hulme, 5–18. San Francisco: Jossey-Bass, 2013.

Bok, Derek. "The Trouble with Shared Governance." *AGB Trusteeship* 21 (2013) 19–24.

Bolles, Richard N. *What Color Is Your Parachute? 2020: A Practical Guide for Job-Hunters and Career-Changers.* New York: Ten Speed, 2019.

Bonhoeffer, Dietrich. *Creation and Fall: A Theological Exposition of Genesis 1–3.* Minneapolis: Fortress, 1997.

Bowman, Nicholas A., and Jenny L. Small. "Exploring a Hidden Form of Minority Status: College Students' Religious Affiliation and Well-Being." *Journal of College Student Development* 53 (2012) 491–509.

Bowman, Nicholas A., and Cynthia Toms Smedley. "The Forgotten Minority: Examining Religious Affiliation and University Satisfaction." *Higher Education* 65 (2013) 745–60.

Bowman, Nicholas A., et al. "Religious/Worldview Identification and College Student Success." *Religion and Education* 41 (2014) 117–133.

Boyer, Ernest L. "From *Scholarship Reconsidered* to *Scholarship Assessed.*" *Quest* 48 (1996) 129–39.

———. *Scholarship Reconsidered: Priorities of the Professoriate.* San Francisco, Jossey-Bass, 1990.

Bryant, Alyssa N., and Christy M. Craft. "The Challenge and Promise of Pluralism: Dimensions of Spiritual Climate and Diversity at a Lutheran College." *Christian Higher Education* 9 (2010) 396–422.

Bryant, Alyssa N., et al. "Developing an Assessment of College Students' Spiritual Experiences: The Collegiate Religious and Spiritual Climate Survey." *Journal of College and Character* 10 (2009) 1–10.

Busteed, Brandon. "This May Be the Biggest Lesson Learned from Online Education During the Pandemic." *Forbes,* March 3, 2021. https://www.forbes.com/sites/brandonbusteed/2021/03/03/this-may-be-the-biggest-lesson-learned-from-online-education-during-the-pandemic/?sh=c6291175086e.

Cahalan, Kathleen A. *The Stories We Live: Finding God's Calling All Around Us.* Grand Rapids: Eerdmans, 2017.

Calhoun, Adele E. *Spiritual Disciplines Handbook: Practices That Transform Us.* Downers Grove, IL: InterVarsity, 2015.

California Baptist University. "Mission." https://calbaptist.edu/about/mission.

Campbell, Heidi. *Exploring Religious Community Online: We Are One in the Network.* New York: Lang, 2005.

Campbell, William, and Megan Lane. "Better Together: Considering Student Interfaith Leadership and Social Change." *Journal of College and Character* 15 (2014) 195–202.

Cannell, Linda. *Theological Education Matters: Leadership Education for the Church.* Newburgh, IN: EDCOT, 2006.

Cartwright, John, et al. *Teaching the World: Foundations for Online Theological Education.* Nashville: B&H Academic, 2017.

Chandler, Diane, J. "Whole-Person Formation: An Integrative Approach to Christian Education." *Christian Education Journal* 12 (2015) 314–32.
Chen, Clement, et al. "How Online Learning Compares to the Traditional Classroom: Measuring Accounting Course Outcomes." *CPA Journal* 87 (2017) 44–47.
Choy, Susan. *Nontraditional Undergraduates: Findings from the Condition of Education 2002*. Washington, DC: US Department of Education, 2002.
Cook, Lynn, and Marilyn Friend. "Educational Leadership for Teacher Collaboration." In *Program Leadership for Serving Students with Disabilities*, edited by Bonnie Billingsley et al., 421–44. Washington, DC: Department of Education, 1993. https://eric.ed.gov/?id=ED372532.
Council for Christian Colleges & Universities. "2021 CCCU Campus Diversity Stats." https://diversity.cccu.org/wp-content/uploads/2021/01/2021-CCCU-Diversity-Stats.pdf.
Crenshaw, Kimberlé. "Demarginalizing the Intersection of Race and Sex: A Black Feminist Critique of Antidiscrimination Doctrine, Feminist Theory and Antiracist Politics." University of Chicago Legal Forum, 1989. https://chicagounbound.uchicago.edu/uclf/vol1989/iss1/8/.
Cunningham, Aliel. "Envisioning Christian Presence and Practice in Online Teaching Contexts." *International Journal of Christianity and English Language Teaching* 6 (2019) 3–19.
Dey, Eric L., et al. *Engaging Diverse Viewpoints: What is the Campus Climate for Perspective-Taking?* Washington, DC: Association of American Colleges and Universities, 2010.
Dik, Brian, and Ryan Duffy. *Make Your Job a Calling: How the Psychology of Vocation Can Change Your Life at Work*. West Conshohocken, PA: Templeton, 2012.
Dockery, David S., ed. *Faith and Learning: A Handbook for Christian Higher Education*. Nashville: B&H Academic, 2012.
Dockery, David S. *Renewing Minds: Serving Church and Society through Christian Higher Education*. Nashville: B&H, 2008.
Dockery, David S., and Christopher Morgan, eds. *Christian Higher Education: Faith, Teaching, and Learning in the Evangelical Tradition*. Wheaton, IL: Crossway, 2018.
Downey, Deane E. D., and Stanley E. Porter. *Christian Worldview and the Academic Disciplines: Crossing the Academy*. Eugene, OR: Pickwick, 2009.
Duckworth, Angela. *Grit: The Power of Passion and Perseverance*. New York: Scribner, 2016.
Dweck, Carol S. *Mindset: The New Psychology of Success*. New York: Random House, 2006.
Eck, Diana L. *Encountering God: A Spiritual Journey from Bozeman to Banaras*. Boston: Beacon, 1993.
———. "Religious Pluralism." https://www.youtube.com/watch?v=9FseEtkQTPQ.
Edgar, Scott D. "Facilitating Spiritual Formation in Online Education: Practical Lessons and Learning Theories." Paper presented at the Annual Conference of the Society of Professors of Christian Education, Dallas, October 18–20, 2012.
———. "Online Discipleship: Learning Theories and Instructional Practices." Paper presented at the Annual Conference of the Society of Professors of Christian Education, Chicago, October 17–19, 2013.

———. Review of *Building a Culture of Faith: University-Wide Partnerships for Spiritual Formation* by Cary Balzer and Rod Reed. *Teaching Theology and Religion* 16 (2013) 302–3.

———. "Toward an Ecosystem of Spiritual Formation: Elements for Growth in Online Education." Paper presented at the Annual Conference of the Society of Professors of Christian Education, October 23, 2020.

Edwards, Richard, and Robin Usher. "Lifelong Learning: A Postmodern Condition of Education." *Adult Education Quarterly* 51 (2001) 273–87.

Eisenberg, Daniel, et al. "Promoting Resilience, Retention, and Mental Health." *New Directions for Student Services* 156 (2016) 87–95.

Ferguson, Kristen A. *Excellence in Online Education: Creating a Community on Mission*. Nashville: B&H, 2020.

Fosnacht, Kevin, and Cindy Broderick. "An Overlooked Factor? How Religion and Spirituality Influence Students' Perception of the Campus Environment." *Journal of College and Character* 21 (2020) 186–203.

Free Methodist Church of America. "We Believe." https://fmcusa.org/webelieve.

Freire, Paulo. *Pedagogy of the Oppressed: 30th Anniversary Edition*. New York: Bloomsbury, 2014.

Garverick, Paul. "Remaining Christ-Centered and Mission-Focused." Seminar presented to faculty at Indiana Wesleyan University, May 19, 2020.

Gearhart, Christopher C., and Graham D. Bodie. "Active-Empathic Listening as a General Social Skill: Evidence from Bivariate and Canonical Correlations." *Communication Reports* 24 (2011) 86–98.

Ginder, Scott, and Christina Stearns. "Web Tables: Enrollment in Distance Education Courses, by State: Fall 2012." National Center for Education Statistics. https://nces.ed.gov/pubs2014/2014023.pdf.

Global Learning Partners. https://www.globallearningpartners.com/.

Goetzman, Darlene M. *Dialogue Education Step by Step: A Guide for Designing Exceptional Learning Events*. Global Learning Partners, 2012.

Goheen, Michael W., and Craig G. Bartholomew. *Living at the Crossroads: An Introduction to Christian Worldview*. Grand Rapids: Baker Academic, 2008.

González, Justo L. *The Story Luke Tells: Luke's Unique Witness to the Gospel*. Grand Rapids: Eerdmans, 2015.

Gresham, John. "The Divine Pedagogy as a Model for Online Education." *Teaching Theology and Religion* 9 (2006) 24–28.

Guinness, Os. *The Call: Finding and Fulfilling the Central Purposes of Your Life*. Nashville: Word, 1998.

Hannaford, Ronald Geoffrey. "A Model of Online Education Effecting Holistic Student Formation Appropriate for Global Cross-Cultural Contexts." PhD diss., Fuller Theological Seminary, 2012.

Hanshaw, George, and Janet Hanson. "Using Microlearning and Social Learning to Improve Teachers' Instructional Design Skills: A Mixed Methods Study of Technology Integration in Teacher Professional Development." *International Journal of Learning and Development* 9 (2019) 145–73.

Harris, Robert A. *The Integration of Faith and Learning: A Worldview Approach*. Eugene, OR: Cascade, 2004.

Himes, Brant. "Connecting Our Story to God's Story." Los Angeles Pacific University. https://www.lapu.edu/sub-resource/our-story-gods-story/.

Hobbs, Tawnell D., and Lee Hawkins. "The Results Are In for Remote Learning: It Didn't Work." *The Wall Street Journal*, June 5, 2020, https://www.wsj.com/articles/schools-coronavirus-remote-learning-lockdown-tech-11591375078.

Holmes, Courtney M., and Christine Reid. "A Comparison Study of On-campus and Online Learning Outcomes for a Research Methods Course." *The Journal of Counselor Preparation and Supervision* 9 (2017) 1–24.

Horst, Becky. "Job, Career, Vocation: The Difference is in the Calling." *Bulletin Alumni Magazine* (2002). https://www.goshen.edu/news/bulletin/02march/job_career.php.

Inoue, Yukiko, ed. *Online Education for Lifelong Learning*. Hershey, PA: Information Science, 2007.

Interfaith Youth Core. "Building Interfaith America." https://ifyc.org/.

Iselin, Darren, and John D. Meteyard. "The 'Beyond in the Midst': An Incarnational Response to the Dynamic Dance of Christian Worldview, Faith and Learning." *Journal of Education and Christian Belief* 14 (2010) 33–46.

Jahnke, Isa, et al. "Unpacking the Inherent Design Principles of Mobile Microlearning." *Technology, Knowledge and Learning* 25 (2020) 585–619.

Jarvis, Peter. *Adult Education and Lifelong Learning: Theory and Practice*. 3rd ed. New York: RoutledgeFalmer, 2004.

Jones, Sandra, et al. "Distributed Leadership: A Collaborative Framework for Academics, Executives and Professionals in Higher Education." *Journal of Higher Education Policy and Management* 34 (2012) 67–78.

Jung, Joanne J. *Character Formation in Online Education: A Guide for Instructors, Administrators, and Accrediting Agencies*. Grand Rapids: Zondervan, 2015.

Kaemingk, Matthew, and Cory B. Willson. *Work and Worship: Reconnecting Our Labor and Liturgy*. Grand Rapids: Baker Academic, 2020.

Kelsey, David H. "Spiritual Machines, Personal Bodies, and God: Theological Education and Theological Anthropology." *Teaching Theology and Religion* 5 (2002) 2–9.

Khan, Mohammad Ayub, and Laurie Smith Law. "An Integrative Approach to Curriculum Development in Higher Education in the USA: A Theoretical Framework." *International Education Studies* 8 (2015) 66–76.

Kimball, Ezekiel, and Susan M. Campbell. "Advising Strategies to Support Student Learning Success: Linking Theory and Philosophy with Intentional Practice." In *Academic Advising Approaches: Strategies That Teach Students to Make the Most of College*, edited by Jayne K. Drake et al., 3–16. San Francisco: Jossey-Bass, 2013.

Kirkpatrick, Donald L., and James D. Kirkpatrick. *Evaluating Training Programs: The Four Levels*. 3rd ed. San Francisco: Berrett-Koehler, 2006.

Klein-Collins, Rebecca. "Strategies for Becoming Adult-Learning-Focused Institutions." *Peer Review* 13 (2011) 4–7.

Knowles, Malcolm. *The Adult Learner: A Neglected Species*. 3rd ed. Houston: Gulf, 1984.

———. *The Modern Practice of Adult Education: From Pedagogy to Andragogy*. Englewood Cliffs, NJ: Cambridge, 1980.

Kosmin, Barry A., and Juhem Navarro-Rivera. "The Transformation of Generation X: Shifts in Religious and Political Self-Identification, 1990–2008." Trinity College, 2012.

Krathwohl, David R. "A Revision of Bloom's Taxonomy: An Overview." *Theory into Practice* 41 (2002) 212–18.

Krathwohl, David R., et al. *Taxonomy of Educational Objectives, Handbook II: Affective Domain*. New York: David McKay, 1965.

Kurzweil, Ray. *The Age of Spiritual Machines: When Computers Exceed Human Intelligence*. New York: Viking, 2000.

Lederman, Doug. "Virtual Learning Will Be Better This Fall. Right?" *Inside Higher Ed*, July 29, 2020. https://www.insidehighered.com/digital-learning/article/2020/07/29/will-virtual-learning-be-better-fall-will-it-be-better-enough.

Lemke, Dale L. "Vocation and Lifelong Spiritual Formation: A Christian Integrative Perspective on Calling in Mid-Career." *Christian Education Journal* 17 (2020) 301–24.

Li, Ning, and William H. Murphy. "Religious Affiliation, Religiosity, and Academic Performance of University Students: Campus Life Implications for U.S. Universities." *Religion & Education* 45 (2018) 1–22.

Liberty University. "LU Shepherd." https://www.liberty.edu/osd/lu-shepherd/.

———. "Yammer." https://www.liberty.edu/online/yammer/.

Longman, Tremper, III. *Genesis: The Story of God Bible Commentary*. Grand Rapids: Zondervan Academic, 2016.

Lopez, Tara. "Coaching 101: New Success Coach Training." Department of Student Success, Los Angeles Pacific University, 2018.

———. "Guiding Spiritual Formation as a Success Coach." Department of Student Success, Los Angeles Pacific University, 2015.

Lopez, Tara, et al. "Active Listening in Spiritual Formation." Department of Student Success, Los Angeles Pacific University, 2019.

Los Angeles Pacific University. "About Us." https://www.lapu.edu/about/.

———. "Accessibility." https://www.lapu.edu/resource/accessibility/.

———. "Career and Vocation Center." https://career.lapu.edu/.

———. "Commitment to Faith, Life, and Learning." https://catalog.lapu.edu/undergrad/info/learning-outcomes/.

———. "Faith, Life, and Learning." https://www.lapu.edu/resource/faith-life-learning/.

———. "Fast Facts." https://www.lapu.edu/resource/institutional-research/.

———. "Institutional Learning Outcomes." https://catalog.lapu.edu/undergrad/info/learning-outcomes/.

———. "Los Angeles Pacific University Wins 2020 Omni Awards for Instructional Media Design." https://www.lapu.edu/2020-06-22/.

———. "Our History." https://www.lapu.edu/about/our-history/.

———. "Student Success." https://www.lapu.edu/about/success-coaches/.

———. "Student Support Services." https://catalog.lapu.edu/undergrad/services/.

———. "The University's Christian Worldview." https://catalog.lapu.edu/undergrad/info/christian-worldview/.

———. "What We Believe." https://www.lapu.edu/about/what-we-believe/.

———. "What We Believe: Faith and Learning." https://www.lapu.edu/about/what-we-believe/faith-and-learning/.

Lowe, Mary. "A Summary of the Findings of the Study: Assessing the Impact of Online Courses on the Spiritual Formation of Adult Students." *Christian Perspectives in Education* 4 (2010) 1–18.

———. "Spiritual Formation as Whole-Person Development in Online Education." In *Best Practices of Online Education: A Guide for Christian Higher Education*, edited by Mark A. Maddix et al., 58–64. Charlotte, NC: Information Age, 2012.

Lowe, Stephen D., and Mary E. Lowe. "Absent in Body: Is Spiritual Formation Possible in Online Christian Education?" *Christianity Today* 54 (May 2010) 14–15.

———. *Ecologies of Faith in a Digital Age: Spiritual Growth through Online Education.* Downers Grove, IL: IVP Academic, 2018.

Lundin, Roger, ed. *Christ across the Disciplines: Past, Present, Future.* Grand Rapids: Eerdmans, 2013.

Maddix, Mark A. "Developing Online Learning Communities." *Christian Education Journal* 10 (2013) 139–48.

Maddix, Mark A., et al. *Best Practices of Online Education: A Guide for Christian Higher Education.* Charlotte, NC: Information Age, 2012.

Maddix, Mark A., and James R. Estep. "Spiritual Formation in Online Higher Education Communities: Nurturing Spirituality in Christian Higher Education Degree Programs." *Christian Education Journal* 7 (2010) 423–34.

Maxwell, Kelly E., and Monita C. Thompson. "Breaking Ground Through Intergroup Education: The Program on Intergroup Relations, 1988–2016." University of Michigan Intergroup Dialogue. https://igr.umich.edu/working-paper-series.

Mayhew, Matthew J., et al. "Silencing Whom? Linking Campus Climates for Religious, Spiritual, and Worldview Diversity to Student Worldviews." *The Journal of Higher Education* 85 (2014) 219–45.

Mayhew, Matthew J., et al. "The Association Between Worldview Climate Dimensions and College Students' Perceptions of Transformational Learning." *The Journal of Higher Education* 87 (2016) 674–700.

McCaulley, Esau. *Reading While Black: African American Biblical Interpretation as an Exercise in Hope.* Downers Grove, IL: IVP Academic, 2020.

McKnight, Scot. *The Blue Parakeet: Rethinking How You Read the Bible.* Grand Rapids: Zondervan, 2008.

McMurtrie, Beth. "Are Colleges Ready for a Different Kind of Teaching This Fall?" *The Chronicle of Higher Education* 66 (2020) 1.

———. "Evangelical Colleges' Diversity Problem." *Chronicle of Higher Education* 62 (2016) A23–A26.

Mezirow, Jack. *Transformative Dimensions of Adult Learning.* San Francisco: Jossey-Bass, 1991.

Middleton, J. Richard. *A New Heaven and a New Earth: Reclaiming Biblical Eschatology.* Grand Rapids: Baker Academic, 2014.

Miller, Kevin D. "Reframing the Faith-Learning Relationship: Bonhoeffer and an Incarnational Alternative to the Integration Model." *Christian Scholar's Review* 43 (2014) 131–38.

Moreland, J. P., and William Lane Craig. *Philosophical Foundations for a Christian Worldview.* Downers Grove, IL: InterVarsity, 2003.

Mount Vernon Nazarene University. "COVID-19 Policies." https://www.mvnu.edu/returntothevern/covidpolicies.

Naisbitt, John. *High Touch High Tech: Technology and Our Related Search for Meaning.* London: Nicholas Brealey, 1999.

Nash, Ronald H. *Life's Ultimate Questions: An Introduction to Philosophy.* Grand Rapids: Zondervan, 1999.

National Center for Education Statistics (NCES). "Fast Facts: Distance Learning." https://nces.ed.gov/fastfacts/display.asp?id=80.

National Student Clearinghouse Research Center. "Current Term Enrollment Estimates: Fall 2020." https://nscresearchcenter.org/wp-content/uploads/CTEE_Report_Fall_2020.pdf.

Naugle, David K. *Worldview: The History of a Concept.* Grand Rapids: Eerdmans, 2002.
Newbigin, Lesslie. *The Gospel in a Pluralist Society.* Grand Rapids: Eerdmans, 1989.
Ní Shé, C., et al., eds. "Teaching Online is Different: Critical Perspectives from the Literature." Dublin City University, 2019.
Otto, Patrick, and Michael Harrington. "Spiritual Formation within Christian Higher Education." *Christian Higher Education* 15 (2016) 252–62.
Palloff, Rena M., and Keith Pratt. *Building Online Learning Communities: Effective Strategies for the Virtual Classroom.* San Francisco: Jossey-Bass, 2007.
Paredes-Collins, Kristin. "Campus Climate for Diversity as a Predictor of Spiritual Development at Christian Colleges." *Religion & Education* 41 (2014) 171–93.
———. "Cultivating Diversity and Spirituality: A Compelling Interest for Institutional Priority." *Christian Higher Education* 12 (2013) 122–37.
Park, Julie J., and Nicholas A. Bowman. "Religion as Bridging or Bonding Social Capital: Race, Religion, and Cross-racial Interaction for College Students." *Sociology of Education* 88 (2015) 20–37.
Patel, Eboo. "Faith is the Diversity Issue Ignored by Colleges. Here's Why That Needs to Change." *Chronicle of Higher Education* 65 (2018) 1.
———. "Preparing Interfaith Leaders: Knowledge Base and Skill Set for Interfaith Leaders." *New Directions for Student Leadership* 152 (2016) 75–86.
Patel, Eboo, and Mary Ellen Giess. "Engaging Religious Diversity on Campus: The Role of Student Affairs." *About Campus* 6 (2016) 8–15.
Patel, Eboo, and Cassie Meyer. "Religious Education for Interfaith Leadership." *Academic Journal of Religious Education* 105 (2010) 16–19.
The Peak Performance Center. "Affective Domain of Learning." https://thepeakperformancecenter.com/educational-learning/learning/process/domains-of-learning/affective-domain/.
Pei, Leisi, and Hongbin Wu. "Does Online Learning Work Better Than Offline Learning in Undergraduate Medical Education? A Systematic Review and Meta-Analysis." *Medical Education Online* 24 (2019). https://doi.org/10.1080/10872981.2019.1666538.
Pew Research Center. "Decline of Christianity Continues." https://www.pewforum.org/2019/10/17/in-u-s-decline-of-christianity-continues-at-rapid-pace.
———. "The Global and Religious Landscape." https://www.pewforum.org/2012/12/18/global-religious-landscape-exec/.
Placher, William C., ed. *Callings: Twenty Centuries of Christian Wisdom on Vocation.* Grand Rapids: Eerdmans, 2005.
Plantinga, Cornelius, Jr. *Engaging God's World: A Christian Vision of Faith, Learning, and Living.* Grand Rapids: Eerdmans, 2002.
Point Loma Nazarene University. "Christian Practice." https://ctl.pointloma.edu/christian-practices/.
Poppinga, Amy, et al. "Building Bridges Across Faith Lines: Responsible Christian Education in a Post-Christian Society." *Christian Higher Education* 18 (2019) 98–110.
Powell, William. "Collaboration." In *Count Me In: Developing Inclusive International Schools.* Washington, DC: Department of State Overseas Advisory Council, 2004. https://2009-2017.state.gov/m/a/os/43980.htm.

Radford, Alexandria Walton, et al. "Demographic and Enrollment Characteristics of Nontraditional Undergraduates: 2011–12." National Center for Education Statistics. https://nces.ed.gov/pubsearch/pubsinfo.asp?pubid=2015025.

Ramsey, Richard. "The Ministry of . . . Grading?" *Christian Education Journal* 9 (2012) 408–19.

Rath, Tom. *StrengthsFinder 2.0.* New York: Gallup, 2007.

READY Education. "The Student Retention Research Report: Impact of a Mobile-First Strategy." https://www.readyeducation.com/student-retention-research-report-digital-engagement.

Rhodes, Terrel. *Assessing Outcomes and Improving Achievement: Tips and Tools for Using Rubrics.* Washington, DC: Association of American Colleges and Universities, 2010.

Rockenbach, Alyssa Bryant, and Matthew J. Mayhew. "How the Collegiate Religious and Spiritual Climate Shapes Students' Ecumenical Orientation." *Research in Higher Education* 54 (2013) 461–79.

———. "The Campus Spiritual Climate: Predictors of Satisfaction Among Students with Diverse Worldviews." *Journal of College Student Development* 55 (2014) 41–62.

Rockenbach, Alyssa N., et al. "Fostering the Pluralism Orientation of College Students through Interfaith Co-curricular Engagement." *The Review of Higher Education* 39 (2015) 25–58.

Ryken, Philip Graham. *Christian Worldview: A Student's Guide.* Wheaton, IL: Crossway, 2013.

Samuel, Joshua. "Re-viewing Christian Theologies of Religious Diversity." *The Ecumenical Review* 71 (2019) 739–54.

Schreiner, Laurie. "The 'Thriving Quotient': A New Vision for Student Success." *About Campus* 15 (2010) 2–10.

———. "Thriving in College." In *Positive Psychology and Appreciative Inquiry in Higher Education,* edited by Peter C. Mather and Eileen Hulme, 41–52. San Francisco: Jossey-Bass, 2013.

Sheffer, Hadass, et al. *The Comeback Story: How Adults Return to School to Complete their Degrees.* Washington, DC: New America, 2020.

Simpson, Elizabeth J. *The Classification of Educational Objectives in the Psychomotor Domain.* Vol. 3. Washington, DC: Gryphon House, 1972.

Sire, James W. *The Universe Next Door: A Basic Worldview Catalog.* 5th ed. Downers Grove, IL: IVP Academic, 2009.

Smith, C. Christopher, and John Pattison. *Slow Church: Cultivating Community in the Patient Way of Jesus.* Downers Grove, IL: InterVarsity, 2014.

Smith, Daryl. G. *Diversity's Promise for Higher Education: Making it Work.* 2nd ed. Baltimore: Johns Hopkins University Press, 2015.

Smith, David I. *On Christian Teaching: Practicing Faith in the Classroom.* Grand Rapids: Eerdmans, 2018.

Smith, David I., and James K. A. Smith. *Teaching and Christian Practice: Reshaping Faith and Learning.* Grand, Rapids: Eerdmans, 2011.

Smith, James K. A. *Desiring the Kingdom: Worship, Worldview, and Cultural Formation.* Grand Rapids: Baker Academic, 2009.

Soares, Louis. "Post-traditional Learners and the Transformation of Postsecondary Education: A Manifesto for College Leaders." American Council on Education, 2013. https://www.acenet.edu/Documents/Post-traditional-Learners.pdf.

Sperling, John, and Robert W. Tucker. *For-Profit Higher Education: Developing a World-Class Workforce*. New York: Routledge, 2017.

Spiritual Transformation Inventory. https://www.spiritualtransformation.org.

Staley, David J., and Dennis A. Trinkle. "The Changing Landscape of Higher Education." *Educause Review* (January/February 2011) 16–32.

Stark, J. David. "Gaming the System: Online Spiritual Formation in Christian Higher Education." *Theological Education* 52 (2019) 43–53.

Stetzer, Ed. "The Big Story of Scripture (Creation, Fall, Redemption, Restoration) In Pictures: Your Input Requested." *Christianity Today Blog Forum*, November 28, 2012. https://www.christianitytoday.com/edstetzer/2012/november/big-story-of-scripture-creation-fall-redemption.html.

Stoltzfus, Tony. *Coaching Questions: A Coach's Guide to Powerful Asking Skills*. Virginia Beach, VA: Tony Stoltzfus, 2008.

Tableau Public Research Center. "Undergraduate Enrollment in Its Steepest Decline So Far Since the Pandemic Began." https://public.tableau.com/profile/researchcenter#!/vizhome/Spring_StayInformed_2/Story1.

Theology of Work Project. https://www.theologyofwork.org/.

Tisdale, Nora Tubbs. "Job and Vocation: Discerning the Difference." *Reflections* (2012).

US Department of Education. National Center for Education Statistics, Integrated Postsecondary System (IPEDS). "Fall Enrollment Surveys." https://nces.ed.gov/ipeds/datacenter/InstitutionByName.aspx?goToReportld=1.

Veith, Gene Edward. *Post-Christian: A Guide to Contemporary Thought and Culture*. Wheaton, IL: Crossway, 2020.

Vella, Jane. *Learning to Listen, Learning to Teach: The Power of Dialogue in Educating Adults*. San Francisco: Jossey-Bass, 2002.

———. *On Teaching and Learning: Putting the Principles and Practices of Dialogue Education into Action*. San Francisco: Jossey-Bass, 2008.

Vesely, Pam, et al. "Key Elements in Building Online Communities: Comparing Faculty and Student Perceptions." *Journal of Online Teaching and Learning* 3 (2007). http://jolt.merlot.org/vol3no3/vesely.htm.

Wall, Robert W., and David R. Nienhuis. *A Compact Guide to the Whole Bible: Learning to Read Scripture's Story*. Grand Rapids: Baker Academic, 2015.

Walsh, Brian J., and Richard J. Middleton. *The Transforming Vision: Shaping a Christian Worldview*. Downers Grove, IL: InterVarsity, 1984.

Wang, C., et al. "The Efficacy of Microlearning in Improving Self-Care Capability: A Systematic Review of the Literature." *Public Health* 186 (2020) 286–96.

WASC Senior College and University Commission. "Commission Action Letter, Seeking Accreditation Visit 1, February 2018 Action." https://wascsenior.box.com/shared/static/xvvfq50ahqn9i5sx1d1itec8ez535vrj.pdf.

———. "Standard 1: Defining Institutional Purposes and Ensuring Educational Objectives." https://www.wscuc.org/resources/handbook-accreditation-2013/part-ii-core-commitments-and-standards-accreditation/wasc-standards-accreditation-2013/standard-1-defining-institutional-purposes-and-ensuring-educational-objectives.

Washatka, John. "Diverse Faith Perspectives," Los Angeles Pacific University. https://www.lapu.edu/sub-resource/diverse-faith-perspectives/.

———. "Practicing Tolerance in Diversity." Los Angeles Pacific University. https://www.lapu.edu/sub-resource/diverse-faith-perspectives/.

Watson, James E. "The Inclusion of Intentional Ethos Enablers in Electronic Distance Learning Opportunities for Christian Institutions." *American Journal of Distance Education* 22 (2008) 195–206.

Wilding, Melody. "Do You Have a Job, Career, or Calling? The Difference Matters." *Forbes*, April 23, 2018. https://www.forbes.com/sites/melodywilding/2018/04/23/do-you-have-a-job-career-or-calling-the-difference-matters/?sh=2772a251632a.

Wilhoit, James C., et al. "Soul Projects: Class Related Spiritual Practices in Higher Education." In *Building a Culture of Faith: University-Wide Partnerships for Spiritual Formation*, edited by Cary Balzer and Rod Reed, 187–215. Abilene, TX: Abilene Christian University Press, 2012.

Williams, Damon A., et al. "Toward a Model of Inclusive Excellence and Change." Washington, DC: Association of American Colleges and Universities, 2005.

Wingard, Robert W. "An Incarnational Model for Teaching in the Church." *Quarterly Review* 2 (2002) 45–57.

Wright, N. T. *Scripture and the Authority of God*. New York: HarperOne, 2011.

www.ingramcontent.com/pod-product-compliance
Lightning Source LLC
Chambersburg PA
CBHW031428150426
43191CB00006B/437